Facilitating a Violence Prevention Support Group

For Kids Who Are Bullied

In the Violence Prevention Series:

Facilitating a Violence Prevention Support Group: For Kids Dealing with Someone Else's Anger (grades K–6)
Facilitating a Violence Prevention Support Group: For Kids Who Are Bullied (grades K–6)
Facilitating a Violence Prevention Support Group: For Kids Who Bully (grades K–6)

Other titles:

Anger Management and Violence Prevention (grades 6–12)
Changing Families (grades 6–12)
Peter the Puppy Talks About Chemical Dependence in the Family (grades K–6)
Tanya Talks About Chemical Dependence in the Family (grades 6–8)
Thomas Barker Talks About Divorce and Separation (grades K–6)

Facilitating a Violence Prevention Support Group

For Kids Who Are Bullied

Teresa M. Schmidt, L.C.S.W., B.C.D.

Hazelden
Center City, Minnesota 55012-0176

1-800-328-9000
1-651-213-4590 (Fax)
www.hazelden.org

ISBN 1-56246-118-4

Hazelden Publishing and Educational Services is a division of the Hazelden Foundation, a not-for-profit organization. Since 1949, Hazelden has been a leader in promoting the dignity and treatment of people afflicted with the disease of chemical dependency.

The mission of the foundation is to improve the quality of life for individuals, families, and communities by providing a national continuum of information, education, and recovery services that are widely accessible; to advance the field through research and training; and to improve our quality and effectiveness through continuous improvement and innovation.

Stemming from that, the mission of this division is to provide quality information and support to people wherever they may be in their personal journey—from education and early intervention, through treatment and recovery, to personal and spiritual growth.

Although our treatment programs do not necessarily use everything Hazelden publishes, our bibliotherapeutic materials support our mission and the Twelve Step philosophy upon which it is based. We encourage your comments and feedback.

The headquarters of the Hazelden Foundation is in Center City, Minnesota. Additional treatment facilities are located in Chicago, Illinois; New York, New York; Plymouth, Minnesota; St. Paul, Minnesota; and West Palm Beach, Florida. At these sites, we provide a continuum of care for men and women of all ages. Our Plymouth facility is designed specifically for youth and families.

For more information on Hazelden, please call **1-800-257-7800.** Or you may access our World Wide Web site on the Internet at **www.hazelden.org**.

12/27/04

This work, and *Facilitating a Violence Prevention Support Group: For Kids Who Bully*, are dedicated to the members of my family: my parents, Marion and William J. McKay; my sisters and brothers, Mandy Christine, Joe, and Michael; and to my husband, Wiltz, and our sons, Matthew and Thomas, and our daughter, Belen. It is also dedicated to the nineteen children who participated in the field testing of these manuals, who let me know what worked in the group sessions, and what didn't work. It is finally dedicated to all of the children with whom I have worked in groups, who have taught me what I need to teach them, and to all of my adult clients who have validated the correctness of what we teach in this manual.

Contents

Acknowledgments   ix
About the Author   x
Introduction   1

Part One   5
Chapter 1: School Violence   7
    Entitlement and Tolerance   8
    Bullies and Victims   9
Chapter 2: Child Development   11
    Personal Level   11
    Family Level: The Effects of Maltreatment on Developmental Tasks   13

Part Two: Establishing a Support Group Program for At-Risk Students   17
Chapter 1: Dynamics of the Group Model   19
    Group Format   20
    Progression of Themes   23
    Displacement Communication   27
    Benefits of Use   28
Chapter 2: Implementing the Group Program   30
    Gaining Administrative Support   30
    Staffing and Training   31
    Developing Referrals   32
    Screening Candidates   35
    Acquiring Informed Parental Consent   36
    Forming and Scheduling the Groups   37
    Behavior Management   38
    Assuring Group Confidentiality   39
    Self-Disclosing by Leaders   40
    Role Modeling by Leaders   40
    Following Up Group Participation   40

Using the Program in Guidance Counseling   41
Using the Program in Family Therapy   41

Part Three: Session Plans   **43**
Group Guide for Daniel the Dinosaur   45
Session 1:   Daniel the Dinosaur Talks about Violent Behaviors in Schools   47
Session 2:   Daniel the Dinosaur Learns Why Some Children Use Violence   64
Session 3:   Daniel the Dinosaur Meets Mrs. Owl   80
Session 4:   Daniel the Dinosaur Learns How to Stand Tall   95
Session 5:   Daniel the Dinosaur Learns How to Use I Statements and
             I Hear You Statements   108
Session 6:   Daniel the Dinosaur Learns New Assertive Behavior Skills   123
Session 7:   Daniel the Dinosaur Practices Assertive Behavior Skills in Situations
             Where He Is Being Teased   138
Session 8:   Daniel the Dinosaur Practices Assertive Behavior Skills and Learns
             Two Other Steps to Take When Being Left Out   150
Session 9:   Daniel the Dinosaur Learns Anger Management   164
Session 10: Daniel the Dinosaur Learns to Resolve Conflict   177
Session 11: Daniel the Dinosaur Presents What He Has Learned and
             Says Goodbye   190

Part Four: Support Materials   **199**
Basic Fact Worksheets (with answers dotted in)   203
Basic Fact Posters   213
Basic Facts List   229
Questions to Help Clarify the Basic Facts   230
Process and Progress Form   235
Progress Notes   236
Self-Referral Group Survey Form   238
Parental Consent Form   239
Screening Interview Outline   240
References and Suggested Readings   241

Support Materials within the Text
Activity Sheets and Handouts (in each session)
Assignments (in each session)
Audience Evaluation Form (in session 11)   195
Basic Fact Worksheets (in each session)
Certificate of Participation (in session 11)   197
Feeling Daniel (in session 2)   76
Group Evaluation Form (in session 11)   196
Group Rules Contract (in session 1)   59

Acknowledgments

I would like to again thank Thelma Spencer, Ed.D., with whom I collaborated to write *Peter the Puppy Talks About Chemical Dependence in the Family*. Thelma and I developed a structured format for school groups in my living room over Christmas vacation in 1988. This book, and *Facilitating a Violence Prevention Support Group: For Kids Who Bully*, are the seventh and eighth books based on that structured format, although there has been a natural evolution of the material based on group and consulting experiences. The current works are solely my responsibility.

I would also like to thank the administration and guidance counselors, Paul Quirk and Miriam Zaknoen, of Maple Elementary School and Pine Tree Elementary School in Avon, Indiana, who graciously provided opportunities for field testing the first draft of these two group manuals. Their assistance was invaluable.

I am still grateful for the help and support of my family. My sons, Thomas and Matthew Schmidt, were in the third grade and fifth grade when Thelma Spencer and I developed *Peter the Puppy*. Matthew is now a senior and Thomas a sophomore in high school, and they have continued to provide consultation and suggestions. They have shown supreme patience with the time I have spent working on these books over the last seven years. My husband, Wiltz Wagner, has taken me to ride motorcycles at the drag strip and at the Bonneville Salt Flats, which has helped me maintain perspective, and has given much love and affection which have enhanced the current writing.

About the Author

Teresa M. Schmidt, M.S.W., L.C.S.W., B.C.D., has been a clinical social worker since 1970. A graduate of the College of William and Mary and the Smith College School for Social Work, Ms. Schmidt has had extensive experience in outpatient settings. Bringing her clinical experience in mental health to Newport News Public Schools, Newport News, Virginia, in 1987, she worked with Dr. Thelma Spencer to develop and implement in a school setting a prevention/intervention group program for children from chemically dependent families. Ms. Schmidt is coauthor with Dr. Spencer of *Peter the Puppy Talks About Chemical Dependence in the Family, Tanya Talks About Chemical Dependence in the Family,* and *Thomas Barker Talks About Divorce and Separation.* Ms. Schmidt's other titles include *Facilitating a Violence Prevention Support Group: For Kids Who Bully* and *Facilitating a Violence Prevention Support Group: For Kids Dealing with Someone Else's Anger* (co-written with Dr. Spencer), which are also a part of the *Violence Prevention Series.* Ms. Schmidt has also written *Anger Management and Violence Prevention* and *Changing Families,* two support group manuals for middle and high school students. Ms. Schmidt currently lives in the cornfields of Indiana, where she maintains a private practice, consults with local school systems on leading support groups, and conducts training workshops for mental health and school professionals on the local, state, and national level.

Introduction

Here is a group of five boys, third to fifth grade, referred to a bullies' group as a result of disciplinary referrals. Billy's mother died of a drug overdose; his father uses drugs and can't hold a job, so Billy lives with relatives. Johnny is on house arrest because he punched another boy, Stephen, in the nose. Bryan picks on kids in the classroom, the rest room, the hallway, the cafeteria. Michael is on probation for fighting. Kevin misses group a lot because of absenteeism. They all know Stephen, a large, somewhat overweight boy, who is in the same class as three of the group members, except for the boy who punched him in the nose who is not allowed to be in the same room as Stephen. The boys say Stephen is a sissy, and they all giggle. Sometimes they tell him that he is so fat that his beeper is as big as a VCR. These boys are frequently disruptive in the group, talking among themselves. Bryan especially seems to see his role as the comedian, making jokes, and entertaining everybody. Most of the boys acknowledge that they have a problem with their behavior because they get into trouble a lot and get sent to the principal's office. The boys sometimes attribute their behavior to anger, but usually they feel overly picked on by the administration, or they blame someone else for starting a fight. Not one of them thinks there is anything wrong with calling Stephen a sissy.

Here is another group of five children, referred to a group for children who are victims of bullies. Katrina is a little third grader, with short blonde hair. She is constantly going to the teacher because the other children call her names or won't let her play. George, a fifth grader, is a boy who is on probation because he broke the nose of a boy in his neighborhood who was messing with him. Simon, a fourth grader, is a boy who laughs when you talk about the rules in the cafeteria. He says rules are great, but nobody is around to make sure the kids follow them. Debra is a fourth grader who looks depressed, and answers questions so quietly you can barely hear her. Brandon is a ten-year-old boy who makes every statement with a question in his voice.

Most people think of school violence as occurring in middle or high school, and they typically describe students bringing guns and knives to school, causing serious injuries or death. But, school violence really begins with children like the boys in the first group just described, in elementary school, feeling justified in calling each other names. Elementary school bullies call others names, tease, won't let other children play, and generally mess with children like the ones in the second group, who know firsthand what it feels like to be the victims of school violence, and who are somewhat cynical about the idea that adults can do anything to change the behavior of the children who are bullies. Rules are meaningless if they are not enforced.

An effective school violence prevention program will need to do more than teach the aggressive children anger management or conflict resolution skills. Since the boys in the group for aggressive children feel *entitled* to make fun of Stephen, and the school administration and faculty have *tolerated* the name calling by not setting limits or enforcing consequences, the boys have learned that it is okay to call names and pick on other children. There may be rules about not calling people names, but they are never enforced. The boys' behavior won't change unless there is a "systemic approach."

The school administration will need to be very clear about a definition of violence that will include name calling, gossiping, spreading rumors, intimidation, and harassment, as well as physical violence. The school leadership must adopt the value that violent behavior is bad, is not acceptable, and will not be tolerated in school. Then, leadership must set clear consequences for violent behavior, with the aim of setting limits on such behavior, but also of teaching the children how to replace their violent behavior with more appropriate behavior. The teachers must increase their awareness of the range of violent behavior and must see themselves as responsible for not tolerating violence, for setting consequences in motion, and when appropriate, for helping the children correct their behavior.

These group manuals, *Facilitating a Violence Prevention Support Group: For Kids Who Bully* and *Facilitating a Violence Support Group: For Kids Who Are Bullied*, are part of the systemic, schoolwide approach necessary to solve the school violence problem. *Facilitating a Violence Prevention Support Group: For Kids Who Bully* has as its two primary goals (1) to establish a definition of violence and the value that it is not acceptable, and (2) to teach violent children the assertive behavior skills that they can use to replace their aggressive behavior. The more that every principal and teacher in the school knows what each manual teaches, the more they can utilize the material to help the children correct their behavior in actual everyday situations.

The companion manual, *Facilitating a Violence Support Group: For Kids Who Are Bullied,* helps victims of children who are bullies learn how to respond in a way that will help them stand up for themselves. They, too, learn the definition of violence and the value that it is not acceptable. They also learn that it is not solely their responsibility to deal with violent children: that adult intervention is needed to set limits and enforce consequences for violent children, thus decreasing the feeling of entitlement and tolerance of violent behavior.

Part One of these manuals contains a brief description of the issues pertinent to school violence and child development issues relevant to bullies and victims.

Part Two contains materials to help you understand the dynamics of the group model, including group format and progression of session themes. It also provides guidelines and materials to help you implement the group in your school or agency.

Part Three contains the complete group guide. The group guide includes the objectives, necessary preparations, background information and guidelines, and detailed step-by-step plans for each of the eleven sessions.

Part Four contains support materials. This section will further help group leaders and other staff make the group process successful and rewarding for everyone involved.

Several other manuals that feature the group model are available from Hazelden.

1. *Peter the Puppy Talks About Chemical Dependence in the Family* meets the needs of children (grades K–6) from chemically dependent families.
2. *Tanya Talks About Chemical Dependence in the Family* is designed for middle school children (grades 6–8) from chemically dependent families.
3. *Thomas Barker Talks About Divorce and Separation* helps children (grades K–6) from divorced, separated, single-parent, or stepfamilies.
4. *Anger Management and Violence Prevention* is a group for middle and high school students who use violence to express anger, whose parents are violent, or who are in a violent dating relationship.
5. *Changing Families* is a group for middle and high school students from separated, divorced, single-parent, and stepfamilies.

And in the Violence Prevention Series:

6. *Facilitating a Violence Prevention Support Group: For Kids Who Bully* is for children (grades K–6) who need to learn to change their aggressive behavior.
7. *Facilitating a Violence Prevention Support Group: For Kids Dealing with Someone Else's Anger* is for children (grades K–6) whose families use violence to express anger and for children who use violence to express anger.

Overall, these manuals provide sound, practical, creative, and innovative ways to help children correct their misconceptions, meet their emotional needs, deal effectively with their problems, and grow to live lives that are much less "at risk."

Part One

Chapter 1: School Violence

Chapter 2: Child Development

Chapter 1

School Violence

School violence is one of the primary issues that schools face, along with substance abuse and the effects on students' learning and social behavior by poverty, divorce, and parental chemical dependence. The increase in violence occurring among young people is well documented. The 1993 Crime Report by the FBI indicated the violent crime arrest rate for juveniles (ages 10–17) rose 27 percent from 1980 to 1990, when it reached 430 per 100,000 juveniles. In the 25-year period from 1965 to 1990, the overall murder arrest rate for juveniles increased 432 percent, from 2.8 per 100,000 to 12.1 per 100,000. During the 1980–1990 decade, there was a 79 percent increase in the number of juveniles who commit murders with guns. The aggravated assault rate rose steadily, and that crime category had the highest number of arrests, indicating that today's youth are inclined to settle a dispute by engaging in a physical altercation.

The National Education Association reports that violence occurs in schools at an alarming rate. As quoted in *Solving Violence Problems in Your School* (Remboldt 1995, 4):

- Every hour of every school day, 2,000 students are physically attacked on school grounds.
- One in five students regularly carries a weapon to school (one in twenty carries a gun).
- Each school day more than 6,000 teachers are threatened with injury and 260 are assaulted.
- Metal detectors are positioned in 25 percent of big city public schools.

Experts agree that comprehensive prevention and intervention programs will be necessary to create any change in school violence. *Respect & Protect* ® by Carole Remboldt and Richard Zimman (1996), also published by Hazelden, is a comprehensive and systematic approach that

- is both adult centered and student centered
- contains both a prevention element (environmental control) and an intervention element (choices, consequences, and contracts)

- is based on the principle that everyone has an obligation to respect and protect the rights of others
- promotes a systemwide school ethos that states in effect: "Violence is not okay. We do not tolerate it here."

By environmental control, the approach does not mean metal detectors or other militant security measures. Rather, environmental control means "creating a school environment that supports adult efforts to intervene in—not ignore—violence when they see it. It also involves policies, programs, and educational approaches that support nonviolent resolution of conflicts and a systematic approach using choices, consequences, and contracts to address problems of bullying and other types of violence."

Entitlement and Tolerance

Two attitudes promote violent behavior in schools: *entitlement* and *tolerance*. In *Solving Violence Problems in Your Schools*, Remboldt (1995, 13) writes,

> Many students feel *entitled* to act violently toward teachers and toward other students, especially passive, weaker, or younger ones. Their lack of sensitivity toward the effect violence has on others inclines many students to think it's perfectly normal and acceptable to express their anger, get their needs met, or fulfill their desires in violent ways. This sense of entitlement to act in violent ways is not being addressed effectively by adults in the schools. In fact, it is being *tolerated* by them. Students by and large ignore adults' warnings regarding violent behavior because adults usually tolerate the behavior and allow students to get away with it.

Most people will readily agree that it is violent to bring weapons to school or to engage in activities that are physically harmful. School personnel do not tolerate such behaviors, and there are usually clear consequences, often involving suspension or expulsion. However, experts in the field of school violence are now seeing violence as including a wide range of behavior, beginning with name calling, spreading rumors, and social exclusion at one extreme, leading to midrange behavior such as pushing, shoving, or intimidation, and ending with weapons and death at the other extreme. While the one extreme of name calling is common beginning in elementary school, the midrange violent behavior of fighting peaks in middle school. Weapons and severe injury are generally more common in high school. Because weapons and death are relatively uncommon in elementary school, school personnel may not believe they have a violence problem, and they often look the other way when they notice name calling, spreading rumors, social exclusion, and perhaps even a mild push or shove. This tolerance perpetuates the violent behavior. Even if school personnel do intervene at the midrange behavior of fighting, it is often too late to change the pattern of aggressive behavior that the children have been getting away with.

The point of environmental control is to eliminate the tolerance that enables violence to exist. School administrators must create a schoolwide policy where violence is clearly defined, with the definition clearly spelling out behaviors like name calling, spreading rumors, intimidating, not letting someone play with you, as well as pushing, shoving, hitting, kicking, and so on.

The Norwegian researcher Dan Olweus (1994), who has written extensively on bullying in schools, describes aggressive behavior as a "negative action when someone intentionally inflicts, or attempts to inflict, injury or discomfort upon another. . . ." He describes three categories of negative actions:

- words—by threatening, taunting, teasing, and calling names
- physical contact—by hitting, pushing, kicking, pinching or restraining another
- acts—making faces or dirty gestures, intentionally excluding someone from a group, or refusing to comply with another person's wishes

Therefore, for children, we adopt a simple all-encompassing definition of violence:

Violence is any mean word, look, sign, or act that hurts another person's body, feelings, or possessions.

The next step in a schoolwide violence prevention program is to declare a safe school policy, where it is clearly spelled out that violent behavior will not be tolerated. A clear system of procedures and consequences for violent behavior must be set up and implemented on a consistent and predictable basis. In-service training to raise the awareness of teachers, and to spell out their responsibilities in setting limits, enforcing consequences, and helping children change aggressive behavior is another necessary component. Affective curriculum, anger management training, and conflict resolution programs should be provided across the board. Special programs to help children who have frequent violent behavior replace their aggressive behavior with more appropriate social skills will also be necessary.

School administrators can use Hazelden programs *Respect & Protect*® and the *No-Bullying Program* to develop a schoolwide violence prevention program.

Bullies and Victims

Affective curriculum, anger management, and conflict resolution programs may succeed in alleviating some school violence problems, but researchers have found another kind of school violence that will not be touched by such programs: bullies and victims. Olweus has studied bullies in Scandinavia for more than twenty years; his programs have been implemented in Britain.

Olweus (1994, 10) points out that bullying involves an imbalance in strength. "The student who is exposed to the negative actions has difficulty defending him/herself and is somewhat helpless against the student or students who harass." Olweus differentiates between direct bullying, with relatively open attacks on the victim and indirect bullying, in the form of social isolation and intentional exclusion from a group.

Hazelden's *StudentView*® Survey finds that a fairly well-defined group of students, slightly more than 4 percent of girls and nearly 14 percent of boys, are involved in beating up people or starting fights three or more times a year, peaking in the seventh grade for boys and in the eighth grade for girls. Because girl bullies are more likely to use verbal attacks, spreading rumors, and social exclusion, they may be underrepresented in this statistic. Olweus (1994, 15) finds that younger and weaker children report being victims of bullies; second graders report the highest rates of being bullied, mostly by older students. Olweus's findings verified that "boys were most often victims and . . . perpetrators of direct bullying . . . but girls were exposed to indirect bullying to about the same extent as boys."

Because the behavior of bullies tends to be driven by the need for power and dominance rather than by anger or an inability to handle conflicts, the typical school solutions to violence—conflict resolution and anger management programs—will not be effective.

Given the research findings in both Olweus and the *StudentView*® Survey, Hazelden has defined bullying in this way:

> **Bullying occurs whenever someone uses his or her power *unfairly* and *repeatedly* to hurt someone.**

Facilitating a Violence Prevention Support Group: For Kids Who Bully can be used as a consequence for children who exhibit bullying behavior. Unlike *Facilitating a Violence Prevention Support Group: For Kids Dealing with Someone Else's Anger,* which helps children who live with violent parents, or who use violence to express their own anger, *Facilitating a Violence Prevention Support Group: For Kids Who Bully* helps children who use violence to meet their needs for material things, or for power or domination.

The material carries out both the prevention and intervention elements of *Respect & Protect*®. By its clear definition of violent behavior, and its strong value judgment that violent behavior is bad, unacceptable, and not to be tolerated, it provides clear limits for children. Second, it provides children with ways they can change their behavior from violent to assertive. It teaches social and assertive behavior skills that they can use to replace their aggressive behavior.

Facilitating a Violence Prevention Support Group: For Kids Who Are Bullied can be used to help children who are typically victims of other children's aggressive behavior learn how to respond in ways that are not aggressive, and that will promote higher effectiveness and self-esteem.

Chapter 2

Child Development

Chapter 1 explored the issues pertinent to school violence, including entitlement and tolerance, and the need for a systemic approach to prevent school violence. Chapter 2 will review the tasks of child development as they relate to bullies and victims.

The theory of lifespan developmental psychology looks at child and adolescent development in a comprehensive way (Coleman and Hendry 1990). While psychoanalytic theory examines child development as an individual task, and sociological theory looks at roles and role changes, the lifespan approach proposes that there is a human ecology: individuals live in families, and both individuals and families develop in the context of their geographical, historical, social, and political settings. Both individuals and families grow and develop and change, and they reciprocally influence each other as they do so. Theorists are increasingly looking at individuals as being producers of their own development: they are active agents in shaping or determining their lives.

The ecological framework used by many researchers consists of four levels: the personal (ontogenetic), the family (microsystem), the social (exosystem), and the societal (macrosystem). The first two of these levels, personal and family, will be examined for bullies and victims.

Personal Level

Thinking and Reasoning: Formal Operational Thinking. The K–6 children who will participate in this group will tend to think in concrete ways rather than in abstract ways, like adults. Jean Piaget describes the stage of **concrete operations,** ages 7 through 11, when children's thought is relational. Children begin to master notions of classes, relations, and quantities. Conservation and seriation is possible, enabling children to formulate hypotheses and explanations about concrete events. Children formulate a hypothesis originating from the concrete data, rather than from internal resources. And, once the hypothesis is formulated, children in concrete operations are reluctant to change the hypothesis, tending instead to alter the data.

As adolescents move into the stage of **formal operations,** they are able to utilize a number of important capabilities: one of these is the "contrary to fact" proposition, which has been described as a shift in thinking from the real to the possible, which facilitates a hypothetico-deductive approach to problem solving and to the understanding of propositional logic. Adolescents develop the ability to think about mental constructs as objects which can be manipulated and to master concepts such as probability and belief.

John C. Coleman and Leo B. Hendry (1990) describe a study of concept-formation where children of 8 to 9 years and adolescents between 13 and 14 were shown pictures of wheeled and nonwheeled tools and vehicles. Shown pairs of a wheeled and nonwheeled object, the child was asked to choose one item, and a light went on when a wheeled item was chosen. Only half of the younger children came to the conclusion that choosing a wheeled object made the light go on, and it took them nearly all of the seventy-two trials. By comparison, all the adolescents solved the problem, and many did so in as few as ten trials. The adolescents thought of hypotheses, tested them, and discarded them if they did not work. The younger children came to a hypothesis based on the data (tool versus nontool or vehicle versus nonvehicle), and were unable to give up the hypothesis even though they failed on most trials. These children were unable to differentiate the hypothesis from reality.

Social Cognition. Social cognition theorists look at the child's concrete thinking and egocentrism, and compare them to the adolescent's formal operational thinking, which allows the adolescent to think about the thoughts of other people. Coleman and Hendry (1990) describe Robert Selman's stage theory of social cognition, which involves role taking, perspective taking, empathy, moral reasoning, interpersonal problem solving, and self-knowledge. Selman's stages describe early adolescence (ages 5–10) as a time when the teen has the capacity for a more complex type of social cognition. The teen moves beyond simply taking the other person's perspective (in a back and forth manner) and is able to see all parties from a more generalized third-person perspective. By age 15, the adolescent may move to a still higher and more abstract level of interpersonal perspective-taking, which involves coordinating the perspectives of society with those of the individual and the group.

Temperament. Researchers have also looked at a child's temperament, and its influence on aggressive behavior. Jerome Kagan, a Harvard researcher, (Reiss and Roth 1993) had found that some children tend to be shy, vigilant, and restrained ("inhibited") when confronted with unfamiliar situations (such as meeting new children or adults). Others tend to be sociable, spontaneous, and relatively fearless in their behavior ("uninhibited"). A fearless, uninhibited early temperament appears to be a risk factor for later aggression and violence. Olweus (1994, 40) has found that: "A child with an active and 'hot-headed' temperament is more likely to develop into an aggressive youngster than is a child with an ordinary or more quiet temperament." Children who tend to be victims of other children's aggressive behavior are more likely to be shy, vigilant, and restrained.

Family Level: The Effects of Maltreatment on Developmental Tasks

Dante Ciccheti and Paul Howes (1991) provide a framework for looking at how families can help children master their developmental tasks. They see development as a series of tasks that are age and stage appropriate, but which remain critical to the child's continual adaptation. For instance, attachment, the major risk of infancy, continues to be relevant as children reach the tasks of later years, such as emotional regulation, autonomy, peer relations, and school adjustment. Cicchetti and Howes believe that some families provide **potentiating,** or **risk factors,** increasing the likelihood of the child developing incompetence, while some families provide **compensatory,** or **protective factors,** which increase the probability of competence in their developmental tasks. Cicchetti and Howes describe the effects of maltreating-parents on the developmental achievements of young children in five areas: attachment, emotion regulation, autonomous self, peer relations, and school adjustment.

Task 1: Attachment

The task of infancy, to form secure attachment relationships with the primary caregiver, is especially affected by the characteristics of the caregiver. An adequate caregiver will be sensitive and responsive to the infant's needs. Mothers who are inconsistent in their accessibility and responsiveness to their infants tend to have babies who are both anxious and angry. Mothers who tend to withhold close bodily contact, especially at times of high infant intensity, have babies who are anxious and avoidant of the mother. Children who have insecurity and fear in these initial relationships may expect maltreatment in later relationships and may continue to express their own anger or avoidant behavior in later childhood and adult relationships (Crittenden and Ainsworth 1989). Olweus (1994) found that parents of bullies tend to have a negative basic attitude, characterized by a lack of warmth and involvement by the primary caretaker. In contrast, victims of bullies tend to have closer contact and more positive relationships with their parents, especially their mothers, which has been perceived as overprotection by some teachers.

Task 2: Emotion Regulation

Emotional self-regulation, the ability to modulate and initiate both positive and negative affect, is another early childhood task that continues to be an important task throughout the rest of the lifespan. Cicchetti and Howes (1991) believe "that the use of emotional language helps one control nonverbal emotional expressions, which in turn enhances regulation of the emotions themselves." Parents who use emotional language by putting feelings into words help their children learn to organize and control their emotional expressions. Maltreated children are overly aware of aggressive stimuli, an adaptive coping mechanism to alert them to signs of immediate danger. However, such awareness of aggressive stimuli is not adaptive when children are in nonthreatening situations. Olweus found that parents of bullies tended to be overly permissive and tolerant, without setting clear limits to aggressive behavior toward peers, siblings, and adults. And, parents of bullies also tend to use authoritarian parenting techniques, such as physical punishment and violent emotional outbursts. Further, bullies have in common with maltreated children a tendency to see aggression in neutral or positive situations. Victims of bullies, in contrast, are cautious, sensitive, and quiet, and react to attack by crying and withdrawing.

Task 3: Autonomous Self

The toddler develops a sense of being a separate individual with personal thoughts, feelings, and behaviors, a foreshadowing of the adolescent move to independence. Maltreated toddlers show evidence of low self-esteem, not smiling when they see themselves in the mirror and talking less about themselves. In a tool use/problem solving situation, maltreated two-year-olds show increased anger, frustration with their mother, and noncompliance, revealing a difficulty in making a smooth transition to autonomy. Maltreated children in grades 1–3 see themselves as more competent and accepted than comparison children, and more competent than their teachers perceive them to be. Such inflated self-perception may reflect unrealistic coping strategies that help them gain a sense of personal competence and control in chaotic home settings, but may eventually cause them to feel like failures. By grades 4–6, maltreated children view themselves as less competent and accepted, and more in accordance with teacher ratings, showing a lower self-worth. Research on bullies show that they have a strong need to dominate others; if male, are physically stronger than boys in general; and have a positive self-esteem, with little anxiety and insecurity. Victims of bullies, in contrast, are more anxious and insecure than students in general; feel ashamed, stupid, and unattractive; feel like failures; and have low self-esteem. If male, they tend to be physically weaker than boys in general.

Task 4: Peer Relationships

Positive peer relationships can be buffering factors in the lives of maltreated children. However, maltreated children tend to display more disturbed patterns of interaction with peers, showing higher levels of physical and verbal aggression in interaction with peers and a higher degree of withdrawal from interaction. Both patterns lead to increasing isolation and peer rejection. Bullies contrast with maltreated children by having an average or slightly below average level of popularity. Victims, on the other hand, are lonely and abandoned at school, often without one good friend.

Task 5: Adaptation to School

This final task of childhood involves integration into the peer group, acceptable performance in the classroom, and appropriate motivational orientations for achievement. Maltreated children may have unmet physical needs, may have concerns over safety, and may tend to search for acceptance. They may show dependence on teachers, score low on tests of cognitive maturity, and show less readiness to learn in school. In contrast, the optimum state for the child is a secure readiness to learn: a dynamic balance between establishing secure relationships with adults and feeling free to explore the environment in ways that will promote cognitive competence. Bullies tend to show a more generally antisocial and rule-breaking ("conduct-disordered") behavior pattern that will cause them difficulty in adaptation to school. Olweus shows that both bullies and victims may tend to have lower grades in school.

James Garbarino (1989) describes three parenting styles. **Authoritarian families** are paternalistic and harsh, and use rigid and domineering styles of child rearing. Parents tend to avoid feelings and use high levels of force. Authoritarian parents tend to allow their children little freedom, and there is increased conflict over spending money, friends, social life, and activities outside the home. If the parental discipline has been severe without much love and affection, children may become overtly aggressive, and may seek peer acceptance from membership in a delinquent gang.

    Permissive families tend to be overindulgent, making few demands upon children, setting few limits, and demanding a high level of emotional gratification from children. Some permissive parents tend to be too protective and overinvolved, hampering the drive for emotional independence.

    In contrast, **authoritative families** grant just enough autonomy so the child can develop a sense of self-governship and control; they also provide enough structure so that the child is not overwhelmed with responsibility or lost with no direction. Authoritative parents use negotiation techniques, are flexible, and are able to adapt general principles and techniques ("set rules," "offer encouragement") to their particular children.

    Children who are bullies tend to come from families who combine authoritarian with permissive parenting styles. Schools would do well to take notice of these three parenting styles. Schools should look to provide an authoritative environment for children: clear and firm expectations for behavior, clear guidelines, stated consequences which are then imposed, with the purpose being the correction of the child's behavior rather than punishment.

The group manuals in the Violence Prevention Series help children decrease aggressive or passive behavior in a way that also helps them meet the developmental tasks of childhood.

School Violence

1. The group provides a clear definition of violent behavior: violence is any mean word, look, act, or sign that hurts another person's body, feelings, or possessions.
2. The group provides a clear value judgment: violence is bad and unacceptable, and will not be tolerated.
3. The group provides many assertive behavior skills that children can use to replace aggressive behavior or passive behavior.

Child Development

1. Children think concretely. They can identify easily with the appealing stuffed animal characters used in the bibliotherapy.

2. Elementary-aged children can only see their own point of view. In *Facilitating a Violence Prevention Support Group: For Kids Who Bully,* the lesson on empathy in session 5 helps them, in a concrete way, begin to see the point of view of the other person.

3. The group leader will provide an attachment opportunity with the group members, by accepting them with warmth and consistency, while setting limits on behavior.

4. In the weekly feelings check-in, the children learn emotion regulation: they learn to identify, validate, tolerate, and express their feelings appropriately.

5. The small group experience helps children who are victims of other children's aggressive behavior see that they are not alone and allows them opportunities to create a support system that expands to school and neighborhood.

6. The small group experience allows children to improve their peer relationships as they practice the assertive behavior skills they can use to replace their aggressive or passive behavior.

7. Group experiences have shown to help children improve their adaptation to school.

This material was drawn from the following sources:

Cicchetti, D., and V. Carlson, eds. 1989. *Child maltreatment: Theory and research on the causes and consequences of child abuse and neglect.* New York: Cambridge University Press.

Cicchetti, D., and P. W. Howes. 1991. Developmental psychopathology in the context of the family: Illustrations from the study of child maltreatment. *Canadian Journal of Behavioral Science* 23 (July).

Coleman, J. C., and L. Hendry. 1990. *The Nature of adolescence.* New York: Routledge.

Crittenden, P. M., and M. D. S. Ainsworth. 1989. Child maltreatment and attachment theory. In Cicchetti and Carlson, eds. *Child maltreatment: Theory and research on the causes and consequences of child abuse and neglect.* New York: Cambridge University Press.

Garbarino, J. 1989. Troubled youth, troubled families: the dynamics of adolescent maltreatment. In Cicchetti and Carlson, eds. *Child maltreatment: Theory and research on the causes and consequences of child abuse and neglect.* New York: Cambridge University Press.

Olweus, D. 1994. *Bullying at school.* Cambridge, Mass.: Blackwell Publishers.

Reiss, J., and J. Roth, eds. 1993. *Understanding and preventing violence.* Washington, D. C.: National Academy Press.

Remboldt, C. 1995. *Solving violence problems in your school: Why a systematic approach is necessary.* Minneapolis: Johnson Institute.

———. 1995. *Violence in schools: The enabling factor.* Minneapolis: Johnson Institute.

Sharp, S., and P. Smith, eds. 1994. *Tackling bullying in your school.* New York: Routledge.

Part Two

Establishing a Support Group Program for At-Risk Students

Chapter 1: Dynamics of the Group Model

Chapter 2: Implementing the Group Program

Chapter 1

Dynamics of the Group Model

The group model used in the Violence Prevention Series is a dynamic process that helps meet the needs of children by providing structure, consistency, predictability, and fun. It incorporates a structured format that remains the same for all group sessions. The group model also presents a specific and definite progression of themes that fosters nonjudgmental education about the particular issue at hand, corrects misconceptions that children commonly have regarding the issue, and teaches children effective assertive behavior skills to help them change their behavior.

All this takes place through the medium of stories told by a make-believe animal. The children can easily identify with these "characters" without being defensive about their own behavior. Trevor and Tiffany, the Tyrannosaurus Twins, are the animal characters with whom those in the group for kids who bully, the Trevor and Tiffany group, can identify. Children in the group for victims of kids who bully, the Daniel group, are able to identify with Daniel the Dinosaur. The groups enable children who are aggressive or who are victims of other children's aggressive behavior to recognize that they're not alone, that other children have behaviors and feelings just like theirs, and that, above all, they can learn to manage their feelings and change their behavior in order to get along with others better.

Perhaps the most effective and practical setting for this group model is in the school. This is the case for a variety of reasons. First, most children who exhibit aggressive behavior have such strong defenses that they don't consider it a problem, and they don't seek help to change it. Children who are victims of other children's aggressive behavior are often ashamed or embarrassed, fear retaliation, or have been told to stop provoking or to toughen up. They often give up asking for adult help. Schools have access to the greatest number of children who have aggressive behavior or who are victims of other children's aggressive behavior, since those children may not attend a community center or mental health facility, or may not yet be involved in the court system. Better than any other setting, schools are in a position to offer prevention services—like this program—to the many children who use aggressive behavior or who are victims of other children's aggressive behavior.

Schools can offer the group model's services as part of a comprehensive prevention program or a schoolwide violence prevention program implemented by pupil services personnel, which include clinical and school social workers, school psychologists, guidance counselors, and chemical dependence counselors. Teachers can be trained to provide these groups. Student Assistance Programs (SAPs) and Core Teams will also find the program's group model ideal to use and easy to implement.

Although the school is a valuable setting for this group model, it may be used elsewhere: in mental health centers, in private practice, in chemical dependence treatment centers that provide family services, in battered women's shelters, in community centers and agencies, and through the court system.

A comprehensive support-group program offers groups for at-risk children from separated, divorced, or step-families, as well as from families experiencing chemical dependence or violence. *Facilitating a Violence Prevention Support Group: For Kids Who Bully* and *Facilitating a Violence Prevention Support Group: For Kids Who Are Bullied* help children who have problems with aggressive behavior, and children who are victims of children with aggressive behavior. This section provides information on implementing these groups in your school, agency, or other counseling setting, whether or not it's part of a schoolwide violence prevention program. The section includes information on acquiring administrative support, recruiting and training staff, developing a referral network, screening candidates, forming and scheduling groups, and behavior management. You will also find information on informed consent, confidentiality, and self-disclosure on the part of group leaders. The section will also point out effective ways to follow up on the individual, group, and system levels.

Group Format

The group model presented in these manuals follows a structured format for each group session that is both educationally and clinically sound. The three-part format includes the same components.

1. Beginning the session
   - Group rules (reviewed in the first several sessions and in later sessions if necessary)
   - Centering exercise
   - Feelings check-in
   - Review of basic facts (beginning with session 2)
   - Review of homework assignment (beginning with session 2)
2. Exploring the story
   - Story (the heart of the session)
   - Group discussion
   - Follow-up activity
   - Worksheet for reinforcing basic facts
   - Homework assignment
3. Wrapping up
   - Repetition of centering exercise
   - Affirmation
   - Closing activity

Since the format and its components remain virtually constant through all the sessions, these components deserve a closer look.

Group Rules and Rules Contract. Creating an atmosphere in which a group of children feel secure and willing to share thoughts and feelings is a major undertaking. Many children will have never participated in a group process before, so they'll be unaccustomed to the expectations and the boundaries of a group. Group rules ensure that all group members will be treated with the dignity and respect they deserve. Group rules also establish a standard of behavior for group members. They establish the expectation that children can be responsible for their behavior and their participation in the group. Review the material under Screening Candidates and Behavior Management in the next chapter for information on how to set limits and enforce consequences regarding the group rules.

The group leader presents the rules in contract form during the initial screening interview, makes sure the child understands them, and obtains a commitment from the child to follow them in group. Then, in the first group session, the group leader has all the children discuss and commit themselves to following the rules by signing their names to the contract. Rules are displayed in the group meeting room. For the first several sessions, the leader reviews them, making sure that the children understand them all. If the children's behavior deteriorates, then the leader can review the rules in the next sessions. The rules remind the children that they're safe in group, that the rules serve to protect them, and that all group members will behave as they've agreed to behave by signing the contract.

Centering Exercise. This exercise sets the stage for group work in a positive way. The techniques learned in the centering exercise, which include deep breathing and tensing and relaxing muscles as well as guided imagery, are not limited to group work only. Once mastered, children can use them in "real-life" situations. Repeated toward the end of a group session, the centering exercise not only reinforces learning but also enables the children to calm down—especially if intense feelings arose during the session—and helps them to get ready to return to their regular classroom. Some school boards have forbidden the use of guided imagery in counseling situations. If that is the case, you can teach the children the techniques of deep breathing and tensing and relaxing muscles without added imagery.

Feelings Check-in. During the feelings check-in the children learn to identify, own, and express feelings in appropriate ways. The group leader validates, accepts, and tolerates the children's feelings. For example, responding to a child who says he wants to hit his classmate, the group leader might say, "It sounds like you're feeling very angry. Can you tell us what you're angry about?" After the child responds, the group leader could continue, "Many children feel angry when a child does what Kenneth did. But it's not okay to use aggressive or violent behavior. Let's see if we can think of an assertive behavior skill that you could use; we'll be learning many of them in this group."

By accepting and validating feelings and by helping the children identify helpful ways to express feelings, the group leader consistently teaches that feelings aren't bad or dangerous, that they can be felt and expressed, and that they will pass. Thus, the feelings check-in functions both as a corrective and a therapeutic experience for the children. Even though children who are bullies tend to act not in anger but out of a need for power and domination, they tend to identify themselves not as bullies, but as having problems with anger. It's helpful to use that framework when teaching them how to replace aggressive behavior with assertive behavior. Many children who are victims of bullies are amply supplied with anger. They may be provocative victims who are aggressive themselves. The feelings check-in serves to help both groups of children learn better ways to handle feelings.

Review of the Basic Facts. Beginning with session 2, the basic facts learned in previous sessions are reviewed for understanding. When a child reads the basic fact, ask him or her to explain it. It the child cannot, use the Questions to Help Clarify the Basic Facts (see pages 230–234) to make sure the key concepts with each basic fact are covered. The clarification is provided to make the group more user-friendly for the group leader. This regular repetition and clarification is an effective technique to help even very young children learn and use the key concepts presented in the sessions.

Homework Assignment Review. In each session, you will give the students a homework assignment, which is designed to help them understand or practice what they have learned. The assignments are based on cognitive-behavioral theory and the principal of starting behavioral change by observing current behavior. Some assignments require group members simply to observe themselves, their friends, and their families, to see if anybody uses violent behavior. Others ask them to practice using the assertive behavior skills they have learned. The assignment is given at the end of each session, and it is reviewed at the beginning of the next session. The review, a go-around where the students report what they have observed or practiced, is an important component of this group. Being expected to put what they see or do into words will force the group members to be more observant. And hearing how other group members are trying to use their new skills provides encouragement and motivation for all. If a child has not done the homework, ask him or her to look back at the last week, think of one instance relevant to the homework, and do the assignment now in retrospect. Remember that behavior change starts with the smallest, concrete steps. Be sure to reinforce the students' ability to observe their violent behavior. Review the Behavior Management section on pages 38–39 if you want to use positive reinforcement to encourage the children to bring in completed homework assignments.

Story (Bibliotherapy). Bibliotherapy simply means "healing story." The story or bibliotherapy uses an appealing make-believe animal to present basic facts about violence. Most of the children will be able to identify easily with the characters without losing face. Even tough, streetwise children experience fun, warmth, and affection with the characters.

Discussion. Each session's story is followed by questions the leader may use to initiate group discussion. In the discussion, the children have the chance to process the story, and the group leader has the chance to make sure they understand the concepts and issues presented.

Activity. The activity in each session reinforces the material presented in the story. In a non-threatening way, it encourages the children to express their idea of violence, and helps them learn how to use the assertive behavior skills.

Basic Fact Worksheet. The Basic Fact Worksheet is a verbal, visual, and auditory tool that reinforces the basic facts the story has presented and the children have discussed. The worksheet is a cumulative learning tool, representing and adding to the basic facts each time the group meets. The worksheet also serves to build the children's self-esteem. Unlike worksheets the children might receive in a regular class in school (for example, an arithmetic worksheet), these worksheets are "fail-safe," designed to enable the children to get the "right" answer every time.

Homework Assignment. As described above, the homework assignment also reinforces the main objectives of the group session, by having the children observe their own behavior, or by asking them to practice an assertive behavior skill.

Affirmation. This gives the children a chance to end the group sessions on a positive note, even if intense feelings arose during the session. The affirmation reinforces the content presented in the session and helps the children learn to use assertive behavior skills.

Closing. The closing exercise helps the group develop a sense of bonding, cohesiveness, acceptance, and sharing. It allows for physical touch in a safe, nonthreatening atmosphere, which may be a new experience for many of the children. The same closing exercise concludes each session.

This structured format encourages the children to participate as fully as possible in the group process. Go-arounds, where everybody has a chance to describe art work and practice assertive behavior skills, are used extensively to make it easy for group members to share in a safe, nonthreatening way. Although the children are never forced to take part and are given the right to "pass," the format allows each group member at least three opportunities per session to speak and other, nonverbal opportunities to participate as well. The repeated structure in all group sessions provides a sense of predictability and consistency that is helpful in setting boundaries for these children.

Progression of Themes

In sessions 1 and 2 in the Trevor and Tiffany group, the program presents a new definition of violence, describes the characteristics of children who use aggressive behavior and of children who are victims of others who use aggressive behavior, and tells what is likely to happen to children when they grow up if they don't stop their use of aggressive behavior. In session 3, an adult intervenes in a situation common to bullies, and the children meet Mrs. Owl, who gives the value judgment that violent behavior is bad and will not be tolerated in schools. In sessions 4 through 8, the group program introduces guidelines to help children stop their aggressive behavior, and teaches nine assertive behavior skills to replace aggressive behavior, with many opportunities to practice them. Sessions 9 and 10 teach anger management and conflict resolution plans, and in session 11, the children have an opportunity to teach others what they have learned and have a small party to celebrate the end of the group.

Sessions 1 through 3 are nearly identical in both the Trevor and Tiffany group and the Daniel group. In the Daniel group, sessions 4 through 6 introduce the same nine assertive behavior skills that are introduced in Trevor and Tiffany, although much more emphasis is made on changing passive behavior to assertive behavior. In session 4, children are given a structured opportunity to practice standing tall, using body language in an assertive way. Sessions 7 and 8 give the children examples to use the assertive behavior skills in situations where they are being teased or left out. Sessions 9 through 11 are identical to those in the Trevor and Tiffany group.

These themes combine to create a program where violent behavior common to elementary school children is clearly described and labeled as bad and unacceptable, in a way that allows the children, both the bullies and victims, to save face. The group leader never describes Trevor and Tiffany as bad *dinosaurs*; instead, the leader describes their *behavior* as bad, and gives them many opportunities to learn to replace the aggressive behavior with more socially acceptable assertive behavior. Daniel is not described as weak or wimpy; instead he is described as peace-loving and as not having many alternatives to passive behavior.

The Trevor and Tiffany group program has the following sessions:

Session 1:   Trevor and Tiffany, the Tyrannosaurus Twins, Talk about Violent Behaviors in Schools
Session 2:   Trevor and Tiffany Learn Why Some Children Use Violence
Session 3:   Trevor and Tiffany Meet Mrs. Owl
Session 4:   Trevor and Tiffany Learn to Stop and Think, Check It Out, and Choose to Use Helpful Ways
Session 5:   Trevor and Tiffany Learn to Stand in Daniel's and Della's Shoes
Session 6:   Trevor and Tiffany Learn to Replace Their Aggressive Behavior with Assertive Behavior
Session 7:   Trevor and Tiffany Learn New Assertive Behavior Skills
Session 8:   Trevor and Tiffany Learn Assertive Body Language and Practice Assertive Behavior Skills
Session 9:   Trevor and Tiffany Learn Anger Management
Session 10: Trevor and Tiffany Learn to Resolve Conflicts
Session 11: Trevor and Tiffany Present What They Have Learned and Say Goodbye

In session 1, Trevor and Tiffany give the new definition of violence—*any mean word, look, sign, or act that hurts another person's body, feelings, or possessions.* They describe the behaviors typical of children who bully, behavior which is usually tolerated by schools: name calling, spreading rumors, yelling, threatening other children, tripping them, bumping into them, not letting them play. Finally, they describe the consequences of violent behavior: someone usually is hurt, either in their body, feelings, or possessions.

In session 2, Trevor and Tiffany describe characteristics and families of children who are violent, as well as children who are victims of other children's aggressive behavior. They describe the usual sequelae in adult life: poor performance in school and on jobs, alcohol or other drug use, bad marriages, and criminal records. They point out the reasons why children who are victims often do not tell adults of the behavior of other children.

In session 3, an adult, Mrs. Owl, intervenes when she sees Daniel being teased, setting a role model for teachers and school personnel. She tells Trevor that his behavior is violent, and is bad and will not be tolerated in school. She goes on to present three rules that all children can follow to prevent violent behavior in their school.

In session 4, Trevor and Tiffany describe the defenses (excuses) typically used by children who use aggressive behavior, and teach three guidelines to help children stop their aggressive behavior: Stop and Think, Check It Out, and Choose to Use Helpful Ways.

Session 5 introduces Trevor and Tiffany to the idea of empathy. The children are given the opportunity to stand in Daniel's and Della's shoes, to see what it feels like to be the victim of aggressive behavior. This is another factor in giving them a reason to change their behavior.

In session 6, Trevor and Tiffany learn the difference between passive, aggressive, and assertive behavior, and learn the assertive behavior skills of I Statements and Kill-Them-With-Kindness Sandwiches to help them begin to replace aggressive behavior with assertive behavior.

In session 7, Trevor and Tiffany learn six new assertive behavior skills: I Hear You Statements, Apologizing, Humor, Sound Bites, Nice Replies, and Broken Records, and in the activity are given opportunities to practice using them.

Session 8 introduces the assertive behavior skill of body language and gives the children an opportunity to change aggressive behavior to assertive behavior.

Session 9 teaches the children a plan for anger management; Session 10 teaches a plan for conflict resolution and provides a rehearsal for the presentation of session 11.

In session 11, the children present the basic facts to an audience of your choosing and then have a small party to celebrate the end of the group. The presentation is a simple way to meet a number of objectives. When children teach someone else the basic facts they have learned, their own learning increases, as does their self-esteem. The children's presentation also helps to raise the level of the audience's learning (whether the audience is a principal, a colleague, or a class of children and their teacher) about the issue of violence, and teaches them assertive behavior skills; it also encourages future referrals. The presentation is a powerful prevention tool. It allows the children to "save face" by having them present the basic facts as ways they, and everybody else in the school, can decrease school violence.

The Daniel group program has the following sessions.

Session 1:   Daniel the Dinosaur Talks about Violent Behaviors in Schools
Session 2:   Daniel the Dinosaur Learns Why Some Children Use Violence
Session 3:   Daniel the Dinosaur Meets Mrs. Owl
Session 4:   Daniel the Dinosaur Learns How to Stand Tall
Session 5:   Daniel the Dinosaur Learns How to Use I Statements and I Hear You Statements
Session 6:   Daniel the Dinosaur Learns New Assertive Behavior Skills
Session 7:   Daniel the Dinosaur Practices Assertive Behavior Skills in Situations Where He Is Being Teased
Session 8:   Daniel the Dinosaur Practices Assertive Behavior Skills and Learns Two Other Steps to Take When Being Left Out
Session 9:   Daniel the Dinosaur Learns Anger Management
Session 10: Daniel the Dinosaur Learns to Resolve Conflicts
Session 11: Daniel the Dinosaur Presents What He Has Learned and Says Goodbye

In session 1, Daniel gives the new definition of violence—*any mean word, look, sign, or act, that hurts another person's body, feelings, or possessions.* He describes the behaviors typical of children who bully—behavior that is usually tolerated by schools: name calling, spreading rumors, yelling, threatening other children, tripping them, bumping into them, not letting them play. Finally, he describes the consequences of violent behavior: someone usually is hurt in his or her body, feelings, or possessions.

In session 2, Daniel describes characteristics and families of children who are violent, as well as children who are victims of other children's aggressive behavior. He describes the usual sequelae in adult life: poor performance in school and on jobs, alcohol or other drug use, bad marriages, and criminal records. He points out the reasons why children who are victims often do not tell adults of the behavior of other children.

In session 3, an adult, Mrs. Owl, intervenes when she sees Daniel being teased, setting a role model for teachers and school personnel. She tells Trevor that his behavior is violent and is bad and will not be tolerated in his school. She goes on to present three rules that all children can follow to prevent violent behavior in their school.

In session 4, Daniel learns the difference between passive, aggressive, and assertive behavior, and learns how to stand tall. He learns the assertive body language of posture, eye contact, and tone of voice.

Session 5 clarifies for Daniel when he should go to an adult for help and when he should use an assertive behavior skill when someone is treating him violently. Daniel also learns the assertive behavior skills of I Statements and I Hear You Statements.

In Session 6, Daniel learns six new assertive behavior skills: Kill-Them-With-Kindness Sandwiches, Apologizing, Humor, Sound Bites, Nice Replies, and Broken Records; in the activity he is given opportunities to practice using them.

Session 7 provides Daniel with opportunities to use each of the assertive behavior skills in situations when he is being teased or called names.

Session 8 gives Daniel the chance to use the assertive behavior skills in situations when he is being left out and teaches two other steps he can use to take care of himself.

Session 9 teaches the children a plan for anger management; session 10 teaches a plan for conflict resolution and provides a rehearsal for the presentation of session 11.

In session 11, the children present the basic facts to an audience of your choosing and then have a small party to celebrate the end of the group. The presentation is a simple way to meet a number of objectives. When children teach someone else the basic facts they have learned, their own learning increases, as does their self-esteem. The children's presentation also helps to raise the level of the audience's learning (whether the audience is a principal, a colleague, or a class of children and their teacher) about the issue of violence and teaches them assertive behavior skills; it also encourages future referrals. The presentation is a powerful prevention tool. It allows the children to "save face" by having them present the basic facts as ways they, and everybody else in the school, can decrease school violence.

Displacement Communication

In its bibliotherapy, the group model uses a therapeutic technique called displacement communication (Kalter 1990) to help children learn to change their aggressive behavior while allowing them to save face. Since children who exhibit aggressive behavior have strong defenses, it is easier for them to realize that what other children (like Trevor and Tiffany, the dinosaurs) are doing is wrong, than to realize that they are showing bad behavior. Learning through the displacement of what Trevor and Tiffany learn, and through the situations and scenarios in the story and activities, the children can learn to put the assertive behavior skills into use in a way that doesn't threaten them. It is only when they do the homework assignment that they are encouraged to start changing their own behavior. Similarly, the displacement allows the children who are victims of other children's aggressive behavior to avoid embarrassment or humiliation by describing what happens to them.

Benefits of Use

Using this group model for aggressive children or children who are victims of aggressive children can benefit your school on a number of levels, including the logistics level, the individual level, and the system level.

The Logistics Level. Logistically, the model provides structure for new and untrained group leaders. The materials contained in the manual provide everything a leader will need to implement a group, including a self-referral group survey form for classroom surveys, a parental consent letter, a screening interview outline, and complete guidelines and all materials for each session.

The structure of the group format cuts down considerably on behavior problems during group session. Generally, children in elementary school enjoy participating in these groups and eagerly recommend them to their friends.

The Individual Level. Children who participate in the program have benefited in a variety of ways, including the following: (1) children's behavior in school improved, as evidenced by fewer trips to the office and fewer suspensions, and (2) children integrated concepts taught in the group into other situations. One classroom which had about five aggressive children was the audience for a presentation. Children from this class were in both the Trevor and Tiffany group and the Daniel group. The children reported that the entire class improved in decreasing and handling aggressive behavior after the presentation. One third-grade child in a Trevor and Tiffany group came up with one of the Nice Replies used in the manual: he said to a kindergarten child, "I'd like to fight with you, but you're too small for me to fight with. You'll have to get someone your own size." Another group member, a fifth-grade child who was a provocative victim in a Daniel group, came up with this Nice Reply: "I'd like to fight with you because you're messing with me, but I'm on probation, and I'm not allowed to fight." Children in the initial sessions of the Daniel group who looked very depressed, who could barely be understood, or who were dependent upon adults blossomed. They looked less depressed, could be understood clearly, and became much more independent by the end of the group. They were eager to give a presentation and did an excellent job.

The System Level. Since the group model recommends in-service programs for administrators and teachers about school violence, the entire system can benefit from using this group model.

The program will probably be more effective if the school has a schoolwide prevention plan in place. Teachers will already be using the same definition of violence described here; plans for intervention, for where to send the aggressive children, and for what to offer them to help them change their behavior will already be in place. This group is one program that will help them change behavior.

If the school does not have a schoolwide prevention plan, then an in-service will be a good way to raise the awareness and education levels of teachers and administrators about school violence. It may be an impetus for starting a schoolwide violence prevention plan. Feel free to use the Basic Facts List and the Assertive Behavior Skills as handouts.

Chapter 2

Implementing the Group Program

This chapter will help you implement the group program in your school, agency, or other counseling setting. The chapter includes information on acquiring administrative support, recruiting and training staff, developing a referral network, screening candidates, forming and scheduling groups, and behavior management. You will also find information on informed consent, confidentiality, and self-disclosure on the part of the group leaders. The chapter will also point out effective ways to follow up on the individual, group, and system levels. Finally, it will outline ways you can use the program in guidance counseling and family therapy.

As mentioned earlier, although schools may be able to reach the largest numbers of children, the program may be used in a variety of other settings as well. After deciding where it will best fit in your school's (or agency's) situation, you must undertake the task of getting it started. The first step in doing that is gaining administrative support.

Gaining Administrative Support

You need administrative support. Without it, the program can't exist, let alone prosper. Most administrators will be well aware of the need for groups for children who exhibit violent behavior, although some are offended by the term *bully*. Although the word *bully* is included in the manual, it is not used with the children in either group to avoid stereotyping. Because of the strong defenses, these children may not describe themselves as bullies, but most admit to getting into trouble and having trouble with anger. Describing this as a group to stop school violence and to help children replace aggressive behavior with assertive behavior should make it noncontroversial for principals, students, and their parents who will give permission for them to be in the group.

If a school is to support the program, the principal's backing is necessary. If principals establish this and other support groups as a priority, they will direct teachers to allow children to be removed from the classroom in order to participate. Likewise, principals will also be prepared to answer questions from parents who wonder why their child is being offered a chance to participate in a group to help children replace aggressive behavior with assertive behavior.

If necessary, offer an in-service to raise awareness levels. Use the Basic Facts List on page 229 as the basis for the information you give teachers and administrators. Describe the new definition of violence; why it is necessary for adults to intervene, even when the behavior is just name calling or social exclusion; and some of the assertive behavior skills you will be teaching. Most teachers will readily see how they can gain if their students decrease aggressive behavior. School staff members will feel good about referring students to groups that really work. Good groups will give both administrators and classroom teachers more free time to do their jobs. Refer to the implementation handbook for the *Respect & Protect*® program published by Hazelden for more information about in-services.

If you're blessed with wholehearted administrative approval, but you're in a school without a violence prevention program, it's still a good idea to provide in-service sessions for school personnel to acquaint them with the issues described above. The more adults in the school environment can help an aggressive child or a victim of an aggressive child process what he or she could have done instead of acting aggressively or passively, the more quickly the child will be able to change his or her behavior.

Staffing and Training

The authorization to provide prevention and intervention services for aggressive students can come from the superintendent or school board in the form of violence prevention. The program will be enhanced if implemented by and with trained personnel. Effective staff may include members of Student Assistance Programs and Core Teams, social workers, psychologists, guidance counselors, chemical dependence counselors, nurses, and teachers—all of whom can be trained to lead groups to help aggressive children. Although you'll have to depend on the staffing patterns of your school or agency, keep in mind that the needs of the children will be better met if personnel from various helping professions work together—not engage in territorial battles—to provide services.

The better trained your personnel, the better they'll be able to meet the needs of aggressive children. Training should include the following:

- information about the goals of the program
- education about the definition of violence
- information about how schools have tolerated violent behavior
- the characteristics of families of aggressive children and the children who are victims of aggressive children
- why it is important to help children change their behavior now, since otherwise they will continue to be violent when they grow up
- the need for school personnel and other adults to intervene when they see nonphysical violent behavior
- the assertive behavior skills that children will use to replace aggressive behavior
- instruction on how to lead groups
- ongoing supervision

One training model might require twenty hours of in-service on violence and eleven hours of supervised experience leading groups. Another model might consist of fifteen hours of experiential in-service, during which staff members lead and participate in the program's group session together. After this experience, they would be ready to co-lead a group with a certified worker. A third model might have a trainer provide staff development for new group leaders and in-services for school faculty at the beginning of the school year. The trainer then can assist new group leaders in developing referrals and screening potential group members. The trainer also leads a group, with a new leader observing. When the group is repeated during the second half of the school year, the new leader facilitates the group, with the trainer observing and providing supervision.

A fourth model meets the needs of professionals who are implementing this program by themselves. This model combines the expertise of different professionals as group co-leaders: for example, a teacher can lead a group with an agency therapist. The complementary nature of skills, training, and experience will again better serve the needs of children.

Finally, you can also check your local resources for facilities that provide training. These may include state and local health and education departments, colleges and universities, and social welfare agencies. You can also find help by turning to a national organization, such as Hazelden, which specializes in training.

Developing Referrals

Once you've gained administrative support and have begun training group leaders for the program, begin to develop a list of children who could benefit from being part of a group. If your school has implemented a comprehensive violence prevention plan, referral procedures should already be in place.

If not, you can build this list by looking to a number of referral sources, including the following:

- school counseling/social work case histories
- teachers and administrators and other school staff
- disciplinary referrals
- parents
- schoolchildren themselves
- broader community

School Counseling/Social Work Case Histories. Ask school counselors or social workers to recommend potential group members from their case loads.

Teachers and Administrators. Look for referrals from any and all members of the school staff: building administrators, teachers, maintenance personnel, secretaries, Core Teams, school nurses, and bus drivers. With the help of your in-service, all school staff will be able to recognize children who use aggressive behavior. By understanding how the group program operates and what it teaches, staff can refer children appropriately.

Disciplinary referrals. Again, schools with a systemwide plan in place will automatically refer children who have had repeated referrals for aggressive behavior. If not, the group leader can ask the principal to look through the disciplinary referrals for appropriate group referrals.

Parents. Some referrals will come directly from parents who might disclose during an interview or conference their stress over their child's aggressive behavior or their child's victimization by other children. Remember that parents of children who have aggressive behavior (1) tend to lack a close, nuturing relationship with their child; (2) do not set limits on their child's aggressive behavior toward adults or toward peers; and (3) tend to discipline by overreactive emotional and physical outbursts. Some parents will welcome the chance to have their children learn to replace aggressive behavior with assertive behavior and might benefit themselves from a parenting class to learn how to set limits appropriately for their children. Parents of victims tend to be overprotective. They may not know the assertive behavior skills to teach their children.

Schoolchildren themselves. Another referral source is your school's student body. Self-referrals are likely to begin as soon as youngsters become aware of the Daniel group and the Trevor and Tiffany group because students will recognize the programs' value. Also offer classroom presentations on the Della the Dinosaur group, which is for children from violent families. Once the children understand what the groups are about, they'll find it easier to self-refer.

Simply arrange to visit a classroom. Begin your presentation by announcing to the children that you will be offering some groups during the school year and that you want the children to know about them. To give the children a taste for what happens in group, lead them in a centering exercise (for example, "Stop and Breathe to Five," page 52).

Introduce Trevor and Tiffany and Daniel by showing the children the stuffed toy dinosaurs you purchased to use when leading the groups. Describe some things about Trevor and Tiffany: they go to Swamp Elementary School and take the Dinosaur school bus to get there. Trevor likes math and Tiffany likes social studies. At school, they have to stand in the lunch line to wait for their lunches; Trevor's favorite school lunch is caveman pizza. The boy dinosaurs play Dinosaur Dodge Ball during recess, and the girl dinosaurs practice jump rope. Trevor and Tiffany are the strongest and almost always the meanest (every child who has seen *Jurassic Park* knows that velociraptors are the meanest) dinosaurs in the swamp. Trevor and Tiffany like to be the boss, and sometimes they use violence to get their way. Trevor sometimes yells at the other dinosaurs, especially a new dinosaur named Daniel, a brontosaurus, who just moved to Swamp School. Once Trevor yelled at Daniel and threatened him to get him to move out of *his* seat on the bus. Sometimes he trips Daniel when they play Dinosaur Dodge Ball. Sometimes he cuts in front of Daniel in the lunch line and steals his caveman pizza. Tiffany calls Daniel's sister Della names, like Scaleface, and tells the other dinosaur girls that Della has the disease of Scaleface. Then, Tiffany and the other girls won't let Della jump rope with them.

Ask the children for some examples of violence they have seen in school. Expect the children to describe hitting and kicking, and bringing guns or knives to school. Tell the children that they are correct, but the things that Trevor and Tiffany do are violent as well. Violence is any mean word, look, act, or sign that hurts another person's body, feelings, or possessions. Say that there is one main consequence of violent behavior: someone, like Daniel, gets hurt.

Describe how once Trevor and his friends Stevie Stegosaurus and Michael Triceratops were teasing Daniel, calling him Brontostupid. But this time, Mrs. Owl (show the children your stuffed owl, on whom you have placed pearls and a pair of glasses) saw Trevor and his friends teasing. She made them stop teasing Daniel and then she taught them that what they were doing was violent. She said that violent behavior is bad and is unacceptable at their school. Then, she worked with both Tiffany and Trevor and taught them how to change their behavior from being violent to being assertive. Explain that assertive behavior is a way to stand up for yourself without hurting anyone else. Some of the assertive behavior skills she taught them were I Statements, when you say how you feel, I Hear You Statements, when you tell the other person you heard how they feel, and Kill-Them-With-Kindness Sandwiches, when you say something nice, say no, or state your point of view, and then say something nice again. They also learned to use Sound Bites, and Nice Replies, like "I'd like to fight with you, but I'm on probation, and I'm not allowed to get into any more fights."

Say that Mrs. Owl also worked with Daniel, and taught him these and other assertive behavior skills, like Body Language—talking clearly while you stand up straight and look the other person in the eye in a friendly way. Using these assertive behavior skills helped Daniel to feel better about himself, and he was able to remove himself from the things Trevor did to him. He also learned that it was okay to tell an adult like a teacher or parent when Trevor wouldn't let him alone; it didn't mean he was a tattletale, and it was a way for the adults to let Trevor know his behavior was bad and not acceptable. That was the only way that the adults could help Trevor learn to change his aggressive behavior.

Tell the students that if they want to be in a group to learn how to stop school violence and how to change their aggressive behavior, like Trevor and Tiffany, and to replace it with assertive behavior, they can sign up to be in the group called Trevor and Tiffany, the Tyrannosaurus Twins. If they would like to learn assertive behavior skills so they can stand up for themselves without hurting anyone else, then they can sign up for the group called Daniel the Dinosaur.

Continue the presentation by introducing Della. Point out that Della is Daniel's sister, and the story in the Della group is about Daniel's and Della's family before they moved to Swamp School. Also point out that the Della group is for children who are concerned about violence in the family, or who want to handle their own anger in better ways. Session plans for the Della group are found in *Facilitating a Violence Prevention Support Group: For Kids Dealing with Someone Else's Anger.*

Be sure to bring the various stuffed animals along to the presentation. Children, even upper elementary children, enjoy holding onto the various stuffed animals. Presenting the groups through the animal characters is a form of displacement communication. Children seem eager to refer themselves when the groups are presented in this way.

After you have finished, hand out your Self-Referral Group Survey Form (see page 238).

(Avoid handing them out at the beginning so the children will not make them into paper airplanes.) Ask each child to sign his or her name on the form, and if they want to be in any of the groups, to mark the group or groups they want to be in. If they want to be in more than one group, ask them to number the groups, with number 1 indicating the group they want to be in the most. Since the number of self-referrals tends to be high, be sure to tell the children that not everyone may be in a group right away. You will decide which groups to offer depending on your time and the needs of the children. Also tell the children that you will be meeting with children individually before starting the group.

Broader community. Sharing information about the group program with parents, professionals, and other concerned adults at a community forum regarding violence may lead to referrals from the broader community. For example, once therapists from treatment centers and mental health agencies know about your group program, they will be able to refer some of their clients to it.

When it comes to referrals, the rule of thumb is "the broader the referral network, the better." The broader the referral network, the better the chance aggressive children and their victims will be reached and helped.

Screening Candidates

No matter how children are referred for membership in a Trevor and Tiffany or Daniel group, each candidate should be screened individually before you grant membership. The screening process consists of a brief interview that details demographic factors, that child's adjustment and attitude toward school, and the child's family or living situation. (See Screening Interview Outline on page 240). If the child is self-referred, screening will help gather specific information about the child.

During the screening interview, make the child as comfortable as possible, stress confidentiality, and ask the child his or her reasons for self-referral, reassuring the child that you will not ask such questions in front of other group members. Listen respectfully to the child's reasons for self-referral, remembering that aggressive children may not identify themselves as bullies or as aggressive, but more likely will describe problems with their temper or with anger. Allow them this defense, knowing that one thrust of the group is to label defenses through the displacement, and to decrease their use.

If children are referred because of discipline problems, screen them in order to form a relationship with them before the group begins. Help them see that using aggressive behavior causes them to hurt others and may cause them to have problems later in life. Encourage them to see the group as a way to learn what Trevor and Tiffany learn—how to replace their aggressive behavior with assertive behavior.

Some children who are victims are very open about the hurt and anger they feel when other children tease them or don't let them play. But some are embarrassed or deny or minimize their problems. Allow them their defenses, but encourage them to join the Daniel group to learn ways to get along with others better, ways that would help all children.

If you feel that a child belongs in a group, discuss the group process, including group format and session topics, with the child. Describing the format will prepare the child for what will happen in group and will reassure the child about the safety of the group. Show the child a copy of the Group Rules Contract (see page 59). Explain the rules and tell the child that to be in the group, he or she must make a commitment to attend every group session and to keep all the rules. Tell the child that at the first group session all group members will be asked to sign a copy of the Group Rules Contract. Also take this opportunity to explain the consequences for not following the group rules. You can decide on your own consequences, but one option is to give one warning, and if the bad behavior continues, the child will leave. The child can return the following week, and again will be given one warning for bad behavior. If the behavior continues, the consequence will be that the child will leave the group and will not be able to return. Making these limits and consequences clear at this point sets the stage for good behavior during the group sessions.

Unless this is a mandated group, ask the child if he or she wants to be in the group. If a child is adamant about not wanting to be in the group, it is probably better not to include him or her. Agreeing to be in the group gives the group members a sense of ownership and investment in the group. Although most children agree to be in the group and to follow the rules, the few who are coerced to join a group will tend to remain resistant throughout all the group sessions.

The prospect of screening every group candidate individually may seem a bit daunting. But such screening isn't just for your sake and the program's sake. It's also a valuable experience for the child. The screening may also serve as a case-finding procedure, during which sexual or physical abuse may come to light and can be dealt with properly. Naturally, cases of sexual or physical abuse should be reported immediately to appropriate authorities. The screening may reveal that the child needs a group experience regarding a family issue such as parental chemical dependence, divorce or separation, or violence. If such is the case, you can make the appropriate referral.

Acquiring Informed Parental Consent

To ensure a group's integrity and success, you need to acquire consent from the parents whose children are candidates for group membership. Procedures for acquiring parental consent must consider the children's needs, the parents' rights to privacy, the school's desire to help its students, and the provisions of the law so as to avoid any legal action being taken against the school.

The simplest way to get informed consent is to have the school mail a letter to the parents of all prospective group members that clearly but simply

- describes the program and group process
- encourages parents to allow their child to receive the services the program and group can provide
- provides a permission form that parents can return to the school (see the Parental Consent Form on page 239.)

If you feel that parents will be resistant, visit with them personally to talk about it. Take along the toy animal you will use in group and share with the parents what Trevor and Tiffany or Daniel will learn in a fun and nonjudgmental way from Mrs. Owl. Explain the group format and progression of themes. Explain that you're hoping to help the children reduce aggressive behavior, or in the case of the Daniel group, to help them learn how to stand up for themselves in a way that doesn't hurt anyone else but does help them feel better about themselves. Once the program is explained well to parents, few are likely to refuse permission for their child to take part.

There will be times when you, another group leader, or another school staff member will identify a particular child who could benefit by participating in a group but whose parents refuse to allow it. If you've clearly explained the purpose and format of the program to the parents and they still don't want their child involved, there are still two ways you can help the child. First, make sure that the child is present for any in-school presentation about the program, either one you offer as a recruitment tool or one that students themselves give in the presentation described in session 11. Children can begin to integrate facts, concepts, and specific skills even when the presentation is brief. Second, you can refer that child to the school counseling services for individual assistance. Some parents will give permission for the children to learn this information individually, but not in a group.

Forming and Scheduling the Groups

You know from your own experience that the best groups—of any kind—are made up of different individuals with varying temperaments and personalities. The same is true for the Trevor and Tiffany and Daniel groups. Although the children referred for the Trevor and Tiffany group will all have aggressive behavior, if possible do not form a group with children who are all hyperactive as well as aggressive. Or, try to find a child who has more ability to admit his or her aggressive behavior to temper the children who may be more well defended. In the Daniel group, you may find yourself with a provocative victim mixed in with very quiet, shy children. You will be surprised at how the shy children become more assertive, especially after you teach the skills of body language.

Be careful about mixing children from different grade levels into a single group. It's best not to have a spread larger than one grade level. Kindergarten and first-grade groups can be effective, but kindergarten to second grade is probably too great a spread.

Group size is also determined by the age of group members. Groups of younger children should be smaller, since they require more time, help, and individual attention: no more than four per group if they are kindergarten, first, or second grade. If they are third through sixth grade, five or six is the maximum number recommended for the Trevor and Tiffany and Daniel groups because of the nature of the children and the time needed for each child to practice all of the assertive behavior skills.

The location, size, and atmosphere of a group's meeting room are very important in establishing a safe, welcoming space for children to open up and take risks. Generally, classrooms aren't the most satisfactory places for group meetings; they're almost always too large and are filled with too many distractions. Ideally, the meeting room needs to be small, comfortable, and quiet, a place where interruptions and potential distractions are minimal. Privacy is essential so youngsters won't be afraid that others outside the room can see or hear them. Seating each child at a table will help avoid fidgety behavior and simplify writing and drawing activities.

Survey your school facility for a good place for group meetings. Obviously, such a space is often a premium in a school setting, so remember that your most important considerations are privacy, quiet, and regular availability.

Besides matters of space, scheduling must also deal with matters of time. The group sessions are designed to last approximately forty-five to sixty minutes. Plan to hold them weekly so that the children have time to integrate the insight and support gained from each session. Weekly sessions are also less likely to interfere with the children's studies and other activities. Try to schedule group meetings for elementary-aged children on the same day, at the same time, and in the same place each week.

In all matters of scheduling, administrative support is an invaluable aid to help foster teacher cooperation in releasing students from regular classes. Remember, however, that co-operation is a two-way street. Let children and teachers know that students participate in the group on the condition that they make up all missed work. Give teachers a schedule of group meetings so that they'll know in advance what class a child will miss, won't plan field trips or tests for those times, and can make arrangements for the child to make up missed schoolwork.

Remember when you lead these groups that your preparation should take place before the children arrive for the group. When children enter the group room, they should see you sitting calmly at the table, with each child's folder at his or her place, with all the new materials already placed inside, and a pencil and box of crayons on top of the folder. Leaders who are frantically placing the current week's materials in the folders and reviewing the chapter as the children arrive are setting themselves up for a chaotic group.

Behavior Management

Remember as you lead groups for children who use aggressive behavior and for their victims, that they have already experienced a failure of adults to set clear limits and enforce consequences for them. You do not want to repeat that mistake. When you screen the children and discuss the group rules with them, and obtain a commitment from them to follow the rules, you are setting the stage for good behavior during all the group sessions. The screening interview is also a good time to explain the consequences for not following the rules. You can decide on your own consequences, but one option is to explain that if they break a rule, you will give them one warning. If they continue to break the rule, you will ask them to leave the group for that session. They can return to group the following week, but if they break a rule, they will again be given one warning. If they continue to break the rule, they will be asked to leave, and this time they will not be able to return. Leaders who do not follow through on the consequences they set are guilty of enabling the children to have bad behavior, and the other children in the group wonder why you do not follow through with what you said you were going to do. You should repeat the limits and consequences you have adopted when asking the children to sign the Group Rules Contract on page 59.

Besides setting clear expectations of behavior, and setting limits and enforcing consequences, another way to promote good group behavior is by positive reinforcement. If children have been unruly, at the start of the session review the group rules and tell them that if they can follow the rules more closely today, you will give them a prize (such as pencils, erasers, stickers, and so on) at the end of the group. Some leaders use dinosaur rubber stamps and stamp a child's hand at the end of the session.

The homework assignments in these group manuals are another opportunity to use positive reinforcement. If you want, you can tell the children in session 1 that you will give each child a simple prize when they bring in the assignment completed and will offer a bigger prize (candy bars seem to be good motivators) if they complete a certain number or all of the assignments. If you decide not to provide this reinforcement, the children will probably not bring in completed assignments. However, during the assignment review, you can ask them to look back at the past week and choose one situation to process the homework during the group.

Assuring Group Confidentiality

Confidentiality is the cornerstone of safe and supportive groups. To be able to admit their aggressive behavior, or their feelings about being the victims of other children's aggressive behavior, the children must know that what they say will be kept in confidence, to keep them from "losing face." It's important to realize that the children will not open up if they think that what they share will become common knowledge around school. Group confidentiality, therefore, must be an absolute guarantee.

This group model not only guarantees confidentiality but also adds a "plus" to it. The children's ability to observe their aggressive behavior is considered to be a first step in changing their behavior and replacing it with assertive behavior. The children themselves are never labeled as bad, nor are the animal characters Tiffany and Trevor; rather it is their violent behavior that is labeled bad and unacceptable. The group leaders provide corrective experiences for the children by setting firm limits on aggressive behavior, and especially by teaching them assertive behavior skills. Care is taken not to embarrass or humiliate children who are victims of other aggressive children.

In setting up groups, therefore, take extra care to assure and protect confidentiality. The children must realize that outside of the group sessions they may not discuss who else is in their group or what they say. Children can, however, discuss the facts and information they learn during group. The group leaders must remember their responsibilities as well. Except in cases where the law requires such revelation (for example, where a group leader suspects that a child is being physically or sexually abused, or is suicidal or homicidal), it is inappropriate for a group leader to reveal to others anything a child may share. It's a good idea to inform the children of this at the very first session.

When it comes to sharing information about the group with classroom teachers, follow the same guidelines as for the children: you obviously have to tell teachers who is in the group; feel free to share as much information about what you teach in group as you can. However, it is probably not appropriate to break confidentiality on personal or family issues that children might bring up.

Self-Disclosing by Leaders

Since the children aren't required or asked to self-disclose, should group leaders self-disclose? If used correctly, self-disclosure can be a useful group technique with children in the fourth grade and up. Even so, leaders should be very cautious and think carefully before self-disclosing. Sharing facts about one's personal life is appropriate only if it is positive role modeling or if it will help illustrate a point effectively. However, leaders should never employ self-disclosure for purposes of eliciting the same from children, nor should they use the group for personal therapy. For example, leaders must not express feelings or share experiences that they haven't adequately resolved or dealt with themselves. From a developmental perspective, self-disclosure is a poor device to use with younger children (grades K–3), who are too egocentric to benefit from such information. Group leaders steer a surer course by focusing on the curriculum and listening to what the children have to say. If you're ever in doubt about whether or not to self-disclose, a good rule of thumb is to trust your doubt and don't.

Role Modeling by Leaders

Although group leaders should make their own decision regarding self-disclosure, the program does ask leaders to share of themselves several times during each group session. Leaders act as role models for important components. Leaders begin the go-around for the feelings check-in, the affirmation, and the closing activity of each session. During the feelings check-in, leaders act as role models by sharing appropriate feelings and facts, such as, "I'm glad to see you" or "I'm feeling sad because my dog died." During the affirmation, leaders model observing violent behaviors in schools and show how to use the various assertive behavior skills. Overall, it's important to follow the rule of thumb described above. Never share a feeling or issue that you have not dealt with or resolved adequately. Doing so would be poor role modeling.

Following Up Group Participation

Some children who participate in the program's groups will require further services. Children with severe aggressive behavior will probably require more than one series of group sessions to show real consistent behavior change. Realizing this, be sure to make further help available. That help can come in the form of individual, group, or system follow-up.

Individual Follow-up. A counselor can continue to see the children individually. Follow-up counseling sessions can help them to learn to use the assertive behavior skills in situations they encounter.

Group Follow-up. Many children with aggressive behavior or who are victims of children with aggressive behavior may have other life stresses, such as parental chemical dependence, separation or divorce, or violence. Such children might benefit from participating in a group geared specifically to address those issues.

Be aware, however, that children should probably not participate in more than one group at a time. Instead, encourage them to spread their participation over one or two years.

System Follow-up. Children with particularly intense violent behavior problems may require the services of a schoolwide helping plan as follow-up to their participation in a group. Such services can include any or all of the following: (1) individual counseling; (2) successive group experiences; (3) a proactive schoolwide plan for anger management (see the Background and Guidelines section for session 9 on pages 165–166); (4) participation in a peer counseling program; and (5) frequent consultation between counselor and teachers and other school staff to enable them to help children use the assertive behavior skills instead of aggressive behavior. Of course, recognize that you may want or need to refer a child or family for outside therapy.

Using the Program in Guidance Counseling

In a school that does not have a comprehensive schoolwide violence prevention program, guidance counselors and other professionals can still use this manual's Basic Facts List and assertive behavior skills not only when working with children in groups but also when working with children individually. The manual's clear definition of violence, and clear limits about the use of any kind of violence helps the counselor set clear boundaries for children individually. And the assertive behavior skills help them know what to do to help children change their behavior. Leading these groups tends to empower counselors in individual counseling with children, since the assertive behavior skills are useful techniques for most children, and indeed, for most adults.

Guidance counselors who have led these groups have used the group material in classroom guidance as well. They report that teachers see immediately the usefulness of the definition of violence, and the clear limit setting, as well as of the assertive behavior skills. They report that children who have participated in the program's groups are usually actively involved in the classroom discussion, which reveals that children truly do integrate crucial concepts presented by the program. (For example, "Children who are hurt by other children are often afraid to tell adults; then they let the other children get away with their mean and violent behavior.") Counselors generally report that leading these groups gives them a sense of greater competence, effectiveness, and empowerment.

Using the Program in Family Therapy

The program's group model works not only in schools, mental health facilities, community agencies, and court systems, it also works well in family therapy with families in which children (or parents) exhibit aggressive behavior.

By using the group material, therapists can use the displacement of the stories and scenarios to help parents become aware of their own aggressive behavior and teach them the necessity of setting limits on their children's aggressive behavior. Parents can learn to look at the situation standing in the other person's shoes and learn to use assertive behavior skills, anger management, and conflict resolution themselves. Then, they will be able to reinforce the child using these skills at home.

The group manuals *Facilitating a Violence Prevention Support Group: For Kids Who Bully* and *Facilitating a Violence Prevention Support Group: For Kids Who Are Bullied* were developed for caring professionals like you who want to stem the growth of school violence and the effects of school violence. These group manuals will help you give your students the information they need to begin to change their use of aggressive behavior or their reactions to the aggressive behavior of others. You can be an important positive factor in the lives of children.

Part Three

Session Plans

Group Guide for Daniel the Dinosaur

Group Guide for Daniel the Dinosaur

Daniel the Dinosaur group educates and empowers children in grades K–6 who are the victims of aggressive behavior to replace their passive or aggressive behavior with assertive behavior.

This guide contains eleven group session plans for facilitating a support group for elementary-aged children who are victims of aggressive children.

Session 1:   Daniel the Dinosaur Talks about Violent Behaviors in Schools
Session 2:   Daniel the Dinosaur Learns Why Some Children Use Violence
Session 3:   Daniel the Dinosaur Meets Mrs. Owl
Session 4:   Daniel the Dinosaur Learns How to Stand Tall
Session 5:   Daniel the Dinosaur Learns How to Use I Statements and I Hear You Statements
Session 6:   Daniel the Dinosaur Learns New Assertive Behavior Skills
Session 7:   Daniel the Dinosaur Practices Assertive Behavior Skills in Situations Where He Is Being Teased
Session 8:   Daniel the Dinosaur Practices Assertive Behavior Skills and Learns Two Other Steps to Take When Being Left Out
Session 9:   Daniel the Dinosaur Learns Anger Management
Session 10: Daniel the Dinosaur Learns to Resolve Conflicts
Session 11: Daniel the Dinosaur Presents What He Has Learned and Says Goodbye

Each plan begins with the **Objectives** section. The section sets a clear direction for the group session.

The **Preparation** section, which follows, lists materials needed and gives directions for getting ready for the session. (Note: when directions in this section call for copies of various materials, most may be found in blackline master form at the end of each session. Other support materials, such as the Screening Interview Outline and the Parental Consent Form, are found in part four of this manual, "Support Materials," pages 199–242. Materials provided there include the Basic Fact Posters. These posters make excellent teaching aids when copied and laminated or made into transparencies. They are used to review the basic facts each week.)

The **Background and Guidelines** section will enrich your understanding of the session's focus and key concepts, as well as guide you through the plan itself.

For the most part, the plan's structure follows the same format for each session and unfolds in three stages. **Beginning the Session** is the first stage and includes a review of group rules, a centering exercise, a feelings check-in (session 1 substitutes an icebreaker), and a review of the basic facts learned so far and of the homework assignment (beginning in session 2). The second stage, **Exploring the Story**, includes the story, discussion, activity, new basic facts, and homework assignment. **Wrapping Up** is the third stage and includes a repetition of a centering exercise, an affirmation, and a closing activity.

To ensure the best results in leading the sessions, you'll want to find appealing and cuddly stuffed toy animals to portray Trevor, Tiffany, Daniel, and Mrs. Owl. In the story, Mrs. Owl wears a pair of glasses and a pearl necklace, so you may want to dress your animal or puppet up accordingly.

This format provides the students with a total experience that is structured as well as welcoming and accepting, instructional as well as creative and enjoyable, challenging as well as affirming and fun. Since the format remains the same for each session, it meets the needs students have for structure, consistency, predictability, and fun. Each group session is designed to take approximately forty-five to sixty minutes, but can be shortened or extended to meet local circumstances.

If you are a new group leader, you should follow up each session by filling out a copy of the Process and Progress Form (see page 235). This form enables you to evaluate the session's effectiveness and to track the students' progress. It also serves as a useful tool when training new group leaders. If you are an experienced leader, you may follow up each session by filling out the Progress Notes (see pages 236–237). No matter what your experience is, it is a good idea to keep some form of notes on each session.

In this manual, session 11, the last session, combines a presentation with a small party to celebrate the end of the group. In the presentation, the children present the basic facts they've learned about stopping school violence and replacing aggressive behavior with assertive behavior to an invited audience. Use the Basic Fact Review in session 10 as a practice session to help the group members rehearse their presentation. To guarantee success, read the Background and Guidelines for sessions 10 and 11 now so that you can plan ahead for the presentation.

These session plans have been carefully crafted and tested. Use them carefully, creatively, and confidently. Everything you need is here.

Session 1

Daniel the Dinosaur Talks about Violent Behaviors in Schools

Objectives

To help the students:

- learn a definition of violence
- recognize four violent behaviors that happen in elementary schools
- identify one consequence of violent behavior

Preparation

- If you want to use them, make a copy of each of the fifteen Basic Fact Posters (see pages 213–228). If possible, laminate the posters or make transparencies.
- Make a copy of the Group Rules Contract (see page 59) for each student. To save time at the copy machine, also make copies of each of the Activity Sheets, the Handouts, the Basic Fact Worksheets, and the Homework Assignments for all of the sessions.
- Copy the group rules onto a large sheet of posterboard that you can display in the group meeting space during this and future sessions.
- Have a large manila folder for each student; print the student's name on the folder.
- Include in each student's folder:
  –a 3" X 5" lined index card
  –the Group Rules Contract
  –Activity Sheet 1 (Daniel Puppet), which you may want to pre-cut and glue before the session
  –Activity Sheet 1A (One Consequence of Violent Behavior in Your School)
  –the Basic Facts List (see page 229), stapled to the inside of the folder, on the left side, for easy reference

- Place the folder, a pencil, and crayons or markers at each student's place.
- Make a poster to use during the session's icebreaker. On newsprint, list the following questions:
  –What is your name?
  –Your age?
  –Your grade?
  –What neighborhood do you live in?
  –What is your favorite sport and sports team?
  –What is your favorite food?
  –What is your favorite TV show and movie?
- Have a chalkboard or flip chart available to list answers in the Discussion section.
- Read through the session plan before meeting.

Background and Guidelines

This session serves several functions. First, it introduces the children to the experience of participation in a group. In the screening interview, you will have discussed the group format, the subjects of the sessions, and the group rules, to prepare the children for your expectations of behavior. In this first session, you will want to provide a warm, welcoming atmosphere in which the children know they are safe and can learn new behavior in a protected environment.

Many of the children who will participate in a Daniel the Dinosaur group appear to be meek, passive, and depressed; others will be provocative victims who themselves show agitated and aggressive behavior; others will appear to be dependent and clingy. Because of the entitlement shown by bullies, that they can do anything they want to their peers, and the tolerance of adults, both at home and at school, of allowing bullies to engage in name calling, intimidation, harassment, spreading rumors, gossip, and social exclusion, many of these children show resignation or fatalism about their plight. They may have been told to toughen up, or not to provoke others, or to stop being aggressive themselves. They may not believe that you will be able to teach them anything that will help them.

In contrast, many of the children who participate in a Trevor and Tiffany group for children with aggressive behavior will have had numerous disciplinary referrals. Typically, they will not be able to admit that they use aggressive behavior using the defenses typical of people who have aggressive behavior: *denial* ("I didn't do anything"), *blaming* ("He made me do it"), *rationalizing* ("I only called him a name because he was picking on my sister"), and *minimizing* ("I only swung at him with my jacket; I didn't really hit him"). It's rare for children to describe themselves as bullies; they are more likely to identify that they have a problem with anger. Because the word *bully* tends to have a negative, judgmental connotation, it is not used in either the Daniel or the Trevor and Tiffany group. Instead, violent behavior is clearly defined and described, in an objective way, but also with the clearly stated value judgment that it is wrong to act in a violent way. However, nowhere are Trevor and Tiffany, the aggressive dinosaurs, described as bad; it is their behavior that is described and judged as bad and not acceptable.

In the same way, Daniel is not identified as a victim, which carries a negative, judgmental connotation. Instead, he is described as a dinosaur who is hurt by Trevor, who uses aggressive behavior. He is not described as bad, nor is his passive behavior described as weak or wimpy. But Mrs. Owl does teach Daniel new ways to behave that will help him feel good about himself when he has to deal with an aggressive dinosaur like Trevor.

It is important for you as the group leader to maintain the distinction between a child and his or her behavior. You want to be accepting of the children, while not accepting their behavior, whether they are bullies or victims. It is this acceptance of the children that will enable them to feel safe with you and more open to learning the alternatives to aggressive or passive behavior. The displacement communication provided through the stories, discussion questions, and activities will allow the children to learn and adopt new definitions of violence without feeling threatened. The displacement communication allows you to deal with violent behavior typical of children without attacking their defenses directly.

In this session, it is probably not a good idea to use direct communication, where you comment on the child's behavior directly, unless you are a leader who has worked extensively with the children prior to starting the group and have developed the necessary relationship with them so that they can accept your comments without feeling threatened. In later sessions, as you learn more about the children by their comments before and during the sessions, you may be able to comment on their behavior, comparing it to Trevor's and Tiffany's, or to Daniel's, and processing the skills learned in the group on their experiences. Then, it might be appropriate to label their defenses directly. In the Trevor and Tiffany group, this is easy to do since they are labeled as excuses in the explanation of Basic Fact 7, "No matter what **excuse** they use, it is not okay for children to hurt other children by words, signs, looks, or acts." Children seem able to quickly list excuses for violent behavior typically given by children. If you are a new leader, or are leading this group for the first time, you might want to follow the group material exactly throughout all eleven sessions.

The second major function of session 1 is to help children reconsider their definition of violence. Most children describe violent behavior as bringing guns or knives to school and killing or stabbing someone. They rarely list the "negative action" Olweus (1994) describes: name calling, teasing, ridiculing, threatening, spreading rumors, picking on someone, or not letting someone play with you. In schools where this group is one component of a schoolwide violence prevention program, children will probably have already learned this new, broader, all-encompassing definition of violence. In schools where this group is being used on its own, it will probably be new to the children, their teachers, and parents. If the children disagree with you about labeling name calling and social exclusion as violent, generalize that many people agree that violence only begins with physical damage. But as you will reiterate when you review Basic Fact 1 in future sessions, you are using a new definition, "**Violence** is any mean word, look, sign, or act, that **hurts** a person's body, feelings, or possessions." Children in the Daniel group tend to readily accept this definition.

Whether this group is given as a solo intervention or as part of a schoolwide violence prevention program, you will enhance the learning of the children if you share the material you are presenting in the group with their teachers and parents. In-services for teachers and workshops for parents would offer wonderful opportunities for you to present the material. At minimum, you can give the teachers and parents the Basic Facts List (see page 229) and Handout 7, Assertive Behavior Skills to Use When Being Teased (see pages 146–147).

The last main function of session 1 is to introduce the concept that violent behavior has consequences. Olweus' research shows that bullies have little empathy for their victims, and since much bullying behavior is tolerated by parents and schoolteachers and administrators, the bullies believe there are no consequences for their behavior. Many children will need your explanation to understand consequences, and it will be important to clarify that consequences are not always negative. For instance, the positive behavior of studying for a test usually results in the positive consequence of a good grade. It's also important to clarify that in the case of bullying, or violent behavior, there are two kinds of consequences: one kind is a consequence for the child who is violent; and the other kind is a consequence for the child who is being hurt. Part of the difficulty in helping bullies change their behavior is that there are usually no negative consequences for their behavior: schools usually tolerate name calling, social exclusion, and often threats and intimidation. Instead, the consequences are usually positive: the bullies have a feeling of "being cool," "strong," and "powerful." Many schools only begin to take notice and enforce consequences for the violent acts that involve physical activity: hitting, severe pushing, kicking, and shoving. Victims know that they suffer consequences when other children treat them aggressively, but since they are frequently ignored and the aggressive children usually have no consequences, the second basic fact in this session will be corrective: "A consequence is what happens after you do something, and violent behavior almost always has the bad **consequence** of hurting someone."

In schools taking a systemic approach to violence prevention, there should be clear expectations, limits, and consequences for violent behavior, even at the name calling and social exclusion extreme. It you are conducting this group in such a school, you will be able to offer as an example your school's consequences for such behavior. If you are conducting the group without such support, you may need to reinforce that verbal violence is harmful to others, just as physical violence is. The discussion questions in session 1 begin to introduce empathy, the ability to understand how someone else is feeling, by asking the students how Daniel and Della, Trevor's and Tiffany's victims, feel after they are called names, or threatened, or not invited to play. This discussion should be validating for the Daniel group members. It gives them the message that they will no longer be ignored and that you are breaking down the usual entitlement and tolerance. The discussion plants seeds for changing the misconception that there are no consequences.

Remember that session 1 lays the groundwork for future sessions. You are introducing a new definition of violence as a way to begin to change the children's belief system. In session 3 you will present the value judgment that violent behavior is bad and is not acceptable. Then, in later sessions you will help the children learn alternatives to violent behavior.

Beginning the Session

Welcome the students and have them sit at a table. Explain that this is the group about Daniel the Dinosaur, who learns to stand tall against bullies. Everyone in the group will be able to learn about how to handle the kind of violent behavior that happens in elementary schools and ways to act when other children use violent and mean ways to get what they want. You will teach them ways to protect themselves and to state how they feel. Stress that this is not a class and there will be no grades. You expect everyone in the group to have fun as they learn how to be assertive instead of passive or aggressive.

Group Rules

Prepare the room by placing the folders, pencils, and crayons or markers at each student's place. Ask the children to look at the folders in front of them. Explain that they will use their folders every time they meet and that everything they need will be in these folders. Ask the group members to take their copy of the Group Rules Contract out of their folders. Meanwhile, display the poster you made listing the group rules. Tell the students that their group has rules, just like every group—use examples of groups like Cub Scouts, Girl Scouts, and sports teams. For the group to work well, everyone needs to keep the rules. Even though the children will have encountered these rules in their screening interview, take a moment to go through them now to check for understanding:

1. I will keep what we talk about private. We call this "confidentiality."
2. I will stay in my seat.
3. I will keep my hands to myself.
4. I will wait for my turn to talk, and I will listen carefully when others talk.
5. I won't tease or put down other people.
6. I can "pass" during go-arounds if I want.
7. I will attend every session.
8. I will make up any class work I miss.

Draw attention to the first rule regarding confidentiality. Remind the children that no one will know what they share in group, with some important exceptions. If they share information about suicide, homicide, child abuse, or sexual abuse, you are required by law to report that information to ensure safety. They are not allowed to share the names of other group members or what they say, but they can share the information they learn from Daniel and from you.

Stress the importance of coming to every session, and coming on time; also stress how important it is that they keep up their class work, since you will need the teachers' cooperation to have groups in the future. Remind the children of the consequences you have decided to use for breaking the group rules.

Once children understand this and other rules, have them sign and date their Group Rules Contracts.

Have the children place their contracts in their folders. Explain that they will be using the folders to hold all their group work, that each session new materials will be added to the folders, and that you will keep the folders until the end of the group sessions when they can take them home. Tell the children that they can draw on their folders at the beginning of each session while waiting for the session to begin.

Keep the group rules poster and display it every time the group meets.

Centering Exercise

Since most of the students will be unfamiliar with a centering exercise, give them—and yourself—time to prepare for one. Explain to the group members that you will begin each group session with a centering exercise, a way to relax and let go of the stresses and frustrations they may have encountered during the day. Point out that some of the centering exercises will help reinforce what you teach about feelings and anger management. Also point out that the centering exercises are techniques that the students can use on their own to manage stress, worry, and temper. Explain that some students create their own centering exercises, and that the one called the "Rainbow," which you will be using in a few weeks, was developed by two students in Virginia.

Begin by inviting the students to relax and by telling them that the name of this exercise is "Stop and Breathe to Five."

> Okay, close your eyes. Concentrate on your breathing. First, stop. Now, breathe in slowly for one, two, three counts. Now, hold that breath for one, two, three counts. Now, slowly breathe out for one, two, three counts. That was one Stop and Breathe.
>
> Let's do a second one. Stop. Now, breathe in slowly for one, two, three counts. Hold that breath for one, two, three counts. Now slowly breathe out for one, two, three counts. That was our second Stop and Breathe.
>
> Let's do a third one. Stop. Now, breathe in slowly for one, two, three counts. Make this air that you breathe in calm and peaceful. Hold that calm and peaceful air for one, two, three counts. Now, slowly breathe out your anger for one, two, three counts. That was our third Stop and Breathe.
>
> Let's do a fourth one. Stop. Now, breathe in calm and peaceful air for one, two, three counts. Make sure this air is calm and peaceful. Now, hold that calm and peaceful air for one, two, three counts. Now, slowly breathe out your anger for one, two, three counts. That was our fourth Stop and Breathe.
>
> Let's do a last Stop and Breathe. Stop. Breathe in calm and peaceful air for one, two, three counts. Make sure this air is calm and peaceful. Now hold that calm and peaceful air for one, two, three counts. Now, slowly breathe out your anger for one, two, three counts. That was our last Stop and Breathe.

Tell the children that "Stop and Breathe to Five" is a good exercise to help them gain control of their feelings and their behavior. If they Stop and Breathe five times, it will help them to chill out and to calm down, and then they will be able to think about what they should do next. You expect that they will be able to use it in class, at lunch, at recess, on the bus, in their neighborhood, and at home.

Icebreaker

Involve the children in an icebreaker. Have them get their index cards from their folders. Display the poster you made prior to the session that asks the children to list their name, age, grade, neighborhood where they live, who lives in their house, a favorite food, sport and sports team, and a favorite TV show and movie. Have the children write their answers to the questions. Share the information in a go-around. To role model for the students, begin this exercise by sharing the information about yourself (you can pass on your age if you wish). Then, have each group member share his or her information. (Note: for younger children, you may have to ask the questions and get responses orally.)

This safe and nonthreatening activity helps the children feel comfortable about sharing information and introduces them to the go-around technique, which will be used throughout the eleven group sessions.

Exploring the Story

To get the youngsters ready for the story, show them the cuddly stuffed toy dinosaur you acquired to portray Daniel. Introduce them and explain that Daniel will be with them every time they meet to have fun and teach them how to chill out and get along with other dinosaurs better. Tell the children that each of them will have a chance to hold Daniel during their time together, but that they can also make their own Daniel puppet. Have the children take out the pre-cut and pasted Daniel puppet patterns (Activity Sheet 1) and crayons. Invite the children to color the puppets while they listen to the story. Using the cuddly toy dinosaurs, have Daniel tell the following:

Hi! My name is Daniel the Dinosaur. I'm here to tell you what I've learned about violent behavior in schools.

In a lot of ways I'm a typical dinosaur. I go to Dinosaur school and I take the Dinosaur school bus to get there. I have schoolwork, just like you do. My favorite subject is language arts. I like to read science fiction stories about the future—you know, the kind of stories that tell about strange creatures like boys and girls and cats and dogs, and fantastic machines like airplanes and elevators and space shuttles. At school, we have to stand in the lunch line to wait for our lunches, just like you have to. My favorite lunch is the palm tree burger with fries. Some of the guys like caveman pizza better. After lunch, we go out to recess and play with the other dinosaurs. The boy dinosaurs usually play Dinosaur Dodge Ball. The girl dinosaurs practice their jump rope routines.

I used to go to Everglades Elementary School, and I had a lot of friends there. But then, my dad, who's in the Dinosaur Army, got transferred on his job, and we all had to move. Now I go to Swamp School. I've really had a hard time since we moved, and now I hate school. Let me tell you about it.

On my first day at my new school, I went to the corner to catch the Dinosaur school bus. (You can imagine how big dinosaur school buses are.) Since I'm so big, I went to the back of the bus where there was a lot of space. After a few stops, this tyrannosaurus dinosaur got on the bus, and came to where I was sitting. He gave me a really loud roar. Then he said, "What are you doing in my seat? Who do you think you are? If you don't move out of my seat, I'm going to punch you in the nose." He was such a strong, loud dinosaur that I did what he said. I moved. I was scared that I was going to get in trouble. It was really embarrassing because all the other dinosaur children were watching. It was a terrible way to start my first day at my new school.

When I got to school, I met my teacher, Mrs. Triceratops, and the dinosaurs in my class. It turned out, of course, that the dinosaur who yelled at me on the bus was in my class. His name is Trevor Tyrannosaurus. I could tell that the other dinosaurs were a little afraid of him. I saw him bossing them around.

After I had been at school for about a week, I was playing Dinosaur Dodge Ball during recess. I still didn't know many dinosaurs yet and hadn't made any friends. I wasn't used to how they played Dinosaur Dodge Ball, and I kept getting hit by the ball. It's hard to move fast when you're a brontosaurus, you know. Anyhow, Trevor was in the middle with me, and he called me an idiot. He said I was a stupid brontosaurus. Then, he tripped me. Since I'm such a big dinosaur, when I fall, I make a really big splash. And, I got a really bad scratch and tore my new shirt. All of the other dinosaurs laughed at me when Trevor tripped me. I know they were thinking that they're better Dinosaur Dodge Ball players than I am. It was really embarrassing to go into school after recess because I was all wet. I was ashamed of myself. I was also angry and hurt.

My sister Della was having a hard time too. Trevor's sister Tiffany was in her class. While the boys play Dinosaur Dodge Ball at recess, the girls jump rope. The girl dinosaurs were being really mean to Della, and they wouldn't let her play. Tiffany didn't know Della at all, but she started telling the girl dinosaurs that Della had the disease of Scale-face. They decided that they wouldn't let Della jump rope with them.

You may know some children like Trevor and Tiffany. They are tyrannosaurus dinosaurs—the strongest and meanest in the swamp. Well, almost the meanest. If you've seen *Jurassic Park*, you know that velociraptors are the meanest dinosaurs in the swamp, but tyrannosaurus dinosaurs are a close second. They like to be the bosses of their packs, even if they have to be really mean in order to be the boss. Sometimes dinosaurs—and children—like Trevor and Tiffany use violence in order to get their way. You probably think violence means someone is killing someone, or pulling a gun or a knife on someone, or beating them up. Those are behaviors that are very violent and can cause physical hurt. But behaviors like that don't happen in most elementary schools. The kind of violent behavior that Trevor and Tiffany used was another kind of violence: *any mean word, look, sign, or act that hurts another person's body, feelings, or possessions.* That kind of behavior—the kind Trevor and Tiffany do—happens in schools all the time. I didn't realize it, but when Trevor yelled at me, and threatened me if I wouldn't give him my seat, and when he called me names, and tripped me when we were playing Dinosaur Dodge Ball, he was being violent. When his sister Tiffany called my sister a name like Scaleface, and spread the rumor that she has the disease Scaleface, and when Tiffany and the other girl dinosaurs wouldn't let Della jump rope, she was being violent.

Sometimes dinosaurs and children like Trevor and Tiffany get into a lot of trouble at school. But most of the time, they get away with the bad things they do to other dinosaurs. They think they can do anything they want, since they are tyrannosaurus dinosaurs. It doesn't matter to them that they are mean to the other dinosaurs, as long as they get their way. They always say the other dinosaurs have done something to make them be mean. So, Trevor said it was really my fault he yelled at me and threatened me on the bus because I was in his seat. He blamed me for his behavior.

Now, you may not think what Trevor and Tiffany did was bad. They didn't think so for a long time. They didn't think there were consequences for their actions. A consequence is what happens after you do something. After all, what's the big deal about yelling and threatening someone you don't like anyway, or spreading rumors, or not letting somebody play with you?

But I know their behavior was mean, and violent, and they hurt my feelings, and my sister Della's feelings. I also know that whenever anyone is violent, there is usually at least one consequence—someone else usually gets hurt.

Why don't you talk about what Trevor and Tiffany did? See if you can figure out what the consequences were—what happened after they yelled and threatened, called names, tripped, spread rumors, and didn't let others play?

Discussion

The discussion questions reinforce the meaning of violence and the second major message of this session: violence has bad consequences. Use the discussion questions to help the children verbalize the definition of violence, to identify how Trevor and Tiffany had violent behavior, and to name the bad consequences of their actions. If the children cannot remember the definition of violence, repeat it for them. If they cannot identify Trevor and Tiffany's violent behavior, use the discussion questions to help them do so. If the children cannot name the bad consequences of Trevor and Tiffany's behavior, you will have to identify them.

- What did Trevor do when Daniel sat in his seat on the bus? (He yelled at Daniel and told him to move. He threatened to punch him in the nose if he didn't move.)
- Was Trevor being violent when he yelled at Daniel and told him to move? (Yes, because violence is any mean word, look, sign, or act that hurts a dinosaur's or person's body, feelings, or possessions.)
- When Trevor yelled at Daniel and threatened to punch him in the nose if he

didn't move, was Trevor being mean? (Yes. He was using mean words, and he said the words in a mean way.)

- Did Trevor's mean words hurt Daniel's body, feelings, or possessions? (Yes, Trevor's mean words hurt Daniel's feelings.)
- How do you think Daniel felt when he got on the bus on his first day in a new school, and Trevor yelled at him to move and threatened to punch him in the nose? (Elicit possible feelings from the children and write them on a flip chart or chalkboard. If they cannot come up with any, list feelings such as hurt, angry, sad, rejected, scared, alone.)
- Was Trevor being violent when he tripped Daniel during Dinosaur Dodge Ball and called him names? (Yes, because violence is any mean word, look, sign, or act that hurts a dinosaur's or person's body, feelings, or possessions.)
- When Trevor tripped Daniel during Dinosaur Dodge Ball, was he being mean? (Yes, Trevor's action was mean, because he tripped Daniel and made him fall.)
- Did Trevor's mean action of tripping Daniel hurt Daniel's body, feelings, or possessions? (Yes, Trevor's mean action of tripping hurt Daniel's body and his shirt. He got scratched and he tore his shirt when he fell.)
- How do you think Daniel felt when Trevor tripped him during Dodge Ball, and Trevor and the other dinosaurs laughed at him? (Elicit possible feelings from the children, and write them on a flip chart, chalkboard, etc. If the children cannot come up with any, list the feelings yourself: hurt, sad, scared, angry, embarrassed.)
- Was Tiffany being violent when she spread rumors about Della, Daniel's sister, and told the dinosaur girls that Della had Scaleface? (Yes, because violence is any mean word, look, sign or act that hurts a dinosaur's or person's body, feelings, or possessions.)
- When Tiffany told the dinosaur girls that Della had Scaleface, was she being mean? (Yes, Tiffany's words were mean, because she was telling lies about Della. She also got the other dinosaur girls not to let Della jump rope with them.)
- Did Tiffany's mean words of spreading rumors about Della and the girls not letting Della jump rope hurt Della's body, feelings, or possessions? (Yes, Tiffany's mean words of spreading rumors about Della and the girls' action of not letting Della jump rope hurt Della's feelings.)
- How do you think Della felt when Tiffany spread rumors about her having Scaleface and the other dinosaur girls wouldn't let her jump rope? (Elicit possible feelings from the children, and write them on a flip chart, chalkboard, and so on. If the children cannot come up with any, list the feelings yourself: hurt, sad, scared, angry, embarrassed.)

In the discussion, be accepting of the children's right to whatever opinions and beliefs they might have, even if they are the beliefs you are trying to change. Some students may have very strong beliefs that it is okay to use violence to get your way, or to express a feeling.

Acknowledge that some people think that way, but they tend to have lots of trouble in getting along with others.

As the group discusses, you can use the go-around technique: go around the group, making sure that each student has an opportunity to add to the discussion. Encourage participation, but don't force it. Remember the sixth group rule, which allows a student to pass. Accept all ideas and answers, explaining or clarifying information where necessary to reinforce learning. Afterward, be sure to thank the students for their participation.

Activity

Ask the children to take out Activity Sheet 1A, One Consequence of Violent Behavior in Your School (see page 61), from their folders. Tell the children to draw a picture with their pencils or crayons or markers of one consequence of violent behavior in their school. Remind the children that violence is not only using guns and knives and killing people. Violence is also any mean word, look, sign, or act that hurts a person's body, feelings, or possessions. You want them to draw the kind of violent behavior that might happen in their school. Repeat for the children that the consequence here would be what happens after someone uses a mean word, look, or action in their school. Assure the children that you are not looking for artistic ability; you just want their ideas of consequences. They can use "stick figures" or they can use words to describe one consequence of violent behavior.

When the children finish, have another go-around. Invite each child to explain his or her drawing.

Basic Facts

Ask the children to take out Basic Fact Worksheet 1 (see page 62) from their folders. Tell the group members that each week they will learn new basic facts that carry the message of the session in easy-to-remember sentences. The worksheets will help them learn the new basic facts. Either read out loud the two basic facts yourself, or choose two children to read them, one at a time.

1. **Violence** is any mean word, look, sign, or act that **hurts** a person's body, feelings, or possessions.
2. A consequence is what happens after you do something, and violent behavior almost always has the bad **consequence** of hurting someone.

Briefly discuss each fact, checking for understanding. Correct any misconceptions.

Give the children time to complete the bottom half of the worksheet by filling in the blanks. Then have the entire group read the basic facts aloud. Explain that in each group session to come, you will be going over the basic facts learned so far at the beginning of each session, and that you will ask them to explain what each means. Have the children put their worksheets in their folders along with their Daniel puppets.

Homework Assignment

Tell the children that they will have a homework assignment each week. These assignments will be very easy and won't take much time. They will help the students learn more. This week, the homework assignment is to watch for violent behavior in their school, neighborhood, or home, and each day to write down one example of what they see. Ask them to pull out Homework Assignment 1 (see page 63) from their folders. Ask a child to read the assignment out loud. Tell the students that they will not be graded on their homework, but they will learn more if they do it. If you will be able to institute a positive reinforcement program for homework, tell the students now that they will receive a sticker or pencil every time they bring in the assignments.

Wrapping Up

Repeat the centering exercise from the beginning of the group, "Stop and Breathe to Five" (see page 52). Tell the children that you will ask next week if any of them remembered to use "Stop and Breathe to Five."

Affirmation

Involve the group in an affirmation. Stand and join in a circle with the children, holding hands. Go around and have each child share something he or she liked about the group. Start the affirmation yourself: "One thing I liked about the group today was . . ."

Closing

Remain standing in a circle with the students holding hands and lead the group in the closing activity, "Pass a Silent Wish." You'll use this same activity to end all group sessions.

Tell the students that you're going to make a silent wish for the student on your right. Then when you've made the wish, gently squeeze the student's hand. The student makes a silent wish for the person on his or her right, then gently squeezes the student's hand, and so on. Continue around the circle until a wish and squeeze come back to you. Usually, students follow the lead of group leaders who expect them to perform this activity.

Collect the folders. Explain to the group that you will keep the folders until the next group session.

Fill out a copy of the Process and Progress Form (see page 235) or the Progress Notes (see pages 236–237), if you are an experienced leader, as soon as you can after leading the session.

Group Rules Contract

1. I will keep what we talk about private. We call this "confidentiality."
2. I will stay in my seat.
3. I will keep my hands to myself.
4. I will wait for my turn to talk, and I will listen carefully when other people talk.
5. I won't tease or put down other people.
6. I can "pass" during the go-arounds if I want.
7. I will attend every session.
8. I will make up any class work that I miss.

_____

Name

_____

Date

Activity Sheet 1
Daniel Puppet

1. Cut out Daniel. 2. Color. 3. Cut out rectangle and paste or tape the two ends to use as a finger puppet.

| paste or tape | | paste or tape |

Activity Sheet 1A
One Consequence of Violent Behavior in Your School

Basic Fact Worksheet 1

1. **<u>Violence</u>** is any mean word, look, sign, or act that **<u>hurts</u>** a person's body, feelings, or possessions.

2. A consequence is what happens after you do something, and violent behavior almost always has the bad **<u>consequence</u>** of hurting someone.

_____

1. _____ is any mean word, look, sign, or act that _____ a person's body, feelings, or possessions

2. A consequence is what happens after you do something, and violent behavior almost always has the bad _____ of hurting someone.

Homework Assignment 1

Each day watch for violent behavior in your school, neighborhood, or home. Write down one example every day. Remember, violence is any mean word, look, sign, or act that hurts another person's body, feelings, or possessions.

Day 1 _____

_____

_____

Day 2 _____

_____

_____

Day 3 _____

_____

_____

Day 4 _____

_____

_____

Day 5 _____

_____

_____

Session 2

Daniel the Dinosaur Learns Why Some Children Use Violence

Objectives

To help the students:

- learn that many children who use violence often use violence when they are adults
- describe three reasons why children who are hurt by children who use violence don't tell adults

Preparation

- Display the posterboard copy of the group rules.
- Have available the toy Daniel the Dinosaur and Basic Fact Posters 1 and 2.
- Photocopy the Questions to Help Clarify the Basic Facts (see pages 230–234) to use in this and all further sessions during the Basic Facts Review.
- Staple the children's copies of the Group Rules Contract to the inside back cover of their folders.
- Include in each student's folder:
  –the Feeling Daniel
  –Activity Sheet 2 (One Thing That Might Happen to a Child Who Is Mean and Violent When He or She Grows Up)
  –Basic Fact Worksheet 2
  –Homework Assignment 2
- Place each student's folder, pencil, and crayons or markers at his or her place.
- Read through the session plan before meeting.

Background and Guidelines

Session 2 identifies the characteristics and families of bullies and their victims; points out that many children who are bullies continue to have aggressive behavior as adults, frequently with negative consequences; describes the effects of bullying on victims; and explores why children who are victims are often afraid to tell adults.

Characteristics of Bullies

Olweus (1994) says that the commonly held notion that bullies are anxious, insecure, and have low self-esteem is a myth. He finds that bullies

- have a positive attitude toward violence and are aggressive toward adults as well as toward other children
- are impulsive and have a strong need to dominate others
- if males, are physically stronger than boys in general
- have little anxiety and insecurity, and a positive view of themselves
- are popular at an average or slightly below average level, often with two or three close followers
- have an "active and hot-headed temperament"

Olweus says it is the combination of an aggressive behavior pattern and physical strength that characterizes the male bully. Olweus also finds that boys do more bullying than girls, bullying both boys and girls. When girls do bully, they tend to use more indirect ways to bully—name calling, spreading rumors, social exclusion—rather than physical ways.

Families of Bullies

Olweus looks to the family for the source of the aggressive behavior pattern. He finds that families of bullies have

- a negative basic attitude, characterized by lack of warmth and involvement by the primary caretaker
- overly permissive and tolerant parenting, without setting clear limits to aggressive behavior toward peers, siblings, and adults
- high use of authoritarian parenting techniques, such as physical punishment and violent emotional outbursts

Characteristics of Victims

Olweus describes two varieties of victims: the passive or submissive victim and the provocative victim.
The **passive** or **submissive** victims are

- more anxious and insecure than students in general
- cautious, sensitive, and quiet

- react to attack by crying and withdrawal
- feel ashamed, stupid, and unattractive; feel like failures and have low self-esteem
- are lonely and abandoned at school, often without one good friend
- have a negative attitude toward violence
- if male, tend to be physically weaker than boys in general
- have closer contact and more positive relationships with their parents, especially their mother

In contrast, the **provocative** victim tends to be both anxious and aggressive. This kind of victim may be hyperactive, with attention deficit disorder.

In session 2's story, these characteristics of bullies and victims are presented through Daniel's description of his family and Trevor's family.

The Adult Consequences of Bullying Behavior

In looking at the long-term effects, Olweus found that victims had fairly normal lives, except that they were more likely to be depressed and to have lower self-esteem. Olweus found that being a bully tended to lead to more serious problems: 60 percent of childhood bullies had at least one criminal conviction by the age of 24, while 35 to 40 percent had three or more convictions. The victims had a below-average level of criminality in young adulthood.

Other longitudinal studies of aggressive children corroborate Olweus's findings. Dr. Leonard D. Eron and Dr. Rowell Heusmann studied 870 third-graders beginning in 1960. They found that children who were aggressive at age 8 were more likely to have court records and low academic records than nonaggressive children. Eron says ". . . by the time they were 30, these individuals were much more likely to have been convicted of crimes, and of more serious crimes; to have more moving traffic violations and convictions for drunken driving; to be more abusive toward their spouses; to have more aggressive children; and to have not achieved educationally, professionally, and socially." Further, Eron found that "the most aggressive boys were about three times more likely to be convicted of a crime than their peers; and, were less apt to finish college and have good jobs." He also found that girl bullies grew up to be mothers of bullies.

As you work with bullies, remember the psychological defenses that are commonly used:

Denial: "I didn't do anything."
Projection or blaming: "He made me do it."
Rationalizing: "She likes it when I tease her."
Minimizing: "All I did was swing my jacket; I didn't even touch him."

These defenses are part of the psychological system that allows bullies to continue mean and aggressive behavior. They don't acknowledge that they have any responsibility for their own behavior. Again through the displacement, you will gently point out these defenses. The basic facts in later sessions allow you to continue to point out the defenses, which the children readily identify.

Remember that in childhood, bullies tend to feel powerful, have average popularity, and good self-esteem. Add to that the permissiveness of their parents and the tolerance of school personnel, and you see why bullies have few negative consequences. This serves to perpetuate their behavior. Therefore, a significant part of this group is to correct the idea that bullies have no negative consequences.

A major objective of this session is to correct the myth that bullies have no negative consequences. This is stated clearly in one basic fact for this session, **"Children** who are mean and violent often grow up to be mean and violent as **adults.** They don't have very happy lives." The repetition of this basic fact throughout the following group sessions will provide you an opportunity to drive home the point that there **are** negative consequences for children with aggressive behavior. As you clarify in later sessions, be sure to underline the fact that these negative consequences are a good reason for children like Trevor to change their behavior— so they will have better lives in the future. Remember to make these points through the displacement to avoid direct confrontation.

Effects of Bullying on Victims

Another point of this session is to describe the second kind of negative consequences for engaging in bullying behavior: the effects on the children who are victims of bullies. As Olweus says, "the repeated harassment by peers . . . increased their anxiety, insecurity, and a generally negative evaluation of themselves." They are lonely and abandoned at school. Victims also frequently end up in trouble at school because of truancy or poor grades. They sometimes become offenders to defend themselves. One study showed that one-third of victims of physical attacks occasionally bring weapons to school. In extreme cases, victims of extreme bullying have taken their own, or others' lives (Greenbaum, Turner, and Stephens 1989).

The story in session 2 also details the effects of Trevor's mean and aggressive behavior on Daniel, his victim. Daniel is not aggressive, has no friends at school, and is fearful.

The activity for this session asks the children to draw or write what might happen when a child who is mean and violent grows up. The homework assignment in this session is to have the children look in their school, neighborhood, or family for people who use violent behavior and what the consequences are. Children are usually much more able to identify violent behavior in others than in themselves. Their reports next week during the assignment review should give insight into their lives and how they see themselves as victims of violence.

The fourth major point of this session is to identify reasons why victims do not tell adults about being bullied. Suffering from humiliation and shame, victims may fear being considered a coward or a failure, or may fear that they will be blamed for being teased. They also fear retribution from the bully, either in the form of a physical attack or even more severe ridicule. Finally, they may fear being called a tattletale.

In many schools, the typical response to bullying is for adults to ignore it and fail to intervene when they see bullying, telling the victims to stop being provocative, or just to fight back. Therefore, victims who do dare to tell an adult are often frustrated because they are blamed or brushed off. The tolerance by adults of bullying behavior and the fear of victims to tell adults combine to **enable** bullies to continue their aggressive behavior. It is to correct this combination that the second basic fact in session 2 is: "Children who are hurt by other children are often **afraid** to tell adults; then they let the other children **get away** with their mean and violent behavior." As you discuss this fact, the children will easily give you reasons why victims might be afraid to tell an adult.

These points make it worthwhile to look at the school where you are implementing this group. Schools which do not have a clear school code about violence that includes the entire definition used here (any mean word, look, sign, or act that hurts another person's body, feelings, or possessions) give their teachers no guidelines for when to intervene. And they do not have clear procedures, such as the contracts and consequences necessary to implement a program. Schools without a program such as *Respect & Protect*® will probably intervene only when the violence becomes physical.

This group will be more effective if implemented in a school with a systemic approach, so that the children will know that the rules are changing, and that violent behavior will not be tolerated, and that instead of being ignored, there will be consequences to help the aggressive children change their behavior. Session 3 demonstrates such a program. Pointing out now that not telling lets the bully get away with his or her behavior sets the stage for session 3, where enabling behavior is corrected, and an adult does intervene and give Trevor some consequences.

Beginning the Session

Welcome the students and remind them that they all belong to the Daniel the Dinosaur group so that they can have fun and learn about school violence. Begin with a quick review of the group rules (see page 51). Draw attention to the poster listing the group rules, or have the children look at their own copies of the Group Rules Contract. In a go-around, have the children read the rules one at a time. Check for understanding before moving on.

Centering Exercise

Make certain that the children are comfortable and quiet. Ask if any of them remembered to "Stop and Breathe to Five" in the past week. Remind them that stopping and breathing to five before thinking will help them make good decisions about how to get along with other children. Introduce the new centering exercise, "The Icicle." Tell the group members that this is another centering exercise that will help them calm down, relax, and be able to think if they get angry or upset. They can use this exercise without anyone else knowing.

> Close your eyes. Tighten the muscles in your feet and legs really tight; make your feet and legs as stiff as an icicle. (Pause.) Now let that cold and stiff icicle melt. Let it melt, drip by drip, into a calm, peaceful puddle. Let your legs get loose and very relaxed, and imagine what they would feel like as part of a puddle. (Pause.) Now tighten your chest, stomach, and trunk area; make it as stiff as an icicle. (Pause.) Now let that icicle melt,

slowly, drip by drip, into a puddle. Feel how calm and relaxed all of the muscles in your trunk area, your stomach, and your chest feel. (Pause.)

Now, put your arms straight out in front of you, make fists, and pretend that your arms are icicles. Make them just as stiff as you can. (Pause.) Now let those icicles melt; let them drip into a puddle, and imagine what they feel like as they drip into a calm, peaceful puddle. Let all of your tension and worry drip out of your fingers into a big puddle. (Pause.) Tighten the muscles in your shoulders, neck, and head; tighten them into a stiff, cold icicle. Make them very stiff and tight. (Pause.) Now let all those muscles relax and melt, slowly, very slowly into a puddle. Let all of your tension and anxiety drip out of those muscles. (Pause.)

Now take every muscle in your whole body; make all those muscles just as stiff and tight as you can. Make your whole body into an icicle. (Pause.) Now let yourself melt, from the tip of your toes to the top of your head. Let yourself melt, drip by drip, into a puddle. Let yourself get very loose and relaxed, like smooth water in a puddle. Imagine that your whole body is a calm, quiet, peaceful puddle.

Remind the students that they can use this technique in school, on the bus, at recess, and at home to help them put thinking between their feelings and their behavior.

Feelings Check-in

Do a feelings check-in with the students. Have them take out their Feeling Daniel. Tell the students that every week they will look at the Feeling Daniel and decide how they are feeling that day, and everybody will give a brief description of how they are doing. Direct the children to color in the section on the dinosaur that shows how they're feeling today. For younger children, read the names of the feelings and their colors out loud: angry—red, scared—purple, sad—blue, glad—yellow. Tell the children that they can color in more than one feeling, since it's possible to have more than one feeling at a time. Tell the children that if they're having a feeling that is not named on their dinosaur, they can add a dinosaur spine in any color they choose and write in the name of the feeling.

When the students finish, have a go-around. Begin by sharing your own feelings. Then, invite each student to share his or her name and how he or she is feeling. Be sure to accept each child's feeling(s) and to affirm each child. Afterwards, tell the children that they will be using this same copy of the Feeling Daniel every time they meet, adding colors at each session. Ask the children to put their sheet away in their folders.

Basic Facts Review

To help the students review their last session and the basic facts learned so far, show them Basic Fact Posters 1 and 2.

In a go-around, ask a student to read Basic Fact 1 aloud and to explain what it means. If the student has trouble explaining the fact, don't contradict or judge, simply clarify his or her explanation. It is this clarification that you provide weekly that will help make sure the children understand the message you are trying to teach them. The clarification highlights the key messages about each basic fact that you want the children to remember.

Repeat the procedure for the next basic fact. This review ensures that the students understand and integrate the basic facts that have been taught. It is also easy preparation for the presentation and provides a lead-in for the session material. In this book, the Basic Facts List and Questions to Help Clarify the Basic Facts are printed on pages 229–234.

Assignment Review

Ask the children if they brought their homework assignments from last week. Remind them that every day they were to watch for violent behavior at school, their neighborhood, or home. In a go-around, ask the children to share what they found: what violent behavior did they see? If they want to keep the name of the people who were violent confidential, allow them to do so, but ask them to describe what they saw. The purpose of this assignment is to help children realize that violence is not just using guns and knives and killing people. If the children forgot to do the assignment, ask them to think back to the past week and to see if they can remember any violent behavior they saw.

Exploring the Story

Have the children get comfortable for today's story. Use the toy Daniel and allow him to tell the following:

> Hi boys and girls! It's good to see you again. We're going to learn more today about how dinosaurs act who are mean and violent. We're also going to talk about the dinosaurs who are hurt by other dinosaurs who are mean and violent.
>
> Do you remember Trevor and Tiffany, the Tyrannosaurus Twins? They are the dinosaurs in my school who always like to get their own way, even if they have to be mean—or violent—to get it. Remember that violence is any mean word, look, sign, or act that hurts a person's body, feelings, or possessions.
>
> You may wonder why Trevor and Tiffany act the way they do. They probably act mean and violent for a number of reasons. Their father Jack is a tyrannosaurus dinosaur too, of course, and he likes getting his way even more than Trevor and Tiffany do. He's so mean and violent that he even beats up their mother, Gladys. Jack never admits he does anything wrong, and he always blames everything on Gladys. He believes that "Might Makes Right." Gladys is so scared of Jack that she lets him get away with his violent behavior toward her. She's pretty sad a lot of the time, and Jack spends a lot of his time at the Dinosaur Bar, so neither parent spends much time with Trevor and Tiffany. Their mom doesn't bake the Best Chocolate Cake Ever with them; their dad doesn't take them to basketball practice or practice basketball jump shots with them; neither parent reads and cuddles

with them or plays Dinosaur Monopoly with them. They are pretty much on their own. They can do anything they want. They don't have to keep their rooms neat or help with the dishes or take out the trash. They usually never get grounded even if they're bad. When their dad does pay attention to them, he's usually giving them a really bad spanking and yelling at them very loudly.

Jack was a lot like Trevor when he was in school. He wanted to feel more powerful than the other dinosaurs, and he used his size to boss others around. Like Trevor, he felt it was okay to be mean and violent, and he was also pretty mean to others. You might think life is pretty good for people like Jack. But he didn't get good grades when he was in school, and except for the few dinosaurs who hung around him, most of the other dinosaurs were scared of him and tried to stay away from him. Jack has had a lot of trouble on his jobs, so sometimes he just quits. He always blames the boss, because he doesn't see how he is mean and violent himself. Once, he even had to spend a week in jail for threatening his boss with a gun. He really doesn't have a very happy marriage or family. So dinosaurs like Jack may think they are the toughest dinosaur around, but they really have a lot of trouble in their lives.

Young dinosaurs like Trevor, who use mean words and actions to get their way, may think like Jack that they are the toughest dinosaur kids around. But they don't really have many friends. They have a few dinosaurs who hang around them and try to be mean too. But most of the other dinosaurs are afraid of dinosaurs like Trevor. Trevor doesn't do as well in school as he could. When he always blames others for what he does, that means he isn't taking responsibility for his own behavior, and that will affect how honest he is when he grows up. So, dinosaurs who are mean and violent so they can be boss and get their way often grow up to use mean words and actions when they are adult dinosaurs. Then they may have trouble on the job and may not have happy marriages or families.

I have a very different family from Trevor and Tiffany. My dad, Brad Brontosaurus, used to be like Trevor's dad, and beat up my mom, Becky, a lot. Della and I were really scared. But my mom finally told him she wouldn't live with him anymore unless he stopped using violent behavior. My dad was able to stop his violent behavior, and now our family does a lot of things together. I play basketball a lot with my dad, and we like to watch the Dinosaur NBA games on TV. My favorite player is Shak O'Saurus. I'm close to my mom. She reads to me every night, and I like sitting next to her on the couch.

I've thought a lot about why Trevor picked on me to be mean and violent. As you know, I'm a brontosaurus dinosaur. We don't move fast. Even though we're big, we're actually pretty weak. We are very peace-loving. We don't like to have fights. We're also quiet and tend to get our feelings hurt easily. Although I had friends at Everglades Elementary School, when I moved to Swamp School, I didn't know anybody. When Trevor made me change seats on the bus, and called me names and tripped me during Dinosaur Dodge Ball, all the dinosaur children laughed at me, and then nobody wanted to be my friend. They were afraid Trevor would make fun of them if they were nice to me.

Trevor kept on being mean and violent to me. His seat in the classroom was behind me, and sometimes he would kick my desk. He wouldn't stop, even when I asked him politely. It was really annoying. Sometimes he would sit next to me at lunch. Whenever we had caveman pizza, he would take my pizza, because it was his favorite. He would just steal it off my tray. If I said anything, he told me to "shut up, or I'll punch you in the nose." I knew he would do it, so I just kept quiet. I was really hungry for the rest of the day. Just like he did in the first week of school, he often tripped me or ran into me when we played Dinosaur Dodge Ball. And he called me Brontostupid.

I felt I couldn't say anything to anybody. I was ashamed to tell Mrs. Triceratops or my parents. I didn't want to be a tattletale. I also wanted to be able to solve my own problems. I was afraid my parents would be angry or ashamed of me.

I was afraid to go to school. I spent so much time worrying about what Trevor might do that I didn't do my schoolwork and my grades went down. I got some of the worst grades in the class. Sometimes, I got into trouble at home, because when Trevor tripped me, I fell and tore my new shirt. You can imagine how angry my mother got. After a while, I stopped even playing Dinosaur Dodge Ball. I spent recess by myself in a corner of the school yard.

I didn't realize it, but I was letting Trevor get away with being mean and violent by keeping what he did to myself. But I'll tell you more about that next week.

Discussion

Lead a discussion to help the group members understand what happens to mean and violent children when they grow up. Also, help them describe personalities typical of children who are hurt by others.

- What is the name of Trevor and Tiffany's father? (Their father's name is Jack.)
- Is Jack mean and violent like Trevor and Tiffany? (Yes. He beats up their mother, Gladys. He doesn't spend much time playing with Trevor and Tiffany. When he does, he's usually yelling at them or spanking them.)
- What is the name of Trevor and Tiffany's mother? (Their mother's name is Gladys.)
- Is Gladys mean and violent? (No. But she is sad a lot of the time because Jack is so violent. Gladys doesn't bake cakes with Trevor and Tiffany.)
- What was Jack like when he was in school? (He was mean and violent and used his size to boss around other dinosaurs.)
- Does Jack have a good job? (No. He usually has trouble on the job, and he ends up quitting.)
- Has Jack ever had to go to jail? (Yes, for threatening his boss with a gun.)

- Does Jack have a happy family or marriage? (No, his wife and children are afraid of him.)
- Does Jack ever accept responsibility for his behavior, or does he always blame others for what he does? (Jack always blames everybody else.)
- Does Trevor have a lot of friends? (No. Except for the few dinosaur kids who hang around him; most of the other dinosaurs are afraid of him and stay away from him.)
- Will Trevor grow up to be like his dad, Jack? (Unless Trevor starts to change his behavior, and stops being mean and violent to get his way, he will probably grow up to be like his dad. He probably won't get good grades. He'll have trouble on his jobs. He might have to go to jail. He may end up beating his wife. He probably won't have a happy family or a happy life.)
- What is the name of Daniel's father? (Brad Brontosaurus.)
- Is Brad mean and violent? (Brad used to be violent with his wife, Becky. But she said she wouldn't live with him anymore unless he stopped using violent behavior. So Brad stopped being mean and violent.)
- What does Daniel like to do with Brad? (Daniel plays basketball with his dad, and they watch the Dinosaur NBA games on TV.)
- Is Daniel mean and violent? (No. Daniel is a brontosaurus dinosaur. He is peace-loving and doesn't like to fight. He is big, but he doesn't have a lot of strength.)
- Does Daniel have a lot of friends at Swamp School? (No. He just moved there, and doesn't know any other dinosaurs. The other dinosaur children are afraid Trevor will make fun of them if they are nice to Daniel.)
- What kinds of things does Trevor do to Daniel? (Trevor kicks Daniel's desk; he steals his caveman pizza; he threatens to punch him in the nose; he trips him or runs into him when they play Dinosaur Dodge Ball; Trevor calls Daniel Brontostupid.)
- Does Daniel tell anybody what Trevor does? (No. He's afraid Trevor will treat him worse if he tells. He's ashamed to tell his teacher or his parents, and he's afraid his parents will be angry at him or ashamed of him. Also, he's afraid he'll be called a tattletale.)
- Does Daniel like school? (No. He worries about what Trevor will do. He doesn't study and gets low grades. He gets into trouble at home because of his torn shirt. He spends recess by himself in a corner.)

Activity

Ask the children to take out Activity Sheet 2, One Thing That Might Happen to a Child Who Is Mean and Violent When He or She Grows Up (see page 77), from their folders. Tell the children to draw a picture with their pencils or crayons or markers of one thing that might happen to a child who is mean and violent when he or she grows up. Assure the children that you are not looking for artistic ability; you just want their ideas of consequences. They can use "stick figures" or they can use words to describe what happens to a child who is mean and violent when he or she grows up.

When the children finish, have another go-around. Invite each child to explain his or her drawing.

Basic Facts

Ask the children to take out Basic Fact Worksheet 2 (see page 78) from their folders. Remind them that they will learn new basic facts each week. With younger children, read out loud the two basic facts yourself; with third grade and up, choose two children to read them, one at a time.

1. **Children** who are mean and violent often grow up to be mean and violent as **adults.** They don't have very happy lives.
2. Children who are hurt by other children are often **afraid** to tell adults; then they let the other children **get away** with their mean and violent behavior.

Briefly discuss each fact, checking for understanding. Correct any misconceptions.

Give the children time to complete the bottom half of the worksheet by filling in the blanks. Then have the entire group read the facts out loud. Remind the children that for the rest of the group sessions, you will be going over the basic facts learned so far at the beginning of each session, and that you will ask them to explain what each means. Have the children put their worksheets in their folders.

Homework Assignment

Tell the children that this week, their homework assignment is to see if they know anybody in their family, in their neighborhood, or in their school who uses mean and violent behavior. Then, they are to see if they can tell the consequences of that person's mean and violent behavior. Remind them that they will not be graded on this; you just want them to look and think about what they have learned. Ask them to retrieve Homework Assignment 2 (see page 79) from their folders, and ask a child to read the assignment out loud.

Wrapping Up

Repeat the centering exercise from the beginning of the group, "The Icicle" (see pages 68–69).

Affirmation

Involve the group in an affirmation. Stand and join in a circle with the children, holding hands. Have each child share something he or she learned about the group. Start the affirmation yourself: "One thing I learned from the story today is . . ."

Closing

Remain standing in a circle with the children holding hands and lead the group in the closing activity, "Pass a Silent Wish" (see page 58).

Collect the folders and fill out a copy of the Process and Progress Form (see page 235) or the Progress Notes (see pages 236–237), if you are an experienced leader, as soon as you can after leading the session.

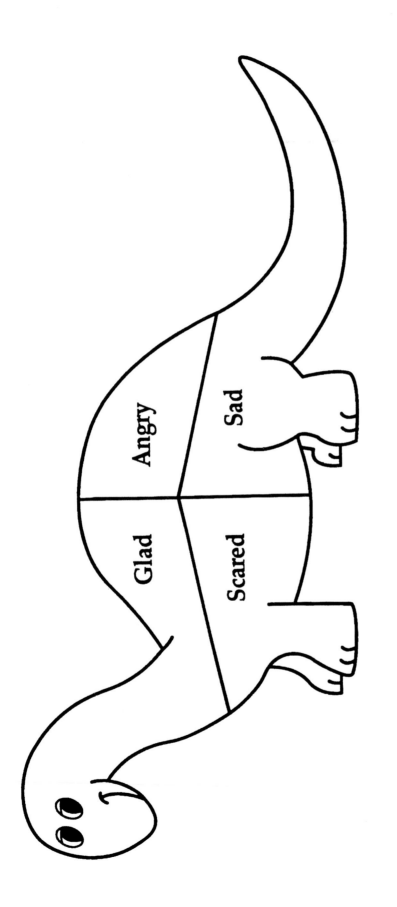

Feeling Daniel

Glad=Yellow   Angry=Red
Sad=Blue   Scared=Purple

Activity Sheet 2

One Thing That Might Happen to a Child Who Is Mean and Violent When He or She Grows Up

Basic Fact Worksheet 2

3. **Children** who are mean and violent often grow up to be mean and violent as **adults.** They don't have very happy lives.

4. Children who are hurt by other children are often **afraid** to tell adults; then they let the other children **get away** with their mean and violent behavior.

_____

3. _____who are mean and violent often grow up to be mean and violent as _____. They don't have very happy lives.

4. Children who are hurt by other children are often _____ to tell adults; then they let the other children _____ with their mean and violent behavior.

Homework Assignment 2

Do you know anybody in your family, in your neighborhood, or in your school who uses mean and violent behavior? See if you can tell the consequences of that person's mean and violent behavior. You don't have to use names. Just describe their mean and violent behavior and the consequences.

_____

_____

_____

_____

_____

_____

_____

_____

_____

_____

_____

_____

_____

Session 3

Daniel the Dinosaur Meets Mrs. Owl

Objectives

To help the students:

- learn that mean and violent behavior in schools is bad and is not acceptable
- learn three rules children can use to decrease mean and violent behaviors in school

Preparation

- Display the posterboard copy of the group rules.
- Have available the toy Daniel the Dinosaur and Mrs. Owl and Basic Fact Posters 1 to 4.
- Add to each student's folder:
  –Activity Sheet 3 (Mrs. Owl puppet) (you may want to pre-cut Mrs. Owl and glue her beak on before the session.)
  –Activity Sheet 3A (Draw One Way to Follow One of the Three Rules to Stop Mean and Violent Behavior in Schools)
  –Basic Fact Worksheet 3
  –Homework Assignment 3
- Have glue available so the children can paste on Mrs. Owl's wings.
- Place each student's folder, pencil, and crayons or markers at his or her place.
- Read through the session plan before meeting.

Background and Guidelines

Session 3 introduces the concept of a schoolwide violence prevention plan, sets the clear standard and value judgment that violent behavior is bad and will not be tolerated, and introduces three rules that children can use to decrease violent behavior in their school. This session addresses the issues of **entitlement** and **tolerance**. Entitlement is the belief by aggressive children that there is nothing wrong with using their power (physical or verbal) to hurt other people or to get what they want. Tolerance refers to the inaction by adults that enables aggressive children to get away with their bad behavior.

As already stated, a comprehensive schoolwide violence prevention program will have components that include

1. a clearly stated policy that violent behavior is unacceptable and will not be tolerated
2. a clear definition of violence that includes name calling, teasing, social exclusion, spreading rumors, and gossiping as well as intimidation and physical acts of violence like pushing, shoving, and hitting
3. teacher in-services to raise their awareness and clarify their roles in enforcing policy
4. a clear system to report all violent behavior
5. a system of choices, contracts, and consequences so that the administrative response is appropriate to the level of violence
6. a wide range of prevention and intervention programs, such as (a) affective and social skills curriculum for all children, (b) anger management and conflict resolution programs for children involved in normal conflict, (c) specific groups for bullies teaching them how to change their behavior, (d) specific groups for victims to teach them to ask an adult for help and how to stand up for themselves, and (e) disciplinary procedures for children who engage in severe or repeated acts of violence.

The program should also include parent education and training and community support.

The intervention program favored by Olweus (1994), focusing only on bully/victim violence, prescribes the following:

General Prerequisites

- Awareness and involvement

Measures at the School Level

- Questionnaire survey
- School conference day on bully/victim problem
- Better supervision during recess and lunch time
- More attractive school playground
- Contact telephone
- Meeting staff and parents
- Teacher groups for the development of the social milieu of the school
- Parent circle

Measures at the Class Level

- Class rules against bullying: clarification, praise, and sanctions
- Regular class meetings
- Role-playing, literature
- Cooperative learning
- Common positive class activities
- Class meeting: teacher and parents/children

Measures at the Individual Level

- Serious talks with bullies and victims
- Serious talks with parents of involved students
- Teacher and parent use of imagination
- Help from "neutral students"
- Help and support for parents (parent folders, etc.)
- Discussion groups for parents of bullies and victims
- Change of class or school

In Basic Fact 6, this group manual incorporates several of Olweus's class rules, to be used by the classroom teacher at the class level:

1. We will not be mean and violent.
2. We will try to help students who are being hurt by other children who are mean and violent.
3. We will include students who are being left out.

The intervention described in this session incorporates several features of Hazelden's *Respect & Protect*® program and some from the Olweus program. First, in Trevor's school, there is a clear policy that violence is bad and not accepted; this is Basic Fact 5: "Mean and violent behavior is **bad,** and is not **acceptable** in our school; it is **never** okay for a child to hurt another child." This is a clear message that no one is entitled to use violent behavior, unless in a life-threatening situation—and life-threatening situations don't happen very often in elementary schools. Second, violence is clearly defined to include mean words and looks as well as actions that hurt another person's body, feelings, or possessions. Third, a school adult intervenes, puts an end to teasing and name calling, and has a "serious talk" with all the parties—Trevor and his friends who are bullying, and Daniel, the victim. This demonstrates how schools can correct their tolerance of aggressive behavior and begin to be more proactive in protecting victims. Then, there is a class meeting introducing the three Olweus class rules.

Remember that children who are victims have often been ignored, told to toughen up, or to stop instigating the bullying. If they are provocative victims, they may have been violent themselves and have been punished for their violent behavior, while the bullies have gotten away with their violent behavior. In this session, this part of the school violence problem—

the tolerance of adults—is corrected when Mrs. Owl steps in and makes Trevor and his friends stop teasing Daniel.

This session makes several distinctions that are repeated in the following sessions. First, it clarifies one reason why bullies pick on specific victims: the victims don't fight back or even stand up for themselves; instead they usually are passive or do nothing, or show fear or burst into tears. In the displacement, Trevor picks on Daniel because he is a good target. He doesn't fight back or even stand up for himself; he cries easily when Trevor teases him. Be sure to understand that victims do not cause the bullies to tease them, but by their passive or fearful reactions, they do give bullies positive reinforcement that encourages the bullies to continue. Again in the displacement, it's clarified that while Daniel does not cause Trevor to tease him, his reaction gives Trevor a positive reinforcement to continue.

In the next several sessions, you will teach the children in the Daniel group nine assertive behavior skills that help them change their usual response to bullies. Instead of being passive and doing nothing, or crying or reacting with fear, they will learn when they should ask an adult or other children for help, or when they should use an assertive behavior skill to stand up for themselves. The new behaviors they learn are not designed to make the bullies stop; rather they are behaviors the children learn to help them change their response and to feel better about themselves. However, we suspect that bullies will decrease their teasing behavior if the victims do not show themselves to be good targets. Beginning in session 5, you can use the review of Basic Fact 7, introduced in session 4, that describes the differences between passive, aggressive, and assertive behavior to drive home these points to the children.

The Trevor and Tiffany group manual can be used as a consequence to help children who are aggressive change their behavior. It can also be used as a demonstration of how school faculty can decrease their enabling behavior.

Beginning the Session

Welcome the students and remind them that they all belong to the Daniel the Dinosaur group so that they can learn how to handle school violence. If necessary, begin with a quick review of the group rules (see page 51). Draw attention to the poster listing the group rules, or have the children look at their own copies of the Group Rules Contract. In a go-around, have the children read the rules one at a time. Check for understanding before moving on.

Centering Exercise

Make certain that the children are comfortable and quiet. Ask if any of them remembered to "Stop and Breathe to Five" or do "The Icicle" in the past week. Remind them that stopping and breathing to five, or tensing and relaxing muscles, and then thinking will help them chill out and make good decisions about how to get along with other children. Introduce the new centering exercise, "The Chill Out." Tell the group members that this is another centering exercise that will help them calm down, relax, and be able to think if they get angry or upset. They can use this exercise without anyone else knowing.

Imagine that it is summer, and you are in the country with some friends. You are walking along a river and are having a good time exploring. But your friends are doing a lot of annoying things, sometimes tripping you, sometimes calling you stupid. You find yourself getting hotter and hotter, and angrier and angrier. You feel like your thermometer is going up to 100 degrees. You feel like telling your friends off, or beating them up.

To chill out, you decide to wade in the river. There's a calm pool—a perfect place to go swimming—and you decide to go in. Luckily, you have a bathing suit on under your shorts. As you put your feet into the river, feel how good the cool water feels. Now, you are in up to your waist. Pretty soon you duck under and get your head wet. Now you feel much cooler, and your temperature is going down. Your muscles are getting more and more relaxed. As your muscles get calmer, you find that your anger is getting calmer too. Now that you have chilled out, you can think better. You realize it won't do any good to beat up your friends or to tell them off. But you can tell them you don't like what they are doing. You find your anger floating away in the wonderful cool water. Imagine again how calm and relaxed your muscles feel, and how cool and calm you feel in the cool water.

Remind the students that they can use this technique in school, on the bus, during recess, and at home, to help them chill out so they can put thinking between their feelings and their behavior, especially if they are angry.

Feelings Check-in

Do a feelings check-in with the students (see page 69). Have them take out their Feeling Daniel and direct the children to color in the section on the dinosaur that shows how they're feeling today. When the students finish, have a go-around.

Basic Facts Review

To help the students review their last session and the basic facts learned so far, show them Basic Fact Posters 1 to 4. The Basic Facts List and Questions to Help Clarify the Basic Facts are printed on pages 229–234.

Assignment Review

Ask the students if they brought their homework assignments from last week. Remind them that they were to look in their family, neighborhood, or school to see if they know anyone who uses mean and violent behavior. Then, they were to look for the consequences of that person's mean and violent behavior. In a go-around, ask the children to share what they found: who are the people they know who have mean and violent behaviors and what are the consequences of those behaviors. If they want to keep the name of the person confidential, allow them to do so, but ask them to describe how the person is mean and violent, and the consequences of that behavior.

If the children forgot to do the assignment, in the go-around ask them to try to think of who they know in their family, or neighborhood, or school, who uses mean and violent behavior, and what are the consequences. Remind the group that you want them to be aware of the different ways children can be mean or violent.

Exploring the Story

Have the children get comfortable for today's story. Use the toy Daniel and allow him to tell the following:

> Hi, boys and girls! It's good to see you again. Today, we're going to learn about what principals, and teachers, and students should do when dinosaurs act mean and violent. Remember last week when I was telling you about what Trevor was doing to me? He kicked my desk, he stole my caveman pizza, he threatened to punch me in the nose, he tripped me and ran into me when we were playing Dinosaur Dodge Ball, and he called me Brontostupid. Remember how scared, and ashamed, and sad I felt? I couldn't tell anyone about what was going on. I was too ashamed, and I was afraid Trevor would find out and make fun of me for being a tattletale. I was afraid telling would just make things worse. Let me tell you about what happened next.
>
> One day Trevor was being his usual horrible self. We were in art class and were supposed to be drawing a picture of something we wear. I'm pretty good at drawing, and I decided to draw my shoes. You can imagine how interesting dinosaur running shoes look. Well, Mrs. Triceratops was out of the room, and Trevor was standing by my desk along with two of his friends, Stevie Stegosaurus and Michael Triceratops. Trevor said, "Look at what Brontostupid is drawing. His picture is awful. He must not have a brain." Stevie and Michael were laughing as hard as they could. I was so embarrassed. I even started to cry. I wished I would just disappear. I knew they would do what they usually do, and stand there and make fun of me and laugh at me for as long as they could. The rest of the class laughed at me, too.
>
> This time, though, something different happened. Mrs. Owl, the lady who comes to school to talk to children about the way they feel, walked into the classroom while Trevor and the guys were making fun of me. [Pull out your stuffed Mrs. Owl, on whom you have placed pearls and a pair of glasses.] She stood in the doorway watching for a few moments, and then she came over to my desk and said, "Trevor, Stevie, and Michael, stop talking and go back to your desks. I'm going to talk to each one of you alone."

[Stop here and ask the children to pull out their Mrs. Owl puppets from their folders. Tell them they have their own Mrs. Owl and they can color her any way they want. They can work on Mrs. Owl while you continue with the story.]

> When Mrs. Triceratops came back, Mrs. Owl talked to her for a little while, and then she took Trevor into her office. Mrs. Owl told Trevor that she noticed he was making fun of me. Trevor told Mrs. Owl that he was just having fun, and that I really liked it when he teased me. And he said it was really Stevie and Michael who were calling me names. Mrs. Owl told Trevor that he was being violent: his mean words were hurting my feelings.

She said that in Swamp School, the principals, teachers, and students do not accept mean or violent behavior toward other children. They think that mean and violent behavior is bad, and they will work to see that mean and violent behavior ends. Trevor could try to pretend he hadn't done anything bad, or blame others for his behavior, but he will still have to stop his violent behavior. It's not okay for him to hurt another dinosaur. She taught him that "Mean and violent behavior is bad and not acceptable in our school."

Mrs. Owl said to Trevor that it sounds like I was having a bad time in school. Trevor knew I wasn't very happy, and he said I was having a bad time because I'm so stupid. Then Mrs. Owl asked Trevor what he could do to help me in this situation. He said he couldn't think of anything. Then, he said it would help if I wasn't so stupid. Mrs. Owl said she wanted to know what **he** could do to help me. Finally, Trevor said he could tell Michael and Stevie to lay off me. Mrs. Owl said, "Excellent. That sounds like a good idea. You try that for a week and then we will meet and see how it went."

Mrs. Owl also met with Michael and Stevie. Then, she met with me. Mrs. Owl is a nice lady who wears glasses and a pretty pearl necklace, but I was still really embarrassed, and I still wished I could disappear. I still didn't want to say anything because I was afraid Trevor would make fun of me for being a tattletale or would punch me in the nose, like he said he would. Mrs. Owl started out by saying, "Hello, Daniel. I saw Trevor and Stevie and Michael calling you names in your classroom. And I talked to Mrs. Triceratops who says you seem pretty sad and spend a lot of time by yourself. Can you tell me what's gone on between you and Trevor?" I didn't say anything. Then Mrs. Owl said that when children call names, or tease, or make fun, or don't let other dinosaurs play, then they are being mean and violent. She told me that Swamp School was working really hard to put an end to mean and violent behavior in our school. But they can't stop mean and violent behavior unless they know what's going on. She said that she knew lots of dinosaurs who are afraid to tell when other dinosaurs hurt their feelings, or their bodies. But then they are just letting the dinosaurs get away with their mean and violent behavior.

I decided to trust Mrs. Owl, and I told her about the first day of school and how Trevor was mean to me on the bus. I told her how he tripped me and ran into me during Dinosaur Dodge Ball, how he kicked my desk, stole my caveman pizza, and called me Bronto-stupid. I told her I had lots of friends at Everglades Elementary School, but I didn't have any friends at Swamp School. Mrs. Owl asked me what I thought I could do to make things better for myself. I told her I couldn't think of anything.

Mrs. Owl said there were several things she could think of. First, she said that when dinosaurs are mean and violent, they often think, like Trevor, that it's okay for them to be mean and violent. They think they have the right to act however they want. And, in some schools, the adults decide to let the children learn on their own the consequences of being mean and violent. However, Swamp School is very concerned about mean and violent behavior, and the principals and teachers here have decided to work very hard to teach that mean and violent behavior is bad behavior and is not acceptable. Dinosaurs like Trevor will have to learn to stop mean and violent behavior while they are at Swamp School.

Mrs. Owl said she would talk to Mrs. Triceratops about having a class meeting to discuss how some dinosaurs are mean and violent, and to teach the class that mean and violent behavior by students is bad behavior and is not acceptable at Swamp School. When Mrs. Triceratops did that, she gave the class the Basic Facts you have already learned. Then we made three rules for our classroom:

1. We will not be mean and violent
2. We will try to help students who are being hurt by other dinosaurs who are being mean and violent
3. We will include students who are being left out.

The first rule says that it is the responsibility of each dinosaur in Swamp School to be sure that they never show mean and violent behavior. Each dinosaur has to watch his or her own behavior and make sure they do not make fun of anyone else, or tease them, or spread rumors about them, or threaten them, or not let them play.

The second rule says that each dinosaur should help other dinosaurs if someone is treating them in a mean or violent way. Otherwise, if a dinosaur like Trevor is teasing someone like me, and the other dinosaurs join in with him and tease me, too, or even just laugh at me, then Trevor will continue his behavior and maybe even get meaner. But if the other dinosaurs come and tell Trevor to knock it off or to pick on somebody as mean as he is, then he will probably stop treating me badly. If all the other dinosaurs do is come and stand near me, then Trevor will probably stop. So, the class rule that dinosaurs can help dinosaurs who are being hurt is a good one that can really help.

The third rule talks about what Tiffany was doing to Della. Tiffany and the girl dinosaurs were not letting Della jump rope with them. It's common for dinosaurs in elementary school to be mean by not letting somebody play. This rule says that we can help stop school violence by including dinosaurs who are being left out in play. They are good rules. Later, you can talk about how you can follow them in your school.

Then Mrs. Owl said she could think of some things she could teach me to help me make my situation in school better. She told me that when I do nothing when Trevor teases me, or when I burst into tears, then Trevor feels like he has a good target, and he continues to be mean and violent. Mrs. Owl asked me if I would like to learn ways to "Stand Tall," to do something besides nothing or burst into tears when Trevor, or someone like him teases me. Mrs. Owl said I don't cause Trevor to tease me by my reaction, but I encourage him to continue. If I learn other, better ways of "Standing Tall," standing up for myself, then I won't give Trevor the response he's looking for. He might still continue his violent behavior, but I will feel much better about myself. I said I would like to learn how to "Stand Tall," and I'll tell you more about that next week. For now, remember the three rules:

1. We will not be mean and violent.
2. We will try to help students who are being hurt by other dinosaurs who are being mean and violent.
3. We will include students who are being left out.

Discussion

Lead a discussion to help the group members understand that mean and violent behavior is not acceptable.

- Who is Mrs. Owl? (The lady who comes to school to talk to dinosaurs about the way they feel.)
- What were Trevor, Stevie, and Michael doing when Mrs. Owl came into the room? (They were making fun of Daniel's drawing of dinosaur running shoes.)
- What did Mrs. Owl do when she saw them making fun of Daniel? (She told them to stop talking, and she sent them back to their seats. She talked to Mrs. Triceratops. Then she met with them, and Daniel, alone.)
- What did Mrs. Owl tell Trevor about his making fun of Daniel's drawing? (She told him he was being violent because his mean words were hurting Daniel's feelings.)
- Is it okay for dinosaurs like Trevor to be violent? (No, it is never okay for one dinosaur to hurt another dinosaur.)
- What will Trevor have to learn? (He will have to learn to stop his mean and violent behavior at school.)
- What can schools like Swamp School do to stop mean and violent behavior? (Schools can set rules that mean and violent behavior is bad and is not acceptable at their school.)
- How did Mrs. Owl teach Daniel's class about mean and violent behavior? (She asked Mrs. Triceratops to have a class meeting. They learned basic facts about violence. Then they decided on three rules.)
- What were the three rules that the class decided on to stop mean and violent behavior? (1. We will not be mean and violent. 2. We will try to help students who are being hurt by other dinosaurs who are being mean and violent. 3. We will include students who are being left out.)
- How can children in your class not be mean and violent? (Expect responses like not teasing others or calling names; not tripping or hitting other children; not spreading rumors or not letting children play with us.)
- How can children in your class help students who are being hurt by other children who are being mean and violent? (We can go and stand near the children who are being hurt; then the children who are being mean might stop.)
- How can children include students who are being left out? (We can ask them to play if other children are not letting them play.)
- What can Daniel learn to help his situation at school? (He can learn to stop being passive or crying when Trevor teases him.)
- Does Daniel cause Trevor to tease him by crying? (No. Trevor is responsible for what he does. But, when Daniel does nothing or cries when Trevor teases him, he does encourage Trevor to tease him worse.)

Activity

Ask the children to take out Activity Sheet 3A, Draw One Way to Follow One of the Three Rules to Stop Mean and Violent Behavior in Schools (see page 92), from their folders. Tell the children to draw a picture with their pencils or crayons or markers of one way they can follow one of the three rules to stop mean and violent behavior. Remind the children that you are not looking for artistic ability; you just want their ideas. They can use "stick figures" or they can use words to describe how they can follow one of the Three Rules.

When the children finish, have another go-around. Invite each child to explain his or her drawing.

Basic Facts

Ask the children to pull out Basic Fact Worksheet 3 (see page 93) from their folders.

>   5. Mean and violent behavior is **bad** and is not **acceptable** in our school; it is **never** okay for a child to hurt another child.
>   6. Children can have three rules to stop mean and violent behavior:
>   a. We will **not** be mean and violent.
>   b. We will try to **help** students who are being hurt by other children who are being mean and violent.
>   c. We will **include** students who are being left out.

Briefly discuss each fact, checking for understanding. Correct any misconceptions.

Give the children time to complete the bottom half of the worksheet by filling in the blanks. Then have the entire group read the facts out loud. Remind the children that you will be going over the basic facts learned so far at the beginning of each session and that you will ask them to explain what each means. Have the children put their worksheets in their folders.

Homework Assignment

Ask the children to pull out Homework Assignment 3 (see page 94) from their folders. Ask one child to read it out loud. Tell the children that you want them to think of a way they can follow one of the three rules every day for the next week and to write down what they have done.

Wrapping Up

Repeat the centering exercise from the beginning of the group, "The Chill Out" (see pages 83–84).

Affirmation

Involve the group in an affirmation. Stand and join in a circle with the children, holding hands. Go ahead and have each child share something he or she liked about the group. Start the affirmation yourself: "One way I can follow one of the three rules to stop mean and violent behavior in school is . . ."

Closing

Remain standing in a circle with the children holding hands and lead the group in the closing activity, "Pass a Silent Wish" (page 58).

Collect the folders and fill out a copy of the Process and Progress Form (see page 235) or the Progress Notes (see pages 236–237), if you are an experienced leader, as soon as you can after leading the session.

Activity Sheet 3
Mrs. Owl Puppet

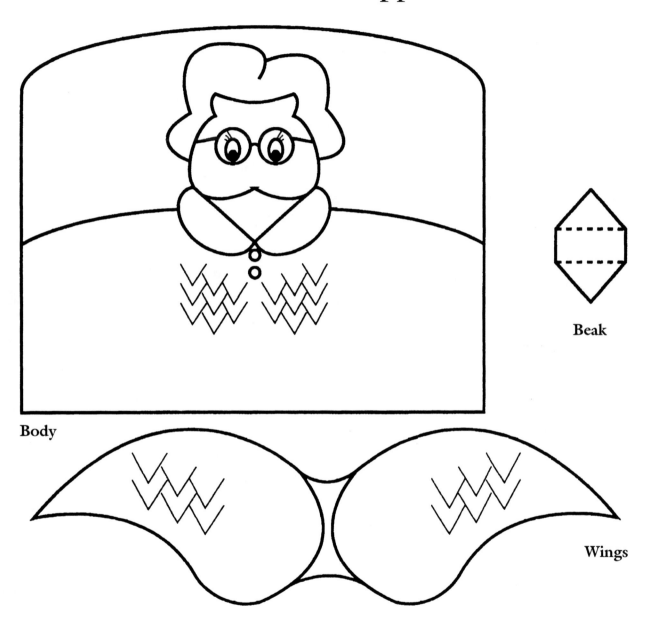

Beak

Body

Wings

1. Color Mrs. Owl with your favorite colors. Color her beak, her body, and her wings.
2. Cut out the body. Print your name on the back. Roll the ends toward the back and tape or paste together.
3. Cut out the beak. Tape or paste the beak onto Mrs. Owl's face.
4. Cut out the wings. Tape or paste them onto Mrs. Owl's back.

Activity Sheet 3A
Draw One Way to Follow One of the Three Rules to Stop Mean and Violent Behavior in Schools

1. We will not be mean and violent.
2. We will try to help students who are being hurt by other children who are being mean and violent
3. We will include students who are being left out.

Basic Fact Worksheet 3

5. Mean and violent behavior is **bad** and is not **acceptable** in our school; it is **never** okay for a child to hurt another child.

6. Children can have three rules to stop mean and violent behavior:
   a. We will **not** be mean and violent.
   b. We will try to **help** students who are being hurt by other children who are being mean and violent.
   c. We will **include** students who are being left out.

_____

5. Mean and violent behavior is _____ and is not _____ in our school; it is _____ okay for a child to hurt another child.

6. Children can have three rules to stop mean and violent behavior:
   a. We will _____ be mean and violent.
   b. We will try to _____ students who are being hurt by other children who are being mean and violent.
   c. We will _____ students who are being left out.

Homework Assignment 3

Every day, see if you can find one way to follow one of the three rules to stop mean and violent behavior in school. Write a short sentence.

1. We will **not** be mean and violent.
2. We will try to **help** students who are being hurt by other children who are being mean and violent.
3. We will **include** students who are being left out.

Day 1 _____

_____

_____

Day 2 _____

_____

_____

Day 3 _____

_____

_____

Day 4 _____

_____

_____

Day 5 _____

_____

_____

Session 4

Daniel the Dinosaur Learns
How to Stand Tall

Objectives

To help the students:

- learn the differences between passive, assertive, and aggressive behavior
- learn the assertive behavior skills of Body Language, including posture, eye contact, and tone of voice

Preparation

- Display the posterboard copy of the group rules.
- Have available the toy Daniel and Mrs. Owl and Basic Fact Posters 1 to 6.
- Add to each student's folder:
  - Handout 4 (Assertive Behavior Skills of Body Language)
  - Basic Fact Worksheet 4
  - Homework Assignment 4
- Place each student's folder, pencil, and crayons or markers at his or her place.
- Read through the session plan before meeting.

Background and Guidelines

The first three sessions described the new, more inclusive definition of violence, the characteristics and families of children who are violent and those who tend to be their victims, and introduced some clear limits that violent behavior is bad, unacceptable, and will no longer be tolerated by the adults in the school. The next three sessions, 4, 5, and 6, introduce nine specific skills to help children change their typical responses (passivity, fear, crying, withdrawal, or in the case of provocative victims, aggression) and replace them with more assertive behaviors. In sessions 7 and 8, the children will have the opportunity to practice these assertive behavior skills in situations such as being teased, called names, or left out. Sessions 9 and 10 will teach anger management and conflict resolution, and session 11 allows the children to solidify their knowledge by presenting it to someone else.

Sessions 4, 5, and 6 introduce nine assertive behavior skills. These are behaviors the children can use when they are being hurt by other children's violent behavior, or when they themselves might have been violent.

You will begin this session by teaching the children the differences between **passive, aggressive,** and **assertive** behaviors. A good way for adults to understand these different behaviors is to imagine that you are about to leave to go to an important meeting and a good friend calls you. If you just listen and miss your meeting, you are acting in a passive way. If you scream at your friend and say, "How dare you call me! Can't you tell I can't talk to you now? Don't ever call me again!" you are acting in an aggressive way. If you tell your friend that you would really like to talk to him or her, but you're on your way out the door and you'll call him or her back tomorrow, then you are being assertive—standing up for yourself in a polite way that does not hurt others.

Expect the word *aggressive* to confuse the group members, many of whom play soccer, basketball, or football, and are coached to be aggressive. Clarify for the children that in sports the word *aggressive* means to play your hardest, to do your best, and to hustle. Here, however, you are using another definition of aggression—violent behavior intended to hurt others. In clarifying Basic Fact 7, "A child can react to another child's violent behavior by being **passive, aggressive,** or **assertive,**" throughout the following sessions, you will need to clarify that in sports it's good to be aggressive, but it's not good to be aggressive when you're trying to get along with others. Remember that aggressive behavior is only justified when your life is being threatened.

The children in the Daniel group, who are referred because they are hurt by other children's violent behavior, tend to have three major reactions. Some are passive, meek, and appear very depressed. Some are whiny and appear very dependent and clingy on adults. Others are provocative victims, who appear intense and angry. Your goal is to help the children replace these kinds of maladaptive behaviors with assertive behaviors, ways they can stand up for themselves politely and take care of themselves. Provocative victims feel justified in their violent reactions to others' aggressive behavior. The value judgment that violent behavior is never justified unless the situation is life-threatening will help them begin to see that their aggressive behavior is just as bad as the child's who started it. We want the children to develop some alternatives to their usual reactions, so that they can choose how they want to respond. There may be some occasions where passive behavior is most appropriate. For instance, if a child accidentally bumps into someone in the hall, doing nothing may be appropriate. If a child repeatedly bumps into someone in the hall, then being passive is not appropriate, but neither is being aggressive since the situation is not life-threatening. So assertive behavior will be the most appropriate. This situation is played out with Daniel and Stevie Stegosaurus in session 5.

It is also important to realize that the goal of using assertive behavior is not to change the behavior of the other person—you can't control anyone else's behavior—you can only control your own behavior. But assertive behavior will help the child feel good about himself or herself because he or she is standing up for himself or herself in a way that doesn't hurt anyone else. You will be repeating this in the clarification of Basic Fact 7 in future sessions.

In this session, and the next two sessions, you will be teaching nine assertive behavior skills—ways the children can stand up for themselves politely without hurting others. The assertive behavior skills, I Statements, and I Hear You Statements, were introduced in the parenting program, *STEP: Systematic Training in Effective Parenting*. Kill-Them-With-Kindness Sandwiches were described by Russell Barkley, author of a training program for parents of oppositional children. Body Language and Broken Records were described in the book *Tackling Bullying in Your School*. Sound Bites were described by Dick Schaefer in *Choices and Consequences* as ignoring skills. He stated that author, counselor, teacher, and lecturer Tom Alibrandi came up with five words or phrases for parents to use to avoid engaging in power trips with their children. They work just as well for children with aggressive behavior and their victims. Apologizing, Humor, and Nice Replies are generally known throughout the population.

You will teach one assertive behavior skill in this session, Body Language, which has three components: posture, eye contact, and tone of voice. This assertive behavior skill is taught first in the Daniel group because so many children have such passive body language that they can't be seen or heard. You will teach them to stand up straight, or to Stand Tall, as Mrs. Owl teaches Daniel; to look at the person to whom they are speaking; and to speak clearly and distinctly so that they can be understood. These three components are broken down in Handout 4. As you help the children practice Standing Tall, or assertive posture, you will remind them to stand up straight, to put their shoulders back, and to stand tall. As you coach them on eye contact, you will ask them to look at the person to whom they are speaking and to look in a friendly way. For tone of voice, you will ask them to speak loudly enough so they can be heard, clearly and distinctly, in a friendly tone, so people can understand them, and as though they mean what they say. These skills are broken down because so many of the Daniel group children mumble, slouch, keep their heads down, and make statements in a very hesitant, questioning tone of voice. Feel free to emphasize any of these skills depending on the characteristics and personalities of the children in your group.

Because these children tend to be meek and passive, an entire session is devoted to helping them learn assertive body language. In the session, you, the group leader, will show them passive, aggressive, and assertive body language by reciting "Mary Had a Little Lamb" in all three ways, for posture, eye contact, and tone of voice. Then you will coach the children to practice saying "Mary Had a Little Lamb" using assertive posture, eye contact, and tone of voice. Use humor as you coach the children, not accepting their efforts until you can hear them speak distinctly, while they are standing up straight looking at you. Children usually enjoy this activity, and it makes an enormous difference that you will see in later sessions. You will be amazed at their ability to teach an audience the Basic Facts in the presentation in session 11 if you do a good job of helping them learn assertive body language skills today and encourage the children to practice them in future sessions. Use the Basic Facts Review and their practicing the assertive behavior skills in the next four sessions as opportunities to practice using assertive body language.

Beginning the Session

Welcome the students. If necessary, begin with a quick review of the group rules (see page 51). Draw attention to the poster listing the group rules, or have the children look at their own copies of the Group Rules Contract. In a go-around, have the children read the rules one at a time. Check for understanding before moving on.

Centering Exercise

Make certain that the children are comfortable and quiet. Ask if any of them remembered to "Stop and Breathe to Five," or used "The Icicle," or used "The Chill Out" in the past week. Remind them that stopping and breathing to five, or tensing and relaxing muscles, and then thinking will help them make good decisions about how to get along with other children. Introduce the new centering exercise, "Defuse the Bomb." Tell the group members that this is another centering exercise that will help them calm down, relax, and be able to think if they get angry or upset. They can use this exercise without anyone else knowing.

> Imagine that someone has just told you that you are stupid. You are really, really angry. You are ready to start to fight. You feel like a bomb ready to explode. You know that if you explode, you will do something bad: something you will get in trouble for or something you will be sorry you did. You decide to give yourself ten seconds to defuse yourself, so that you won't explode, and you will be able to think about what else you can do. Count slowly with me from ten to one. Count slowly and breathe deeply while you count. Ten. Nine. Eight. Seven. Remember to breathe deeply and slowly. Six. Five. Four. Three. Two. One. Now, instead of exploding, see if you have been able to defuse yourself. Now you can "Stop and Think" about what to do next. Congratulations! You have been able to defuse yourself!

Remind the students that they can use this technique in school, on the bus, during recess, and at home to help them relax so they can put thinking between their feelings and their behavior.

Feelings Check-in

Use the Feeling Daniel to do a feelings check-in with the students (see page 69). When the students finish, have a go-around.

Basic Facts Review

To help the students review their last session and the basic facts learned so far, show them Basic Fact Posters 1 to 8. The Basic Facts List and Questions to Help Clarify the Basic Facts are printed on pages 229–234.

Assignment Review

Ask the students if they brought their homework assignments from last week. Remind them of the assignment by reading it: "Every day, see if you can find one way to follow one of the three rules to stop mean and violent behavior in school. Write a short sentence." In a go-around, ask the children to share what they found: ways they could follow one of the three rules every day.

If the children forgot to do the assignment, in the go-around ask them to try to think of one way they followed one of the rules in the past week. If they can't think of anything they did, ask them what they could do in the next week to follow one of the rules. Remind the group that it is only by each individual child in a school following the rules that violent behavior in schools will end.

Exploring the Story

Have the children get comfortable for today's story. Use the toy Daniel and Mrs. Owl and allow Daniel to tell the following:

> Hi, boys and girls! It's good to see you again. Remember last week how Mrs. Owl watched Trevor and Michael and Stevie make fun of my drawing? Then Mrs. Owl met with Trevor and told him he was being mean and violent and that violent behavior was not acceptable at Swamp School. Then Mrs. Owl had a class meeting with Mrs. Tricera-top's class, and they made three rules to stop mean and violent behavior.
>
> 1. We will **not** be mean and violent.
> 2. We will try to **help** students who are being hurt by other children who are being mean and violent.
> 3. We will **include** students who are being left out.
>
> Mrs. Owl said it's good to have those rules, but they won't do any good unless individual dinosaurs like Trevor and Tiffany follow them. She will work with them to help them learn how to change their behavior.
>
> Then Mrs. Owl asked me if I wanted to work with her to learn how to "Stand Tall" so that I can get along with other dinosaurs better, even if nobody is ever mean or violent to me again. I said I would.
>
> First, Mrs. Owl taught me the difference between **passive, aggressive,** and **assertive** behaviors. She used the example of Trevor making fun of my drawing dinosaur running shoes last week. I could react to Trevor by being passive, aggressive, or assertive.
>
> I would be **passive** if I did nothing but sit there and listen to his put downs, probably feeling very hurt and maybe even crying. Mrs. Owl says that when I look really hurt, Trevor knows he has a good target for put downs.

I would be **aggressive** if I did something violent to Trevor: some mean word, look, sign, or act that would hurt Trevor. Sometimes when people use the word *aggressive* they are talking about how hard you try when you play sports like football, basketball, or soccer. In those sports, it's good to play your hardest, to be aggressive. But the way we use the word *aggressive* here is different. We're talking about the kind of aggressive behavior that is like violence: any mean word, look, sign, or act that hurts another dinosaur's body, feelings, or possessions. If I hit Trevor or called him names like Tuba Tyrannosaurus of Tyrannostupid, then I would be aggressive. Mrs. Owl said that what we've learned about it never being okay for a dinosaur to hurt another dinosaur applies to me, too.

So it's good for me to learn **assertive** behavior. Assertive behavior means that you stand up for yourself, no matter what the other dinosaur does. If I said, "Trevor, I feel hurt when you call me Brontostupid," I would be using assertive behavior. Assertive behavior does not change the other person, but it helps me stand up for myself. It helps me feel better about myself. And, if I speak calmly and feel good about what I'm saying, instead of looking afraid and crying, or getting angry and being aggressive back, then I will not be such a good target for Trevor.

Mrs. Owl repeated that it's not okay for me to use aggressive behavior because that would hurt someone else. Being passive usually makes me feel weak and hurt and encourages Trevor to continue his violent behavior. So it will be good for me to learn some assertive behavior skills to use with Trevor.

The first assertive behavior skill I learned was how to **Stand Tall**. Mrs. Owl taught me the assertive behavior skills of **Body Language**. There are three parts to this skill: **posture, eye contact,** and **tone of voice.** Let me explain.

[Ask the children to take out Handout 4, Assertive Behavior Skills of Body Language (see page 105). Ask them to read along with Daniel, or if they are good readers, ask three different children to read the Assertive Behavior Skills of Body Language.]

Posture. Mrs. Owl said my posture shows a lot about me. She showed me three kinds of posture. In the passive kind of posture, she slouched her shoulders, put her head down, and looked kind of afraid.

[The group leader should demonstrate passive posture.]

Then, she demonstrated aggressive posture. She stood up and put her fists out, ready to fight.

[The group leader should demonstrate aggressive posture.]

Then, she demonstrated assertive posture. She stood up straight and put her shoulders back. She kept her head high, but not stuck up. And she looked her tallest.

[The group leader should demonstrate assertive posture.]

She asked me what I think about people who have each kind of posture.

[The leader should demonstrate all three postures again and ask the children what they think about the person with each posture.]

Then Mrs. Owl asked me to practice assertive posture. Here's how I learned to **Stand Tall.**

[The group leader should have the toy Daniel stand tall.]

Eye Contact. Next, Mrs. Owl showed me three kinds of eye contact, you know, how you look at someone. In the passive kind of eye contact, she puts her eyes down and did not look at me and looked kind of afraid.

[The group leader should demonstrate passive eye contact.]

Then she demonstrated aggressive eye contact. She stood up and looked straight at me, with a very mean look in her eyes, like she was ready to fight.

[The group leader should demonstrate aggressive eye contact.]

Then she demonstrated assertive eye contact. She looked me in the eyes, and she looked at me without looking afraid or mean.

[The group leader should demonstrate assertive eye contact.]

She asked me what I think about people with each kind of eye contact.

[The leader should demonstrate all three eye contact behaviors again and ask the children what they think about the person with each kind of eye contact.]

Then Mrs. Owl asked me to practice assertive eye contact. Here's how I learned to make assertive eye contact.

[The leader should have Daniel make good eye contact.]

Tone of Voice. Finally, Mrs. Owl showed me three ways to use my tone of voice, which is how you talk. When she showed me a passive tone of voice, she recited "Mary Had a Little Lamb" in a very weak voice. She did not speak loudly, and she said her words in a way I could barely understand.

[The group leader should demonstrate passive voice by reciting "Mary had a little lamb, its fleece was white as snow, and everywhere that Mary went, the lamb was sure to go," in a passive way.]

Then, she demonstrated an aggressive tone of voice.

[The group leader should recite "Mary" in a mean, hostile tone of voice.]

Then she demonstrated an assertive tone of voice. She recited "Mary Had a Little Lamb" in a tone of voice that was loud enough and clear enough that it was easy to understand. It was a friendly tone of voice, and she spoke as though she meant what she said.

[The group leader should recite "Mary" in an assertive tone of voice.]

Mrs. Owl asked me what I think about people who have each kind of tone of voice.

[The leader should demonstrate all three kinds of tone of voice again and ask the children what they think about the person with each kind of tone of voice.]

Now, let's discuss what we've learned so far.

Discussion

Lead a discussion to help group members understand the differences between passive, aggressive, and assertive behavior and the skills of Body Language. With kindergarten through second-grade children, you may want to describe passive as doing nothing, aggressive as mean, and assertive as standing tall, standing up for yourself in a way that does not hurt anyone else.

- What are three kinds of behavior that Mrs. Owl taught Daniel today? (Passive, aggressive, and assertive.)
- What is passive behavior? Give an example. (Passive behavior is when you do nothing. Sometimes it's good to do nothing until you think about what you should do.)
- What is aggressive behavior? Give an example. (Aggressive behavior is when you look, act, or speak in a mean, violent way to hurt someone's body, feelings, or possessions. Aggressive behavior is mean. This kind of aggressive behavior is different from being aggressive in sports, when you try your hardest to play well.)
- What is assertive behavior? (Assertive behavior is when you stand up for yourself. It may not change the other person, but it will help you feel better about yourself.)
- What are the three skills of Body Language? (Posture, eye contact, and tone of voice.)
- What should you remember in the assertive behavior skill of posture? (Stand up straight; put your shoulders back; lift your head high but not stuck up; stand tall.)

- What should you remember in the assertive behavior skill of eye contact? (Look at the person to whom you are speaking. Have a friendly look in your eyes.)
- What should you remember in the assertive behavior skill tone of voice? (Speak in a loud enough voice. Speak clearly and distinctly. Speak in a friendly tone. Speak so people can understand you. Speak as though you mean what you say.)

Now it's your turn to practice the three assertive behavior skills of Body Language: posture, eye contact, and tone of voice.

Activity

Tell the children that you are going to help them practice all three assertive behavior skills of Body Language: posture, eye contact, and tone of voice. Tell them that they can look at Handout 4 (see page 105) if they want.

Choose a child to go first, and tell him or her that you will coach them on these skills. Have the first child practice the posture of standing tall. First, ask the child to show a passive posture by slouching. Then ask the child to stand in an aggressive way, as though he or she was ready to fight. Then ask the child to stand tall. Remind the child to stand up straight, put his or her shoulders back, lift the head up high, but not stuck up, and stand tall. If the child is using passive or aggressive posture, ask permission to touch, and help the child come to a more assertive posture. Then help the child stand tall without being aggressive.

Then have that child practice eye contact. Gently encourage the child until he or she looks you in the eye. Encourage the child to have a friendly look.

Third, work on tone of voice. Remind the child to speak in a loud enough voice—clearly and distinctly in a friendly tone—so people can understand, and as though the child means what he or she says. Ask the child to recite "Mary Had a Little Lamb" in an assertive tone of voice. You may need to coach the child to attain an assertive tone of voice. Finally, ask the child to put all three Body Language skills together at the same time and recite "Mary" with assertive posture and eye contact with you or the other group members. Be sure to give each child plenty of praise for the improvements he or she makes in these three skills.

Repeat the process with each child in the group.

Basic Facts

Ask the children to take out Basic Fact Worksheet 4 (see page 106) from their folders.

7. A child can react to another child's violent behavior by being **passive, aggressive,** or **assertive.**
8. The assertive behavior skills of **Body Language** include **posture, eye contact,** and tone of **voice** that help you stand up for yourself without hurting anyone else.

Briefly discuss each fact, checking for understanding. Correct any misconceptions.

Give the children time to complete the bottom half of the worksheet by filling in the blanks. Then have the entire group read the facts out loud. Remind the children that you will be going over the basic facts learned so far at the beginning of each session and that you will ask them to explain what each means. Have the children put their worksheets in their folders.

Homework Assignment

Ask the children to pull out Homework Assignment 4 (see page 107) from their folders. Ask one child to read it out loud. Tell the children that you want them to think of a way they can use one of the assertive behavior skills of Body Language, then use assertive posture, eye contact, or tone of voice that will help them stand up for themselves, and write down what they have done.

Wrapping Up

Repeat the centering exercise from the beginning of the group, "Defuse the Bomb" (see page 98).

Affirmation

Involve the group in an affirmation. Stand and join in a circle with the children, holding hands. Go ahead and have each child share an assertive behavior skill of Body Langauge that he or she can use to stand up for himself or herself. Start the affirmation yourself: "One way I can use an assertive behavior skill of Body Language is to . . ."

Closing

Remain standing in a circle with the children holding hands and lead the group in the closing activity, "Pass a Silent Wish" (see page 58).

Collect the folders and fill out a copy of the Process and Progress Form (see page 235) or the Progress Notes (see pages 236–237).

Handout 4
Assertive Behavior Skills of Body Language

Posture

Stand up straight.
Put your shoulders back.
Keep your head high, but not stuck up.
Stand tall.

Eye Contact

Look at the person to whom you are speaking.
Look in a friendly way.

Tone of Voice

Speak in a loud enough voice.
Speak clearly and distinctly.
Speak in a friendly tone.
Speak so people can understand you.
Speak as though you mean what you say.

Basic Fact Worksheet 4

7. A child can react to another child's violent behavior by being **passive**, **aggressive**, or **assertive**.

8. The assertive behavior skills of **Body Language** include **posture**, **eye contact**, and **tone of voice** that help you stand up for yourself without hurting anyone else.

_____

7. A child can react to another child's violent behavior by being _____, _____, or _____.

8. The assertive behavior skills of _____ include _____, _____, and _____ that help you stand up for yourself without hurting anyone else.

Homework Assignment 4

Every day, see if you can use one of the assertive behavior skills of Body Language—posture, eye contact, and tone of voice—that help you stand up for yourself without hurting anyone. Write a short sentence.

POSTURE
Stand up straight.
Put your shoulders back.
Keep your head high, but not stuck up.
Stand tall.

EYE CONTACT
Look at the person to whom you are speaking.
Look in a friendly way.

TONE OF VOICE
Speak in a loud enough voice.
Speak clearly and distinctly.
Speak in a friendly tone.
Speak so people can understand you.
Speak as though you mean what you say.

Day 1 _____

_____

Day 2 _____

_____

Day 3 _____

_____

Day 4 _____

_____

Day 5 _____

_____

Session 5

Daniel the Dinosaur Learns How to Use I Statements and I Hear You Statements

Objectives

To help the students:

- learn when to go to an adult for help and when to use an assertive behavior skill when experiencing violence
- practice the assertive behavior skills of Body Language: posture, eye contact, and tone of voice
- learn the assertive behavior skills of I Statements and I Hear You Statements

Preparation

- Display the posterboard copy of the group rules.
- Have available the toy Daniel and Mrs. Owl and Basic Fact Posters 1 to 8.
- Add to each student's folder:
  –Activity Sheet 5 (Practice Situations for I Statements and I Hear You Statements)
  –Basic Fact Worksheet 5
  –Homework Assignment 5
- Place each student's folder, pencil, and crayons or markers at his or her place.
- Have a red and a black marker and a chalkboard or flip chart available to list different kinds of violent behavior that happen in elementary schools and what to do when they happen to you.
- Read through the session plan before meeting.

Background and Guidelines

This session builds on the concepts of the difference between passive, aggressive, and assertive behavior introduced last week and also clarifies what children should do when they are hurt by other children, depending on the kind of violence they are experiencing. While the *Respect & Protect®* program is built on the idea of environmental control—that adults will no longer tolerate bullying behavior of any kind, not just physical violence—we do not want to make the children completely dependent on adults to handle each situation. This session helps children understand when they should go to an adult and when they should try to think of an assertive response on their own.

To this end, you will begin the session by having the children help Daniel name the different kinds of violent behaviors that happen in school. This should be easy, since the children learned the new more-inclusive definition of violence in session 1, and you have been repeating the specific behaviors in the Basic Facts Review each week. As the children name specific violent behaviors, write them on a chalkboard or flip chart in black marker and place them in four columns. (See the story for examples.) Column 1 should list verbal kinds of violence, such as name calling, put downs, teasing, and not letting someone play. Column 2 should list behaviors such as threatening, intimidation, spreading rumors, trying to take your things, and trying to get you to fight. Column 3 should list physical violence like hitting, pushing, shoving, kicking, choking, and tripping. Finally, column 4 should list severe violence like bringing weapons to school and killing.

You want to emphasize to the children that in cases of possible physical danger, like weapons and hitting, their first concern is getting to a safe place—to leave the dangerous situation and go to an adult. No children should allow themselves to be hurt. You will write on columns 3 and 4 in red marker what they should do in physically violent situations: "Get to a safe place and tell an adult."

Situations typical of those in columns 1 and 2 are more complicated. Whether the child should try to handle these kinds of situations on his or her own depends on the pattern, frequency, and severity of the behavior. For instance, if Jeff and James are friends, and Jeff calls James "Stupid" once, then James should probably handle the situation on his own, using an assertive behavior skill, such as an I Statement. However, if Jeff and James are not friends, and Jeff repeatedly calls James names and makes fun of him, then James should let an adult know so the adult can set limits with Jeff, eventually forcing a consequence to help him change his behavior.

Another reason for a child to ask an adult for help in situations in columns 1 and 2 is if the child has no alternative except to respond in a passive, fearful, timid way, usually by crying; or by reacting as a provocative victim and resorting to violence in return. Then, the child should ask for help so he or she can learn alternative ways of reacting. In such cases, the adult should teach the children assertive behavior skills, for handling future situations on their own. You will write, "Ask an Adult for Help" and "Assertive Behavior Skills" over columns 1 and 2.

Chunking it Down

As you teach the children assertive ways to replace their passive or violent behavior, remember the concept of "chunking it down," although the concept is not used for the children. Keep in mind when you lead these groups that any behavioral change—for children or adults—is usually a process that takes time. In chunking it down, you break behavioral change into small, attainable steps. For changing the behavior of a child who reacts to another child's violent behavior with passive or violent behavior, an example of chunking it down would be for the child to:

1. Learn that violent behaviors are bad and unacceptable; learn that passive behavior, acting fearful, and crying may make you feel bad about yourself and may only encourage the child who is violent toward you to continue his or her violent behavior.
2. Observe his or her own behavior for behaviors like name calling, threatening, and so on, or for behaviors like passive body language and crying.
3. Learn new behaviors, such as assertive behavior skills, to take the place of passive or aggressive behaviors.
4. After acting in a violent or passive way, talk to an adult (a teacher, counselor, or principal) to process the situation: the adult may need to help the child figure out which assertive behavior skill would have been appropriate in that situation.
5. Then, after acting in a violent or passive way, the child can begin to decide on his or her own which assertive behavior skill he or she could have used. The child may decide that being passive was the best choice in that particular situation.
6. Finally, the child can eventually begin to implement the assertive behavior skills.
7. Even then, there will probably be times when the child uses passive or aggressive behavior—then the child may need help to process what he or she should have done.

The more people who understand this process, the more opportunities the child will have to get adult assistance in figuring out which assertive behavior skill he or she should use to replace passive or aggressive behavior. Instead of getting angry at the child for passive or violent behavior, set the standard that passive behavior may only encourage the violent child and that violent behavior is bad and unacceptable and will not be tolerated. Then look at the situation as an opportunity to help the child use his or her new skills.

I Statements

I Statements are ways to express your feelings politely without hurting others. In contrast, You Statements are accusations—"You're an idiot. You shouldn't have done that." The person who hears a You Statement is likely to feel attacked, while the person who hears an I Statement is less likely to feel attacked.

I Statements are broken into three sections to make them easier for children, and if you want, you can refer to them as "I Feel Statements" to make them easier for children to remember:

I feel . . . (say how you feel)

when you . . . (say what the other person did)

because . . . (say why you feel the way you do).

An example of an I Statement is given in the story. This is a skill that children usually need help to master, and they do it through practice. The activity gives them three chances to formulate an I Statement. Some children may need your questioning to help them fill in the blanks. Then, Activity Sheet 5 (see pages 119–120) calls for each child to repeat his or her I Statement, along with the I Hear You Statement they will formulate. This practice, saying the assertive behavior skills out loud, is a way to help the children master the skills.

I Hear You Statements

I Hear You Statements are called "Reflective Listening" in *STEP, Systematic Training in Effective Parenting,* a term too difficult for children to understand, as was the concept until a two-part formula was developed. While an I Statement is a way for a child to send a message to describe the way he or she feels, an I Hear You Statement is a way to receive a message, to let the other person know that the child hears and understands. In an I Hear You Statement, the child says

I can tell that you feel or think . . .

because . . .

The child is not necessarily agreeing with the other person or telling them that he or she is right. But by letting the other person know that the child heard and understood him or her, the child can help to de-escalate (cool off) rather than escalate (heat up) a potentially violent situation.

An example of an I Hear You Statement is given in the story, and Activity Sheet 5 provides three opportunities for the children to formulate one of these. Again, they will probably need your help in formulating an I Hear You Statement.

You will use these skills in sessions 7 and 8 when you teach how they can be used in specific bullying situations like being teased and being left out. The children will have chances to practice how to use them in those sessions. Remember the idea of chunking it down. Don't expect the children to be able to use these skills right away. The more adults in the child's environment who know these skills and who help the child formulate what they could have said, the easier it will be for the children to understand them and begin to use them on their own.

Beginning the Session

Welcome the students. If necessary, begin with a quick review of the group rules (see page 51). Check for understanding before moving on.

Centering Exercise

Tell the students that you will be repeating the first centering exercise, "Stop and Breathe to Five." This exercise can be found on page 52.

Feelings Check-in

Using the Feeling Daniel, do a feelings check-in with the students (see page 69). When the students finish, have a go-around.

Basic Facts Review

To help the students review their last session and the basic facts learned so far, show them Basic Fact Posters 1 to 8. The Basic Facts List and Questions to Help Clarify the Basic Facts are printed on pages 229–234.

Assignment Review

Ask the students if they brought their homework assignments from last week. Remind them of the assignment by reading it: "Every day, see if you can use one of the assertive behavior skills of Body Language—posture, eye contact, and tone of voice—that help you stand up for yourself without hurting anyone else. Write a short sentence."

In a go-around, ask the children to share what they found: ways they could use the assertive behavior skills of Body Language.

If the children forgot to do the assignment, in the go-around ask them to try to think of one way they used assertive posture, eye contact, or tone of voice in the past week. If they can't think of anything they did, ask them what they could do in the next week to use one of these assertive behavior skills. Remind them that using these skills may not change the other person, but it will help them feel better about themselves.

Exploring the Story

Have the children get comfortable for today's story. Use the toy Daniel and Mrs. Owl and allow Daniel to tell the following:

> Hi, boys and girls! Have you been remembering to Stand Tall? I've been practicing standing as tall as I can, with my shoulders back and my head up. I've also been careful to look at people when I talk to them, and to speak very clearly and distinctly. But Trevor is still being a pain in my dinosaur tail.
>
> I was telling Mrs. Owl about the latest thing Trevor the Terrible Tyrannosaurus did. We were playing Dinosaur Basketball during recess. I guess I got in his way when he was trying to make a shot and he missed. So he tripped me, and then he kicked me. I don't know why he was so mean. I wasn't getting in his way on purpose, and it was only a game.

I asked Mrs. Owl what I should do when Trevor is aggressive with me. If he is mean to me, shouldn't I be mean back to him, by hitting him, or at least calling him names?

Mrs. Owl said, "Daniel, remember our basic fact? Mean and violent behavior is bad and is not acceptable in our school; it is never okay for a dinosaur to hurt another dinosaur. The only time it is okay to use violence is when your life is being threatened, and that doesn't happen very often in elementary school. Remember when we learned about the differences between passive, aggressive, and assertive behaviors last week? Let's look at the different kinds of violent behaviors that Trevor and other dinosaurs like him use at school, and then let's look at whether it's better to be passive, aggressive, or assertive. Then, let's learn some more assertive behavior skills for you to use when Trevor is mean to you."

Mrs. Owl went on, "Now, Daniel, what are some of the violent behaviors that children have in elementary school?"

[The leader should stop here and say, "Let's help Daniel and Mrs. Owl. What are some typical violent behaviors that might happen in elementary schools?" Write the children's answers on the chalkboard or flip chart in black marker. As the children name the typical violent behaviors, try to put them into these categories:

1. Name calling
   Put downs
   Teasing
   Not letting you play
   Spreading rumors

2. Intimidation
   Threatening
   Trying to take your things
   Trying to get you to fight

3. Hitting
   Kicking
   Shoving
   Choking

4. Killing
   Using weapons

If the children do not come up with these ideas on their own, fill them in with the behaviors the children do describe.]

Have Daniel go on:

Thanks for your ideas. You're right, there are lots of different kinds of violent behaviors that children use in elementary school. Here's what Mrs. Owl told me about them. She said, "Now, Daniel, when a dinosaur has a violent behavior like bringing a weapon like a gun or a knife to school, or trying to kill another dinosaur,

[Point to column 4]

then you should never try to handle that situation by yourself. It is too dangerous. You should get yourself to a safe place, and then go to an adult immediately, and let the adult take over. If you're afraid that someone else is going to get hurt, you should still get to an adult as soon as you can and let them handle it."

[Write in red marker, "Get to a safe place and tell an adult," over column 4.]

Mrs. Owl went on, "Now let's look at column 3, which has violent behaviors like hitting, kicking, shoving, and choking. Those are not as serious as killing, but they do cause physical harm. The best thing to do if a dinosaur is trying to physically hurt you is to leave the situation and go to an adult for help, whether that dinosaur is bigger than you or not. You should never let yourself stay in a situation where someone can hurt you."

[Write in red marker, "Leave the situation and tell an adult," over column 3.]

"Now let's look at column 2," said Mrs. Owl. "It has behaviors like intimidation, threatening, trying to get something of yours, or trying to get you to fight. When a dinosaur does things like this, you probably aren't going to get physically hurt, but your feelings will certainly get hurt. And, if somebody is trying to get you to give them your lunch, or your money, or your toys, games, or bike, then your possessions might get hurt.

"Column 1 has behaviors like calling names, put downs, teasing, spreading rumors, and not letting you play. These behaviors won't hurt your body or your possessions, but like column 2, they will certainly hurt your feelings. The behaviors in both column 1 and column 2 hurt your feelings, or your possessions, more than your body.

"Now, Daniel, what do you think you should do if someone is calling you names, or teasing you, or threatening you so you will give them your lunch money, your lunch, your *Nintendo* games, or your bike? How about if they spread rumors about you or won't let you play, or try to get you to fight with them?" asked Mrs. Owl.

She answered her own question: "If someone is doing those things a lot, you should not have to handle that situation on your own. And, if you don't know what to do except be afraid, or cry, or fight back, then you should ask an adult for help. Remember when I saw Trevor and Michael Triceratops and Stevie Stegosaurus teasing your drawing of dinosaur shoes? I made them stop because we do not allow violent behavior like that at

Swamp School. I could also see that you were about to cry. I knew you didn't know any other way to react to their violent behavior but to be passive."

Mrs. Owl went on, "So, if someone is teasing you a lot, or calling you names a lot, or threatening to take your *Nintendo* games or your lunch or lunch money, you should ask for help from an adult.

[Write in red marker "Tell an adult," over columns 1 and 2.]

"But you can also use assertive behavior skills to handle situations like that. For instance, this week we're going to learn two new assertive behavior skills, and next week, we're going to learn six more. One of the ones we'll learn next week is called the Broken Record, when you just keep repeating a polite phrase. So, if Trevor is trying to get you to give him your favorite *Nintendo* game, you can just keep repeating, 'I'm not allowed to lend my games. I'm not allowed to lend my games. I'm not allowed to lend my games.' Usually you only have to repeat the phrase three times for the other person to give up.

"Sometimes it's best just to be passive and do nothing. For instance, if Stevie Stegosaurus bumps into you in the hallway once, then it's probably an accident. It's probably best to do nothing and to be passive. But if Stevie bumps into you over and over again, then being passive will not make him stop, and it will not make you feel good about yourself. Remember that it's not okay to be violent yourself unless the situation is life-threatening, and Stevie bumping into you in the hallway is not life-threatening. So, this is a good opportunity for you to use assertive behavior skills," said Mrs. Owl.

"Remember the assertive behavior skill of Body Language that we learned last week? The assertive behavior skills help you stand tall, stand up for yourself in a way that makes you feel good, but doesn't hurt anyone else. So, when someone like Trevor does one of the things in columns 1 and 2 over and over again, it's good to use an assertive behavior skill. I'll be teaching you two more today, and six more next week. Soon you will have a big bag of assertive behavior skills to hide up your sleeve to use when Trevor is violent to you," said Mrs. Owl.

[Add "Assertive Behavior Skills" to "Tell an Adult" in red marker over columns 1 and 2.]

"Remember, the assertive behavior skills may not make Trevor stop, but they will help you feel better about yourself. If Trevor is hurting you with words by calling you names, teasing you, or putting you down, the skills of I Statements and I Hear You Statements are two good assertive ways to respond," said Mrs. Owl.

I Statement. "There are three parts to an I Statement. They are:

'I feel (say how you feel) _____,
'when you (say what the other person did) _____
'because (say why you feel the way you do) _____.'

"So you could have said, 'Trevor, I feel angry when you trip me and kick me because it hurts me.' When you use an I Statement, you are telling the person the way you feel, but you are doing it in a way that does not hurt them. But you are telling them that their behavior has consequences, and that you count, and that it's not okay if the consequences hurt you. Remember to use the assertive behavior skills of Body Language when you make an I Statement. Remember to Stand Tall, to look the other person in the eye, and to speak clearly and in a loud enough tone of voice. By comparison, a You Statement is accusing: 'Trevor, you are a Tyrannostupid yourself!' If you say that, Trevor is likely to feel attacked and will probably want to fight back.

"In an I Hear You Statement, you repeat what the other person said to let him or her know you heard them, and understand what they said. Say, 'I can tell that you feel (or think) _____ because _____.'

"For instance, if Trevor says something like, 'Daniel, you are a stupid brontosaurus. You always get in my way and make me miss my shot when we are playing Dinosaur Basketball,' you can answer using an I Hear You Statement by saying, 'Trevor, I can tell you are angry at me because you think I made you miss your shot.' Notice that you are not saying he is right; you are just letting him know you heard him and understand what he said. An I Hear You Statement is a good way to cool off a fight. That means that instead of heating the fight up, you cool it off," said Mrs. Owl.

Can you help me figure out some more ways to use the assertive behavior skills of I Statements and I Hear You Statements?

Discussion

Lead a discussion to help the group members understand when to ask an adult for help, when to use an assertive behavior skill, and the assertive behavior skills of I Statements and I Hear You Statements.

- If someone is being violent toward you, should you be passive, aggressive, or assertive? (It depends on the situation.)
- When is the only time that it is okay to use violence? (When your life is being threatened.) If a child is tripping you, or hitting you, is your life being threatened? (No.) If someone is calling you names, is your life being threatened? (No.)
- When should you ask an adult for help? (When someone might physically hurt you. When you don't know what to do except be afraid and cry, or to hit back. When someone keeps on calling you names, or not letting you play, over and over again, and they don't stop, even if you use an assertive behavior skill.)
- What is an I Statement? (It's a way to be assertive, to say what you feel without hurting anyone else. I Statements have three parts:

"I feel (say how you feel) _____,
"when you (say what the other person did) _____
"because (say why you feel the way you do) _____."

- What is an I Hear You Statement? (Another way to be assertive. You repeat what the other person has said, not necessarily agreeing with them. By repeating what they have said, you let them know you heard them and understand what they said. I Hear You Statements have two parts: "I can tell that you feel (or think) _____ because _____." I Hear You Statements are a good way to cool off a fight instead of heating up the fight.)

Activity

Ask the children to take out Activity Sheet 5, Practice Situations for I Statements and I Hear You Statements (see pages 119–120), from their folders. Tell the children to look at the first three situations and to write an I Statement. Then they should look at the last three situations and write an I Hear You Statement for each one. Read Situation 1. Ask the children to figure out the way they would feel in that situation and to fill in the blank, "I feel _____." Then, they should describe what the other person did in the blank, "when you _____." Finally, they should say why they feel the way they do in the blank, "because _____." Repeat the process in Situation 4 for the I Hear You Statements. You may need to help the children individually create both I Statements and I Hear You Statements.

When the children finish, have another go-around. Call on each child, and have the child state out loud the I Statement he or she wrote for Situation 1. You may need to coach them to speak in an assertive way, not passively. Repeat the process for Situations 2 and 3. Do the same for I Hear You Statement Situations 5 and 6.

Basic Facts

Ask the children to take out Basic Fact Worksheet 5 (see page 121) from their folders.

9. Children can **ask** for **help** from an **adult** if another child is being violent toward them.
10. **I Statements** and **I Hear You Statements** are two good assertive behavior skills.

Briefly discuss these facts, checking for understanding. Correct any misconceptions.

Give the children time to complete the bottom half of the worksheet by filling in the blanks. Then have the entire group read the facts out loud. Remind the children that you will be going over the basic facts learned so far at the beginning of each session, and that you will ask them to explain what each means. Have the children put their worksheets in their folders.

Homework Assignment

Ask the children to pull Homework Assignment 5 (see page 122) out of their folders. Ask one child to read it out loud. Tell the children that you want them to think of a way they can use these assertive behaviors every day for the next week and to write down what they have done.

Wrapping Up

Repeat the centering exercise from the beginning of the group, "Stop and Breathe to Five" (see page 52).

Affirmation

Involve the group in an affirmation. Stand and join in a circle with the children, holding hands. Go around and have each child share an assertive behavior skill of an I Statement or an I Hear You Statement that he or she can use to stand up for himself or herself. Start the affirmation yourself: "One way I can use an assertive behavior skill of an I Statement or an I Hear You Statement is to . . ."

Closing

Remain standing in a circle holding hands with the children. Lead the group in the closing activity, "Pass a Silent Wish" (see page 58).

Collect the folders and fill out a copy of the Process and Progress Form (see page 235) or the Progress Notes (see pages 236–237).

Activity Sheet 5
Practice Situations for I Statements and I Hear You Statements

Situation 1

You are walking down the hall. A boy named Matthew bumps into you and knocks down your book.

I Statement

Matthew, I feel (say how you feel)

_____

when you (say what the other person did)

_____

because (say why you feel the way you do)

_____.

Situation 2

You are sitting at your desk. A girl named Karla sits behind you and kicks the back of your desk all during class.

I Statement

Karla, I feel (say how you feel)

_____

when you (say what the other person did)

_____

because (say why you feel the way you do)

_____.

Situation 3

You are in math class. The teacher asks you the answer to

problem number 4 and you get it wrong. Later, at the lunch table, Johnny tells you you're stupid.

I Statement

Johnny, I feel (say how you feel)

_____

when you (say what the other person did)

_____

because (say why you feel the way you do)

_____.

Situation 4

You're playing a video game with your older brother or sister. They get wiped out. They tell you it was your fault and now they are going to punch you.

I Hear You Statement

I can tell that you feel (or think) _____
because _____.

Situation 5

Your team is losing at kickball. Thomas says he'll never play with you again.

I Hear You Statement

I can tell that you feel (or think) _____
because _____.

Situation 6

Your mother is yelling at you because you have not cleaned your room. She says you are grounded forever.

I Hear You Statement

I can tell that you feel (or think) _____
because _____.

Basic Fact Worksheet 5

9. Children can **ask** for **help** from an **adult** if another child is being violent toward them.

10. **I Statements** and **I Hear You Statements** are two good assertive behavior skills.

_____

9. Children can _____ for _____ from an _____ if another child is being violent toward them.

10. _____ and _____ are two good assertive behavior skills.

Homework Assignment 5

Every day, see if you can find one way to use an I Statement or an I Hear You Statement. Write a short sentence.

I Statement
    I feel (say how you feel) _____
    when you (say what the other person did) _____
    because (say why you feel the way you do) _____.

I Hear You Statement
    I can tell that you feel (or think) _____
    because _____.

Day 1 _____

_____

Day 2 _____

_____

Day 3 _____

_____

Day 4 _____

_____

Day 5 _____

_____

Session 6

Daniel the Dinosaur Learns New Assertive Behavior Skills

Objectives

To help the students:

- continue to practice the assertive behavior skills of Body Language: posture, eye contact, and tone of voice
- learn new assertive behavior skills: Kill-Them-With-Kindness Sandwiches, Apologizing, Humor, Sound Bites, Nice Replies, and Broken Records

Preparation

- Display the posterboard copy of the group rules.
- Have available the toy Daniel and Mrs. Owl and Basic Fact Posters 1 to 10.
- Add to each student's folder:
  –Handout 6 (Assertive Behavior Skills)
  –Activity Sheet 6 (Practice Situations for Assertive Behavior Skills)
  –Basic Fact Worksheet 6
  –Homework Assignment 6
- Place each student's folder, pencil, and crayons or markers at his or her place.
- Have a chalkboard or flip chart available to use in the Discussion section.
- Read through the session plan before meeting.

Background and Guidelines

This session introduces six new behavior skills that the group members can use to help them replace passive or aggressive behavior with assertive behavior.

Remember to use the Basic Facts to remind the children who are passive that they can learn assertive behavior skills so they have a choice about how they will react if another child is violent toward them. If they are provocative victims, remind them that violence includes name calling and threatening as well as physically hitting someone and that violent behavior is unacceptable. You want to teach them more assertive behavior skills to replace their aggressive or passive behavior.

Continue to remember the concept of "chunking it down." The homework assignment review is an opportunity for you to help the children figure out how they could have used the two assertive behavior skills they learned last week—I Statements and I Hear You Statements. As in every assignment review, if the child hasn't done the homework, ask the child to think of a situation that he or she had to deal with over the past week. Help the child formulate both an I Statement and an I Hear You Statement for the situation and make sure the child repeats it out loud. Children are usually quite able to recall a suitable situation.

This session's story builds on the previous explanation of the differences between passive, aggressive, and assertive behavior and repeats that assertive behavior will not change the other person's behavior but will help children stand up for themselves in a way that doesn't hurt anyone else. Six new assertive behavior skills are introduced in this session.

Apologies

An apology is a way to cool down a situation by admitting you made a mistake and by saying you're sorry. Nobody's perfect, and sometimes the child is at fault. It helps to develop responsibility to be able to admit that sometimes you have done something wrong. A child can also say, "I'm sorry that happened to you," even if the child is not at fault. Clarify that a child does not have to and should not take responsibility for something he or she did not do.

Kill-Them-With-Kindness Sandwiches

A Kill-Them-With-Kindness Sandwich was first introduced by author Russell Barkley in a workshop on training parents of oppositional children. A Kill-Them-With Kindness Sandwich has three parts:

Say something nice.

Say no, or set a limit, or say your point of view.

Then, say something nice again.

An example of a Kill-Them-With Kindness Sandwich is given in the story, and several opportunities to create one are provided in the activity.

Humor

Humor is another simple assertive behavior skill that can help to de-escalate a potentially violent situation. If you have children in your group who have a good natural sense of humor, ask them to try to think of ways they can brush off a situation by making a joke.

Sound Bites

Sound Bites are a collection of short responses that a child can use instead of attacking and mean statements: 'Yes"; "No"; "Oops!"; "Oh, really!"; "Wow!"; and "Whatever." Keeping their responses short helps them be clear about their role in heating up or cooling down a situation. Children usually enjoy Sound Bites a lot and are quick to offer many suggestions for more Sound Bites they can use such as "Huh"; "Not!"; "Wipe Out!"; "See you"; "Awesome"; "Oh, cool"; "Oh, great"; and "Okay."

Nice Replies

Nice Replies are similar to Kill-Them-With-Kindness Sandwiches. These are good ways for children to get out of potentially violent or other kinds of situations by taking charge and politely saying why they don't want to fight. Children have come up with ideas like saying, "I'd really like to fight with you since you are messing with me, but I'm on probation and I'm not allowed to fight." Or, "I'd really like to fight with you but you are too small (or big) for me to fight with." Or, "I'd really like to fight with you, but I've already been to the principal's office too many times this year," or, ". . . but I haven't been to the principal's office at all and I don't want to spoil my record."

Broken Records

The last assertive behavior skill taught in this session is the Broken Record, where the child creates a short declarative statement and just keeps repeating it over and over again. Most children understand the concept although they may be more familiar with tapes and CDs than with records. Examples of Broken Records are "I can't lend my video games," "I'm not allowed to fight," and "I don't like it when you call me an idiot." Encourage the children to remember to use assertive body language, and to speak in a calm, neutral tone of voice when they say Broken Record statements. Saying a neutral or polite statement in a loud, mean, or attacking tone of voice will change this assertive behavior skill into aggressive behavior. Saying these statements in a passive way will make them less effective. As a matter of fact, it's a good idea to coach the children to say each assertive behavior skill, remembering to use assertive body language.

There is a lot of information in this session, so remember not to expect the children to master these skills right away. Activity Sheet 6 gives six situations where the children can think of which assertive behavior skill they could use. If the children are good writers, have them write down the appropriate statement. Then, have each child say what he or she wrote out loud. If they are not good writers, work with them to formulate a statement they could use for each situation, say it for them, and then have each child repeat it individually. You will do the same when you review the homework assignment next week. Remember, your helping them formulate an assertive behavior is a step in chunking it down, helping the children get one step closer to being able to do it on their own.

Beginning the Session

Welcome the students. If necessary, begin with a quick review of the group rules (see page 51). Check for understanding before moving on.

Centering Exercise

Make certain that the children are comfortable and quiet. Ask them if they remembered to do "Stop and Breathe to Five," "The Icicle," "The Chill Out," or "Defuse the Bomb" in the past week. Remind them that stopping and breathing to five, or tensing and relaxing muscles, and then thinking will help them make good decisions about how to get along with other children. Introduce the new centering exercise, "Lower Your Temperature." Tell the group members that this is another centering exercise that will help them to calm down, relax, and be able to think if they get angry or upset. They can use this exercise without anyone else knowing.

> Imagine that a boy in your class has just threatened you. He says he is going to beat you up. You find you are getting angry, very angry. Feel how hot you are. Your face is turning red. Your heart is pounding fast and hard, making you even hotter. You are breathing fast and can hardly catch your breath. Your temperature is almost at the boiling point.

> Now, it's time for you to lower your temperature, from top to bottom. Take a deep breath. Imagine the blood in your brain cooling off. Your head feels cooler. Now, imagine your chest cooling off. You breathe deeply and you breathe in cool air that helps you lower your temperature. You breathe slowly and deeply and that helps your heart to calm down and not pound so hard and fast. Now, your head and your chest feel much cooler. Continue to breathe deeply. Now, your legs and feet begin to cool off. Your heart is still beating, but not so fast. You are still breathing, but now you are breathing deeply and slowly.

> You have lowered your temperature, and now you are not so hot. You feel cool, and you feel calm. Imagine how cool you feel. Because you have cooled down, you will be able to think better, so you can decide what to say to the boy who threatened you. You will be able to think of a good reply, since you worked to lower your temperature.

Remind the students that they can use this technique in school, on the bus, during recess, and at home to help them relax so they can put thinking between their feelings and their behavior.

Feelings Check-in

Using the Feeling Daniel, do a feelings check-in with the students (see page 69). When the students finish, have a go-around.

Basic Facts Review

To help the students review their last session and the basic facts learned so far, show them Basic Fact Posters 1 to 10. The Basic Facts List and Questions to Help Clarify the Basic Facts are printed on pages 229–234.

Assignment Review

Ask the students if they brought their homework assignments from last week. Remind them of the assignment by reading it: "Every day, see if you can find one way to use an I Statement or an I Hear You Statement. Write a short sentence."

In a go-around, ask the children to share what they found: ways they could use the assertive behavior skills of I Statements or I Hear You Statements.

If the children forgot to do the assignment, in the go-around ask them to try to think of one way they used an I Statement or an I Hear You Statement in the past week. If they can't think of anything they did, ask them what they could have done in the past week to use one of these assertive behavior skills. Remind them that using these skills may not change the other person, but it will help them feel better about themselves.

Exploring the Story

Have the children get comfortable for today's story. Use the toy Daniel and Mrs. Owl and allow Daniel to tell the following:

Hi, boys and girls! I hope you had a good time practicing all of your assertive behavior skills. Have you been remembering to Stand Tall—to use assertive posture, eye contact, and tone of voice? And how about your I Statements and I Hear You Statements? Today we're going to learn some new assertive behavior skills to use with dinosaurs like Trevor and Tiffany.

One of the things that Trevor did to me a lot was to threaten me. Remember how he threatened to beat me up the first time I ever laid my dinosaur eyes on him, when I sat in what he said was his seat on the bus? Well, as you might expect, Trevor uses a lot of threats. Let me give you an example. One day, Trevor sat across from me at lunch. I was talking with the other dinosaurs about the neat new video game I bought—Super Stegosaurus Brothers. I was the first one in my school to get this game. When Trevor heard that I had it, he said he wanted me to give him my game so he could play it. He said if I didn't give it to him tomorrow, he would really beat me up.

Mrs. Owl saw me looking down later in the day, and asked me what was wrong. When I told her about Trevor's threat, she said, "Daniel, how would you like to learn some new assertive behavior skills to use when someone tries to threaten you or get you to do something you don't want to do, like lend your favorite video game?" Of course I said I'd like to learn what to say to Trevor.

Here's what Mrs. Owl taught me.

[Ask the children to take out Handout 6 (see page 133) from their folders and to read along with Daniel. Tell the children that this handout includes the assertive behavior skills they learned in the last two weeks.]

You've already learned about the first three assertive behavior skills, **Body Language, I Statements,** and **I Hear You Statements.**

Today, Mrs. Owl started by teaching me about making an **Apology.** "Nobody's perfect," said Mrs. Owl, "and sometimes you do things that are just wrong, sometimes by accident, and maybe even sometimes on purpose. In an apology, you admit you made a mistake and you say you're sorry. Sometimes you can say you're sorry that things don't go well for the other person, even if it's not your fault. Saying 'Sorry,' is a good way to cool the other person off if they are getting hot with anger."

Mrs. Owl also taught me about **Kill-Them-With-Kindness Sandwiches.** "In a Kill-Them-With-Kindness Sandwich, first you say something nice to the other person. Then, you state your point of view, or you set a limit, or you say no. Then, you close by saying something nice again. So, you could have said, 'Trevor, I would like to be able to lend you my new game, Super Stegosaurus Brothers, but I'm not allowed to lend video games, but I'm sorry you'll be disappointed."

Then, Mrs. Owl said, "Daniel, **Humor** is another assertive behavior skill that can work very well to cool off what may become a fight. Suppose Trevor would say, 'Daniel, if you don't want to fight with me, it means you're a chicken!' A really good way to respond is to make a joke, or to do something funny to draw his attention away from what he is starting a fight about. If he calls you a chicken, you could start waving your arms, and clucking like a chicken. Everyone will laugh so much that Trevor will look foolish if he keeps wanting to fight."

"Another good assertive behavior skill is a collection of short responses that I call **Sound Bites,**" said Mrs. Owl. "Here are some very short responses that you can use no matter what Trevor says: 'Yes'; 'No'; 'Oops!'; 'Oh really!'; 'Wow!'; and 'Whatever.' So, if Trevor says 'Are you sitting in my seat?' you could just answer 'Yes.' If Trevor says 'Give me your caveman pizza!' you could just answer 'No.' If Trevor says 'I'm going to beat you up,' you could just answer 'Oh really!' or 'Wow!' or 'Whatever.' That way, you won't be heating up the fight: you'll be cooling it off."

"**Nice Replies** are a fourth assertive behavior skill that work really well in situations where someone is trying to start a fight or get you to do something you don't want to do," Mrs. Owl said. "Michael, a third-grader I know, used to get into a lot of fights with the kindergarten dinosaurs. He used to get into a lot of trouble. Now, when they try to start a fight with him, he just says to them, 'You're too small for me to fight with you.

You'll have to get somebody your own size to fight with.' If they call him chicken, he just clucks, and waves his arms, and starts laughing. He doesn't let them get him mad. Another Nice Reply that you could use if Trevor tries to start a fight with you is to say, 'Trevor, I'd like to fight with you, but I've spent too much time in the principal's office this year. You'll have to find somebody else to fight with.' Nice Replies are just nice ways to say no without hurting the other person."

The last assertive behavior skill Mrs. Owl taught me is called the **Broken Record.** "When you give Trevor an answer, and he keeps trying to get you to change your mind, Daniel, you can just pretend you are a broken record and keep on repeating the same thing. For instance, if Trevor keeps asking you for Super Stegosaurus Brothers, you could just say, 'I can't lend video games.' And, you could just keep repeating that, over and over again— 'I can't lend video games.' Eventually, Trevor will get tired because you haven't changed your mind.

"Remember, these assertive behavior skills may not make Trevor change his behavior, but they will help you feel better about yourself. If you are afraid he is really going to hurt you, it's best to go to an adult. If it's not a dangerous situation, one of these assertive behavior skills will probably be good for you to use," said Mrs. Owl. "If he never stops, then you should still go to an adult. The adult may need to work with Trevor to teach him that his violent behavior is not acceptable.

"Can you help me figure out some more ways to use the assertive behavior skills of Apologizing, Kill-Them-With-Kindness Sandwiches, Humor, Sound Bites, Nice Replies, and Broken Records?"

Discussion

Lead a discussion to help the group members understand these new assertive behavior skills.

- What is a Kill-Them-With-Kindness Sandwich? (First, you say something nice to the other person. Then, you state your point of view, or you set a limit, or you say no. Then, you close by saying something nice again.) Can you give an example? ("Trevor, I'd like to give you the answer to the math homework, but I don't have it myself, so maybe we can figure it out together.")
- What is an Apology? (In an Apology, you admit you made a mistake and you say you're sorry. Sometimes you can say you're sorry that things don't go well for the other person, even if it's not your fault.)
- How can you use Humor as an assertive behavior skill? (Sometimes, if you do or say something funny, or if you make a joke, it cools down what could become a fight instead of heating it up.)
- What are Sound Bites? (A collection of short responses that you can use no matter what the other person says: "Yes"; "No"; "Oops!"; "Oh, really!"; "Wow!";

and "Whatever.") Can you think of other Sound Bites? (The children may come up with responses like, "Huh"; "Not!"; "Wipe Out!"; "See you"; "Awesome"; "Oh, cool"; "Oh, great"; "Okay.") [Write these on a flip chart and save for future sessions.]

- What are Nice Replies? (Nice Replies are just nice ways to say no without hurting the other person.) Can you give an example? ("I'm sorry, but you're too small for me to fight.") Ask the children if they can come up with any other Nice Replies.
- What is the assertive behavior skill of a Broken Record? (In a Broken Record, you just pretend you are a broken record and keep on repeating the same thing.) Can you give an example? ("I can't lend my video game. I can't lend my video game. I can't lend my video game.") Ask the children if they can come up with any other ideas for the Broken Record.

Activity

Ask the children to take out Activity Sheet 6, Practice Situations for Assertive Behavior Skills (see page 135), from their folders. Tell the children to look at each situation and to write how they could use any of the assertive behavior skills on Handout 6 (see pages 133–134). If the children cannot do this activity on their own, ask a child to read Situation 1. Ask the children to figure out which assertive behavior skill might work in this situation. When the children finish, have a go-around. Call on a child to read the assertive behavior skill they used for Situation 1. Repeat for each group member. If the children cannot think of any assertive behavior skills, help them. For your convenience, examples of assertive behavior skills to use are given under each situation. Have each child say one response for Situation 1, even if they all repeat the same response. Repeat the process for Situations 2 through 6. If you want, allow the children to role-play these situations.

Situation 1
Charles says you took his pencil.
> *Examples:*
> I Hear You Statement: "I hear that you think I took your pencil. But I didn't."
> Sound Bites: "Oops!"; "Oh, really!"; "Wow!"; or "Whatever."
> Broken Record: "I didn't take your pencil. I didn't take your pencil. I didn't take your pencil."

Situation 2
Patrick cuts in front of you in the lunch line.
> *Examples:*
> I Statement: "Patrick, I get angry when you cut in front of me."
> Kill-Them-With-Kindness Sandwich: "I know that you are hungry, but there are no cuts in the lunch line. Don't worry, though; there will be plenty of food left for you."

Sound Bites: "Oops!"

Nice Replies: "Excuse me, I think you took my space."

"I'm sorry, there are no cuts allowed in the lunch line or I would let you in."

Situation 3

Joanna or Jeff, your best friend, sits next to you, and during a test, asks you for the answer to Question 6.

Examples:

Kill-Them-With-Kindness Sandwich: "I'd like to help you, but if I tell you the answer, I'll get an F, so I can't help you."

Sound Bites: "Not."

Nice Replies: "Sorry, I haven't gotten there yet."

Broken Record: "Will you please leave me alone? Will you please leave me alone? Will you please leave me alone?"

Situation 4

You are playing kickball at recess. Robby says you cheated.

Examples:

Kill-Them-With-Kindness Sandwich: "Sorry, but I'm not cheating. I just want to play the game."

Sound Bites: "Whatever."

Nice Replies: "I didn't cheat. It was just part of the game."

Situation 5

You are playing basketball. You are a good blocker and Bobby misses. He tries to punch you.

Examples:

I Hear You Statement: "Bobby, I can tell that you are angry that you missed your shot."

Apology: "Sorry, I was just trying to make a good defense."

Kill-Them-With-Kindness Sandwich: "Bobby, I really like to play basketball with you, but I was just playing the game when I blocked your shot, so please don't get angry with me when you miss your shot."

Nice Reply: "It's okay. It's just a game."

Situation 6

Your sister Jennie left her headphones on the couch. You sit on them and break them. Jennie says you have to pay for them.

Examples:

I Hear You Statement: "I can hear that you are upset that your earphones are broken."

Apology: "I'm sorry I sat on your earphones and broke them."

Kill-them-with-Kindness Sandwich: " I know how much you enjoy your earphones, but you shouldn't have left them on the couch, and I can't afford to buy you new ones."

Sound Bites: "Oops!"; "Oh, really?"; "Whatever."

Basic Facts

Ask the children to take Basic Fact Worksheet 6 out of their folders.

> 11. **Kill-them-with-Kindness Sandwiches, Apologizing, Humor, Sound Bites, Nice Replies,** and **Broken Records** are more good assertive behavior skills to use.

Briefly discuss this fact, checking for understanding. Correct any misconceptions.

Give the children time to complete the bottom half of the worksheet by filling in the blanks. Then have the entire group read the fact aloud. Remind the children that you will be going over the basic facts learned so far at the beginning of each session, and that you will ask them to explain what each means. Have the children put their worksheets in their folders.

Homework Assignment

Ask the children to pull out Homework Assignment 6 (see page 137) from their folders. Ask one child to read it out loud. Tell the children that you want them to think of a way they can use one of these assertive behaviors every day for the next week and to write down what they have done.

Wrapping Up

Repeat the Centering Exercise from the beginning of the group, "Lower Your Temperature" (see page 126).

Affirmation

Involve the group in an affirmation. Stand and join in a circle with the children, holding hands. Go around and have each child share an assertive behavior skill that he or she can use to stand up for himself or herself. Start the affirmation yourself: "One way I can use an assertive behavior skill of Kill-Them-With-Kindness Sandwich, Apologizing, Humor, Sound Bites, Nice Replies, or Broken Records is to . . ."

Closing

Remain standing in a circle with the children, holding hands, and lead the group in the closing activity, "Pass a Silent Wish" (see page 58).

Collect the folders and fill out a copy of the Process and Progress Form (see page 235) or the Progress Notes (see pages 236–237).

Handout 6
Assertive Behavior Skills

Body Language. Includes posture, eye contact, and tone of voice.

Posture: stand up straight, put your shoulders back, keep your head high, but not stuck up, and stand tall. *Eye contact:* look at the person to whom you are speaking, and look in a friendly way. *Tone of voice:* speak in a loud enough voice, clearly and distinctly. Speak in a friendly tone, so people can understand you, and speak as though you mean what you say.

I Statements. A way to say what you feel without hurting anyone else. There are three parts to an I statement.
First, you say how you feel:
"I feel _____."
Then you say what the other person did:
"when you _____."
Then you say why you feel the way you do:
"because _____."

Example: "Trevor, I feel angry when you trip me when I miss the ball in Dinosaur Dodge Ball. It's only a game."

I Hear You Statements. You repeat what the other person has said, not necessarily agreeing with them. By repeating what they have said, you let them know you heard them and understand what they said. I Hear You Statements have two parts: "I can hear that you feel (or think) _____ because _____." I Hear You Statements are a good way to cool off a fight instead of heating up the fight.

Example: "Trevor, I can hear that you are upset that I missed the ball when we played Dinosaur Dodge Ball."

Apologies. In an Apology, you admit you made a mistake and you say you're sorry. Sometimes you can say you're sorry that things don't go well for the other person, even if it's not your fault.

Example: "Trevor, I'm sorry that our team lost."

Kill-Them-With-Kindness Sandwiches. First you say something nice to the other person. Then, you state your point of view, or you set a limit, or you say no. Then, you close by saying something nice again.

Example: "Trevor, I'd like to give you the answer to the math homework, but I don't have it myself; maybe we can figure it out together."

Humor. Sometimes, if you do or say something funny, or if you make a joke, it cools down what could become a fight instead of heating it up.

Example: If somebody calls you chicken, start flapping your arms and make clucking noises. You probably won't fight.

Sound Bites. A collection of short responses that you can use no matter what the other person says: "Yes"; "No"; "Oops!"; "Oh, really!"; "Wow!"; and "Whatever."

Example: If someone says they will hit you, say "Oh, really!"

Nice Replies. Nice Replies are just nice ways to say no without hurting the other person.

Example: "I'm sorry, but you're too small for me to fight."

Broken Records. In a Broken Record, you just pretend you are a broken record and keep on repeating the same thing.

Example: "I can't lend video games. I can't lend video games. I can't lend video games."

Activity Sheet 6
Practice Situations for
Assertive Behavior Skills

Situation 1

Charles says you took his pencil.

Situation 2

Patrick cuts in front of you in the lunch line.

Situation 3

Your best friend, Joanna, sits next to you, and during a test, asks you for the answer to question 6.

Situation 4

You are playing kickball at recess. Robby says you cheated.

Situation 5

You are playing basketball. You are a good blocker and Bobby misses. He tries to punch you.

Situation 6

Your sister Jennie left her earphones on the couch. You sit on them and break them. Jennie says you have to pay for them.

Basic Fact Worksheet 6

11. **Kill-Them-With-Kindness Sandwiches, Apologizing, Humor, Sound Bites, Nice Replies,** and **Broken Records** are more good assertive behavior skills to use.

_____

11. Kill-Them-With- _____ Sandwiches, _____, _____, Sound _____, _____ Replies, and Broken _____ are more good assertive behavior skills to use.

Homework Assignment 6

Every day, see if you can find one way to use one of the assertive behavior skills of Kill-Them-With-Kindness Sandwiches, Apologizing, Humor, Sound Bites, Nice Replies, or Broken Records. Write a short sentence.

Day 1 _____

_____

_____

Day 2 _____

_____

_____

Day 3 _____

_____

_____

Day 4 _____

_____

_____

Day 5 _____

_____

_____

Session 7

Daniel the Dinosaur Practices Assertive Behavior Skills in Situations Where He Is Being Teased

Objectives

To help the students:

- apply the assertive behavior skills learned so far in situations where they are being teased

Preparation

- Display the posterboard copy of the group rules.
- Have available the toy Daniel and Mrs. Owl and Basic Fact Posters 1 to 11.
- Add to each student's folder:
  –Handout 7 (Assertive Behavior Skills to Use When Being Teased)
  –Basic Fact Worksheet 7
  –Homework Assignment 7
- Place each student's folder, pencil, and crayons or markers at his or her place.
- Have a chalkboard or flip chart available.
- Read through the session plan before meeting.

Background and Guidelines

This session helps the children learn how to apply all of the assertive behavior skills in situations when they are being teased or someone is calling them names.

You will reiterate in this session that if children are in physical danger from another child's violent behavior, they should go to an adult. If the other child's violent behavior is teasing or calling names, then using the assertive behavior skills should help the children feel better. However, the point is repeated in the story that if the violent child continues to call names, then the victim should tell an adult. That is the only way that adults can intervene and set limits with the violent child and arrange to teach the violent child ways he or she can change the violent behavior.

The story in this session is minimal, allowing most of the session time for practicing the assertive behavior skills in the handout. The main point of this session is to apply these assertive behavior skills in teasing situations. If the children can apply these skills themselves, allow them to do so. If they cannot, examples of how to use each assertive behavior skill in name calling or teasing situations are given in the handout for your convenience. Since saying these assertive behavior skills using assertive body language is a new experience for most of the children in the Daniel group, be sure to give each child in the group an opportunity to say each skill. Be sure to coach each child to use assertive body language when they say each example. Remember the principle of chunking it down. Practicing these skills in the safe group setting puts the children one step closer to being able to use them on their own.

One component of this session is to list the names that children typically call each other. Children in elementary school usually come up with many, many names. They may ask your permission to list the swear words that children use. Allow them to do so, labeling them as such. Seeing all the names that children use in such a list seems to detoxify them. This activity also points out the usefulness of working with children who are being hurt by other children in a group. They realize that they are not the only ones who are hurt by other children.

Beginning the Session

Welcome the students. If necessary, begin with a quick review of the group rules (see page 51). Check for understanding before moving on.

Centering Exercise

Make certain that the children are comfortable and quiet. Ask if any of them remembered to do "Stop and Breathe to Five," "The Icicle," "The Chill Out," "Defuse the Bomb," or "Lower Your Temperature" in the past week. Remind them that stopping and breathing to five, or tensing and relaxing muscles, and then thinking will help them make good decisions about how to get along with other children. Introduce the new centering exercise, "The Waterfall." Tell the group members that this is another centering exercise that will help them to calm down, relax, and be able to think if they get angry or upset. They can use this exercise without anyone else knowing.

> Close your eyes and relax. Pretend that you're walking on a beautiful path in the mountains. You're taking a hike down the mountain. It's October, and the sky is clear and a deep shade of blue. The air is cool, but the sun is warm. The leaves are changing colors and are beautiful shades of red and orange and yellow. Imagine what they look like as you look up at the sky and see the orange and yellow leaves like lace against the sky. There are also green pine trees, so imagine what the green pine needles look like next to the orange and yellow leaves. It's very quiet on the mountain path. There isn't a teacher or a parent

within a hundred miles, and the only sound that you can hear is the sound of the wind as it whistles through the treetops.

You keep walking down the mountain path until you come upon a waterfall, a beautiful cascading waterfall, a stream tumbling down over huge boulders. You sit on a boulder near the waterfall, and you empty your mind. You empty your mind by paying attention to the sound of the water as it rushes over the boulders and trickles down the stream. You imagine that the water is rushing over you and making you feel clean and refreshed. But you're not cold because you're drinking in the warmth of the sun.

As you sit quietly on the boulder, you see leaves floating down the stream because, re- member, it's October, and the leaves are falling. You decide to put all your worries, problems, and frustrations on the leaves and let them all float away.

So, if you're worried because [use appropriate examples specific to the students in your group, such as: you're worried that you don't have your math homework, or you got into trouble on the bus, or you had a fight with your mother because she didn't like what you were wearing this morning . . .] put that worry on a leaf and let it float away. Let all of your problems and worries float away on leaves.

Put all of your worries, and problems, and frustrations on leaves and let them all float away for right now. When you open your eyes, you'll be able to concentrate on the work we're going to do here, because all your problems have floated away. You can go back and work on those problems later.

Remind the students that they can use this technique in school, on the bus, during recess, and at home to help them relax so they can put thinking between their feelings and their behavior.

Feelings Check-in

Using the Feeling Daniel, do a feelings check-in with the students (see page 69). Have them take out their Feeling Daniel. When the students finish, have a go-around.

Basic Facts Review

To help the students review their last session and the basic facts learned so far, show them Basic Fact Posters 1 to 11. The Basic Facts List and Questions to Help Clarify the Basic Facts are printed on pages 229–234.

Assignment Review

Ask the students if they brought their homework assignments from last week. Remind them of the assignment by reading it: "Every day, see if you can find one way to use an assertive behavior skill of Kill-Them-With-Kindness Sandwiches, Apologizing, Humor, Sound Bites, Nice Replies, or Broken Records. Write a short sentence."

In a go-around, ask the children to share what they found: ways they could use the assertive behavior skills of Kill-Them-With-Kindness Sandwiches, Apologizing, Humor, Sound Bites, Nice Replies, or Broken Records.

If the children forgot to do the assignment, in the go-around ask them to try to think of one way they used Kill-Them-With-Kindness Sandwiches, Apologizing, Humor, Sound Bites, Nice Replies, or Broken Records in the past week. If they can't think of anything they did, ask them what they could have done in the past week to use one of these assertive behavior skills. Remind them that using these skills may not change the other person, but it will help them feel better about themselves.

Exploring the Story

Have the children get comfortable for today's story. Use the toy Daniel and Mrs. Owl and allow Daniel to tell the following:

Hi, boys and girls! I hope you have had a good time practicing all of your assertive behavior skills. It's hard to remember all of them, and it's even harder to use them. Have you been remembering to Stand Tall—to use assertive posture, eye contact, and tone of voice? And how about your I Statements and I Hear You Statements? Have you been using Kill-Them-With-Kindness Sandwiches, Apologizing, Humor, Sound Bites, Nice Replies, or Broken Records? Today we're going to look at some situations we might come across to practice using these assertive behavior skills with dinosaurs like Trevor and Tiffany, especially in situations where we're being teased or called names.

One of the things that Trevor did to me a lot was to pick on me, tease me, and call me names. Let me tell you about one especially awful situation.

One time, Trevor was calling me Brontostupid. I finally lost my temper, and I called him Tryannostupid. He kept on calling me names, and he wouldn't stop. So, I kept on calling him names, like Tuba Tyrannosaurus and Trevor the Terrible. Trevor told me he was going to beat me up. Then, he told me that his sister could beat me up. Then, he told me that I was a sissy. I wished I was dead.

When I told Mrs. Owl about this situation, she said, "Daniel, did that hurt your feelings when Trevor called you a sissy?" I said I felt very hurt and embarrassed. Mrs. Owl said, "Let's look at the assertive behavior skills again and figure out which ones you can use in situations where someone is calling you names or teasing you."

[Ask the children to pull out Handout 7 (see pages 146–147).]

First Mrs. Owl said, "Daniel, in this situation, Trevor was calling you 'Brontostupid.' When you called him names, you were being violent yourself. The situation heated up.

It got worse. Trevor got even more aggressive. He threatened to beat you up, and he teased you that his sister could beat you up and called you a sissy. So, we see that being aggressive yourself made the situation worse, and you were in the wrong and looked bad, too.

"Daniel," said Mrs. Owl, "calling names is one of the most common forms of violent behaviors that dinosaurs have. Let's look at the list of Assertive Behavior Skills and see which ones work in situations where someone is calling names."

Mrs. Owl went on, "Daniel, how could you have used an **I Statement** when Trevor called you names?" I thought, and then I said, "I could have said, Trevor, I feel hurt and angry when you call me a sissy or when you say your sister could beat me up because it hurts my feelings."

[Ask a child to repeat the I Statement, "Trevor, I feel hurt and angry when you call me a sissy or when you say your sister could beat me up because it hurts my feelings." Coach the child to use assertive body language. Give the student the opportunity to create an I Statement of his or her own. Have each child make up an I Statement of his or her own, or repeat yours and practice saying it out loud.]

"How could you have used an **I Hear You Statement**?" asked Mrs. Owl. "In an I Hear You Statement, I could have said, 'Trevor, I can tell that you are really angry at me because you are trying to hurt me by calling me a sissy.' By saying that, I would be letting Trevor know that I understand how angry he is and I would also be letting him know that I can tell he is trying to hurt me," I answered.

[Coach a child to repeat the I Hear You Statement, "Trevor, I can tell that you are really angry at me because you are trying to hurt me by calling me a sissy." Remember to coach the child to use assertive body language. Give the student the opportunity to create an I Hear You Statement of his or her own. Have each child make up an I Hear You Statement of his or her own, or repeat yours and practice saying it out loud.]

Mrs. Owl went on. "Daniel, how could you have used a **Kill-Them-With-Kindness Sandwich**? Remember, in a Kill-Them-With-Kindness Sandwich, first you say something nice to the other person. Then, you state your point of view, or you set a limit, or you say no. Then, you close by saying something nice again. So, you could have said, 'Trevor, I know you want to fight, but I don't fight. But I won't call you any more names.' Another example of a Kill-Them-With-Kindness Sandwich to use in this situation is, 'Trevor, I know you like to call me names and tease me, but I don't like it when you do that. I'm going to stop calling you names, and I want you to stop calling me names. I don't want to fight with you.'"

[Have a student repeat the Kill-Them-With-Kindness Sandwich, "Trevor, I know you want to fight, but I don't fight. So I won't call you any more names." Coach the child to use assertive body language. Do the same with "Trevor, I know you like to call me names and tease me, but I don't like it when you do that. I'm going to stop calling you names, and I want you to stop calling me names. I don't want to fight with you." Give the child the opportunity to create a Kill-Them-With-Kindness Sandwich of his or her own. Have each child say out loud his or her Kill-Them-With-Kindness Sandwich, or repeat yours and have them practice saying it out loud.]

> "Daniel," said Mrs. Owl, "since you made a mistake and called Trevor 'Tyrannostupid,' maybe you should make an **Apology**." I thought, and said, "I could tell Trevor, 'I'm sorry I called you a name.'"

[Coach a child to say the Apology, "I'm sorry I called you a name." Give the child the opportunity to create an Apology of his or her own. Have each child say out loud his or her Apology, or repeat yours and have them practice saying it out loud.]

> Then Mrs. Owl said, "Daniel, **Humor** is another assertive behavior skill that can work very well when someone calls you names or teases you. Sometimes you can exaggerate the name they are calling you. So, if Trevor calls you a Brontostupid, you could pretend to be dumb and say, 'Duh, what is a Brontostupid?' Sometimes it helps to think of all the mean names someone can call you, so you won't be hurt when it happens. Let's stop right now and think of all the names that children might call you."

[Ask the students to list all the names that the children in their home, school, and neighborhood use to be mean to other children. If possible, think of humorous responses to use if called these names. Tell the children that just being aware of the names will help them stay calm and not be hurt by the names.]

> "Now let's look at whether you could have used one of the **Sound Bites**," said Mrs. Owl. "Remember those very short responses that you can use no matter what Trevor says: 'Yes'; 'No'; 'Oops!'; 'Oh, really!'; 'Wow!'; and 'Whatever.' So, if Trevor says 'You're a sissy!' you could just say 'No'; 'Oh, really?'; 'Wow!'; or 'Whatever.' If you can use one of the Sound Bites in a very calm tone of voice, you won't be heating up the fight: you'll be cooling it off."

[Coach a child to say "No"; "Oh, really?"; "Wow!"; or "Whatever," again coaching them to use assertive body language. Ask the children if they can think of any other Sound Bites. Have each child say out loud his or her Sound Bite, or repeat yours and have them practice saying it out loud.]

> "How about **Nice Replies**?" said Mrs. Owl. "Could you think of a nice way to stand up for yourself without hurting Trevor when he calls you names?" I thought for a while, and then I said, "I could tell him, 'Trevor, I know you'd like to spend some more time calling me names, but I have to go to the library.'"

[Coach a child to say the Nice Reply, "Trevor, I know you'd like to spend some more time calling me names, but I have to go to the library." Coach the child to use assertive body language. Give the child the opportunity to create a Nice Reply of his or her own. Have each child say out loud his or her Nice Reply, or repeat yours and have them practice saying it out loud.]

"Let's think of a good phrase to use in a **Broken Record**," said Mrs. Owl. I decided I could say, "Trevor, you can call me names, but I won't fight with you. It's not worth fighting over," and just keep repeating the sentence. "Good," said Mrs. Owl, "That's a good sentence to use in a Broken Record. Remember in a Broken Record, you just keep repeating the assertive statement you have chosen to use."

[Coach a student to say, "Trevor, you can call me names, but I won't fight with you. It's not worth fighting over." Ask the child to repeat the statement several times, again using assertive body language. Give the child an opportunity to create a different statement to use in a Broken Record. Have each child say out loud his or her Broken Record, or repeat yours and have them practice saying it out loud several times to make it a Broken Record.]

Then Mrs. Owl said, "Remember again, Daniel, these assertive behavior skills may not make Trevor change his behavior, but they will help you feel better about yourself. If you are afraid he is really going to hurt you, it's a good idea to get away from him and go to an adult. If it's not a physically dangerous situation, one of these skills will probably be good for you to use. They should help you from getting your feelings hurt so much. Of course, if Trevor continues to call you names or tease you, you should tell Mrs. Triceratops or another teacher. Remember that at Swamp School all of the adults are trying to help all children stop their mean and violent behavior. If the adults don't know that Trevor is being violent toward you by calling you names or teasing you, then they can't teach him that such behavior is violent and not acceptable. They also won't be able to teach him ways he can change his aggressive behavior. So, if you tell an adult that Trevor is being violent toward you, you will be helping yourself, but you will also be helping Trevor."

Let's hope you can figure out some more ways to use the assertive behavior skills of Body Language, I Statements, I Hear You Statements, Kill-Them-With-Kindness Sandwiches, Apologizing, Humor, Sound Bites, Nice Replies, and Broken Records when someone is being teased.

Discussion

Lead a discussion to help the group members understand how these assertive behavior skills can be used when being teased.

- Give an example of how to use Body Language when being teased.
- Give an example of how to use an I Statement when being teased.
- Give an example of how to use an I Hear You Statement when being teased.
- Give an example of how to use a Kill-Them-With-Kindness Sandwich when being teased.
- Give an example of how to use an Apology when being teased.
- Give an example of how to use Humor when being teased.
- Give an example of how to use a Sound Bite when being teased.

- Give an example of how to use a Nice Reply when being teased.
- Give an example of how to use a Broken Record when being teased.

Basic Facts

Ask the children to take out Basic Fact Worksheet 7 (see page 148) from their folders.

> 12. The assertive behavior skills help you **stand** up for yourself when someone is teasing you or calling you names.

Briefly discuss this fact, checking for understanding. Correct any misconceptions.

Give the children time to complete the bottom half of the worksheet by filling in the blanks. Then have the entire group read the fact aloud. Remind the children that you will be going over the basic facts learned so far at the beginning of each session, and that you will ask them to explain what each means. Have the children put their worksheets in their folders.

Homework Assignment

Ask the children to pull out Homework Assignment 7 (see page 149) from their folders. Ask one child to read it out loud. Tell the children that you want them to think of a way they can use one of these assertive behaviors when someone is being teased every day for the next week and to write down how.

Wrapping Up

Repeat the exercise from the beginning of the group, "The Waterfall" (see pages 139–140).

Affirmation

Involve the group in an affirmation. Stand and join in a circle with the children, holding hands. Go around and have each child share an assertive behavior skill that he or she can use when being teased. Start the affirmation yourself: "One way I can use an assertive behavior skill when I'm being teased or called names is . . ."

Closing

Remain standing in a circle with the children holding hands and lead the group in the closing activity, "Pass a Silent Wish" (see page 58).

Collect the folders and fill out a copy of the Process and Progress Form (see page 235) or the Progress Notes (see pages 236–237).

Handout 7
Assertive Behavior Skills to Use When Being Teased

Body Language. Includes posture, eye contact, and tone of voice.

Posture: stand up straight, put your shoulders back, keep your head high, but not stuck up, and stand tall. *Eye contact:* look at the person to whom you are speaking, and look in a friendly way. *Tone of voice:* speak in a loud enough voice, clearly and distinctly. Speak in a friendly tone, so people can understand you and speak as though you mean what you say.

Example: When you say the following assertive behavior skills, stand tall, look at the person to whom you are speaking, and speak clearly, distinctly, and as though you mean what you say.

I Statements. A way to say what you feel without hurting anyone else. I Statements have three parts: *I feel* (say how you feel) _____ *when you* (say what the other person did) _____ *because* (say why you feel the way you do) _____.

Example: "Trevor, I feel hurt and angry when you call me a sissy or when you say your sister could beat me up because it hurts my feelings."

I Hear You Statements. You repeat what the other person has said, not necessarily agreeing with them. By repeating what they have said, you let them know you heard them and understand what they said. An I Hear You Statement has two parts: "I can tell that you feel (or think) _____ because _____." An I Hear You Statement is a good way to cool off a fight instead of heating up the fight.

Example: "Trevor, I can tell that you are really angry at me because you are trying to hurt me by calling me a sissy."

Kill-Them-With-Kindness Sandwiches. First you say something nice to the other person. Then, you state your point of view, or you set a limit, or you say no. Then, you close by saying something nice again.

Example: "Trevor, I know that you want me to fight, but I don't fight. I won't call you any more names."

Another example: "Trevor, I know you like to call me names and tease me, but I don't like it when you do that. I'm going to stop calling you names, and I want you to stop calling me names. I don't want to fight with you."

Apologies. In an Apology, you admit you made a mistake and you say you're sorry. Sometimes you can say you're sorry that things don't go well for the other person, even if it's not your fault.

Example: "Trevor, I'm sorry I called you a name."

Humor. Sometimes, if you do or say something funny, or if you make a joke, it cools down what could become a fight instead of heating it up.

Example: "Duh, what is a Brontostupid?"

Sound Bites. A collection of short responses that you can use no matter what the other person says: "Yes"; "No"; "Oops"; "Oh, really!"; "Wow!"; and "Whatever."

Examples: "No"; "Oh, really!"; "Wow!"; or "Whatever."

Nice Replies. Nice Replies are just nice ways to say no without hurting the other person.

Example: "Trevor, I know you'd like to spend some more time calling me names, but I have to go to the library."

Broken Records. In a Broken Record, you just pretend you are a broken record and keep on repeating the same thing.

Example: "Trevor, you can call me names, but I won't fight with you. It's not worth fighting over." Repeat this statement several times.

Basic Fact Worksheet 7

12. The assertive behavior skills help you **<u>stand</u>** up for yourself when someone is teasing you or calling you names.

_____

12. The assertive behavior skills help you _____ up for yourself when someone is teasing you or calling you names.

Homework Assignment 7

Every day, see if you can find one way to use an assertive behavior skill of Body Language, I Statements, I Hear You Statements, Kill-Them-With-Kindness Sandwiches, Apologizing, Humor, Sound Bites, Nice Replies, or Broken Records when someone is being teased. Write a short sentence.

Day 1 _____

_____

_____

Day 2 _____

_____

_____

Day 3 _____

_____

_____

Day 4 _____

_____

_____

Day 5 _____

_____

_____

Session 8

Daniel the Dinosaur Practices Assertive Behavior Skills and Learns Two Other Steps to Take When Being Left Out

Objectives

To help the students:

- apply the assertive behavior skills learned so far in situations where they are being left out
- learn two steps to take in situations where they are being left out

Preparation

- Display the posterboard copy of the group rules.
- Have available the toy Daniel and Mrs. Owl and Basic Fact Posters 1 to 12.
- Add to each student's folder:
  - Handout 8 (Assertive Behavior Skills to Use When Being Left Out)
  - Activity Sheet 8 (Practice Situations for Being Left Out)
  - Basic Fact Worksheet 8
  - Homework Assignment 8
- Place each student's folder, pencil, and crayons or markers at his or her place.
- Have a chalkboard or flip chart available. Write the following:
  - I Statement: "I feel hurt that you won't let me go . . . (or play)."
  - Kill-Them-With-Kindness Sandwich: "I know that you don't want to include me, but I would really like to join in. Won't you let me play (or go) too?"
  - Nice Reply: "I would really like to play."
  - Broken Record: "Please let me go along. Please let me go along. Please let me go along."
  - Another example is "Please let me play, too. Please let me play, too. Please let me play, too."

> –Step One: Ask someone else to play.
> –Step Two: Find something else you like to do.
* Read through the session plan before meeting.

Background and Guidelines

This session is similar to session 7; it helps the children learn how to apply all of the assertive behavior skills in situations when they are being left out by other children. It also teaches two other steps they can take if they are being left out.

Just as in last session, you will reiterate in this session that if children are in physical danger from another child's violent behavior, they should go to an adult. If the other child's violent behavior is leaving them out, then using the assertive behavior skills should help the children feel better. In the discussion, remember to point out, however, that if the violent child continues to exclude, then the victim should tell an adult. That is the only way that adults can intervene, set limits with the violent child, and arrange to teach the violent child ways he or she can change the violent behavior.

The story in this session is again minimal, allowing most of the session time for practicing the assertive behavior skills in Handout 8. The main point of this session is to apply the assertive behavior skills in situations where a child is being left out. If the children can apply these skills themselves, allow them to do so. If they cannot, examples of how to use each assertive behavior skill in situations where they are being left out are given in Handout 8 for your convenience. Again remind the children to use assertive body language when saying each skill and be sure to give each child in the group an opportunity to say each skill. Children are usually able to come up with ideas on their own for the Practice Situations on Activity Sheet 8. If they can't, examples of how to use I Statements, Kill-Them-With-Kindness Sandwiches, Nice Replies, Broken Records, and the two steps are provided. Write them on a flip chart or chalkboard so the children can see them easily and decide which one they would like to use.

The point is made in the story that sometimes children are left out for violent reasons: the children who are leaving them out are being violent. In other situations, however, children may not be asked to play because they are not good athletes. In those situations, using an assertive behavior skill or asking to join in may not be effective. We want the children to be able to do something else that may help them feel better. So, we teach them to ask someone else to play, or to do something else they enjoy. Children who participate in the Daniel group probably have a long list of things they can do on their own. They are often eager to implement the step of asking someone else to play.

Again, the story and group point out the universality of these problems, which is very comforting to children.

[Note: If you have not thought about arranging an audience for the presentation in session 11, begin to do so now. Read the Background and Guidelines sections for session 10 and session 11 and begin to make plans for a suitable audience.]

Beginning the Session

Welcome the students. If necessary, begin with a quick review of the group rules (see page 51). Check for understanding before moving on.

Centering Exercise

Make certain that the children are comfortable and quiet. Introduce the new centering exercise, "The Rainbow."

> Close your eyes and imagine that you're asleep, and in your sleep, you're dreaming. In your dream, you can fly. You soar way, way up in the sky, and you decide to land on a white, fluffy cloud. You lie back and relax on that cloud as it floats lazily across the deep blue sky. You feel safe and warm. You look down and see other clouds below you. Far beneath those clouds is the earth. The cars and people and buildings on earth look very small.
>
> You decide to reach into your pocket and pull out all your worries and sadnesses. You decide to drop them one at a time on the clouds that float below you, one worry, one sadness per cloud. Soon, the clouds change your worries and sadnesses into rain that falls gently to the ground. It falls gently at first, and then it starts to pour. The rain washes away all the dust and dirt and makes everything look clean. It also makes the rivers and lakes beautiful, and helps the plants and flowers and trees to grow.
>
> As the rain stops, the sun comes back out, and there is a beautiful rainbow. You float over on your cloud and sit on top of the rainbow. You smile to yourself because you know that you made that beautiful rainbow. Rainbows can only come after a rain. Without your worries and sadnesses, the clouds couldn't have made the rain. And there would be no beautiful rainbow now. You think to yourself, "Before there can be a rainbow, there must be a cloud and a storm."
>
> Then, because you like to have fun, you slide down the rainbow. There is a pot of happiness at the end of the rainbow. You reach in and fill your pockets full of happiness, and whenever you are feeling sad, you can reach in your pocket for the memory of this rainbow.

Tell the children that two children in Virginia made up this centering exercise.

Feelings Check-in

Using the Feeling Daniel, do a feelings check-in with the students (see page 69). When the students finish, have a go-around.

Basic Facts Review

To help the students review their last session and the basic facts learned so far, show them Basic Fact Posters 1 to 12. The Basic Facts List and Questions to Help Clarify the Basic Facts are printed on pages 229–234.

Assignment Review

Ask the students if they brought their homework assignments from last week. Remind them of the assignment by reading it: "Every day, see if you can find one way to use an assertive behavior skill of Body Language, I Statements, I Hear You Statements, Kill-Them-With-Kindness Sandwiches, Apologizing, Humor, Sound Bites, Nice Replies, or Broken Records when someone is being teased. Write a short sentence."

In a go-around, ask the children to share what they found. If the children forgot to do the assignment, in the go-around, ask them to try to think of one way they could have used the assertive behavior skills of Body Language, I Statements, I Hear You Statements, Kill-Them-With-Kindness Sandwiches, Apologizing, Humor, Sound Bites, Nice Replies, or Broken Records when someone was being teased in the past week. If they can't think of anything they did, ask them what they could do in the next week to use one of these assertive behavior skills. Remind them that using these skills may not change the other person, but it will help them feel better about themselves.

Exploring the Story

Have the children get comfortable for today's story. Use the toy Daniel and Mrs. Owl and allow Daniel to tell the following:

> Hi boys and girls! Have you been remembering to use your assertive behavior skills? Have you been remembering to Stand Tall—to use assertive posture, eye contact, and tone of voice? And how about your I Statements and I Hear You Statements? Have you been using Kill-Them-With-Kindness Sandwiches, Apologizing, Humor, Sound Bites, Nice Replies, or Broken Records? Today we're going to practice using these assertive behavior skills in situations where we're being left out.

> Well, Mrs. Owl asked Della how she felt when the other dinosaurs wouldn't let her play. Della said her feelings were hurt, and she was embarrassed, and ashamed. Mrs. Owl said, "Let's look at the assertive behavior skills again and figure out which ones you could use in situations where other children are not letting you play. Della, some of the assertive behavior skills will be good to use if you want to join in the play. Others will be good ways for you to tell the other children how you feel when they don't let you play."

[Ask the children to pull out Handout 8 (page 159–160).]

> Mrs. Owl said, "Now, Della, how could you have used an **I Statement** when Tiffany called you Scaleface and the other dinosaurs wouldn't let you play jump rope?" Della

thought and then she said, "I could have said, 'Tiffany, I feel sad and angry when you won't let me play.'" "Good," said Mrs. Owl. "That I Statement is a good way to let the other dinosaurs know how you feel when they won't let you play."

Why don't you practice this yourself?

[Give each child the opportunity to create an I Statement of his or her own. If they cannot, have each child say the example under I Statement, "Tiffany, I feel sad and angry when you won't let me play," out loud themselves, making sure they remember to use assertive posture, eye contact, and tone of voice.]

"How could you have used an **I Hear You Statement**?" asked Mrs. Owl. "In an I Hear You Statement, you say, 'Tiffany, I can tell that you are probably angry at me because you won't let me jump rope.' By saying that, you are letting Tiffany know that you understand that she is probably angry, and you are letting her know that you can tell she is trying to hurt you."

Why don't you practice this yourself?

[Give each child the opportunity to create an I Hear You Statement of his or her own. If they cannot, have each child say the example under I Hear You Statement, "Tiffany, I can tell that you are probably angry at me because you won't let me jump rope," out loud themselves, making sure they remember to use assertive posture, eye contact, and tone of voice.]

Mrs. Owl went on. "Della, how could you have used a **Kill-Them-With-Kindness Sandwich**? Remember, in a Kill-Them-With-Kindness Sandwich, first you say something nice to the other person. Then, you state your point of view, or you set a limit, or you say no. Then, you close by saying something nice again. So you could have said, 'Tiffany, I know you like to jump rope with your friends. I just want to play too. I won't take your friends away.' That Kill-Them-With-Kindness Sandwich is a good way to ask to join in."

Why don't you practice this yourself?

[Give each child the opportunity to create a Kill-Them-With-Kindness Sandwich of his or her own. If they cannot, have each child say the example under Kill-Them-With-Kindness Sandwich, "Tiffany, I know you like to jump rope with your friends. I just want to play too. I won't take your friends away," out loud themselves, making sure they remember to use assertive posture, eye contact, and tone of voice.]

"Now," said Mrs. Owl, "let's see if we can figure out how to use the assertive behavior skill of **Apologizing** in this situation. Even though you haven't done anything wrong, Della, you could soften Tiffany up by saying 'Sorry' before you tell her an assertive statement. For example, you could say 'Tiffany, I'm sorry you don't want me to play, but the rules are that everybody gets a chance to play.' That would be another good way to ask to join in."

Why don't you practice this yourself?

[Give each child the opportunity to create an Apology of his or her own. If they cannot, have each child say the example under Apology, "Tiffany, sorry you don't want me to play, but the rules are that everybody gets a chance to play," out loud themselves, making sure they remember to use assertive posture, eye contact, and tone of voice.]

Then Mrs. Owl said, "Della, when you are being left out, it may be hard to use the assertive behavior skills of **Humor** or **Sound Bites**." Can anyone think of a way to use Humor or Sound Bites when being left out? Remember, Humor is making a joke out of the situation. The Sound Bites are "Yes"; "No"; "Oops"; "Oh, really!"; "Wow!"; and "Whatever."

[Give the children an opportunity to come up with ideas. If they cannot, move on to the next paragraph.]

"Let's move on to **Nice Replies** and **Broken Records**," said Mrs. Owl. "Could you think of a nice way to stand up for yourself when you are being left out?" Della thought for a while, and then she said, "I could tell her, 'Tiffany, everybody gets to play.'" "Good," said Mrs. Owl, "maybe you can combine that with a Broken Record, and just keep repeating that Nice Reply. Remember in a Broken Record, you just keep repeating the assertive statement you have chosen to use. This is another good assertive behavior skill to ask to join in."

Why don't you practice this yourself?

[Give each child the opportunity to create a Nice Reply to use in a Broken Record on his or her own. If they cannot, have each child say the example under Broken Record, "Tiffany, everybody gets to play," out loud themselves, making sure they remember to use assertive posture, eye contact, and tone of voice.]

Then Mrs. Owl said, "Now, Daniel and Della, these assertive behavior skills are not the only ways to cope with being left out. There are other ways that will also help you feel better in this situation. When you are being left out, you can try to figure out why. Sometimes the children who are leaving you out are just being mean or violent to you. If you respond by being hurt, they know they have a good target, and they will continue their behavior. The assertive behavior skills help you stand up for yourself without using mean or violent ways yourself. Sometimes, you may not be asked to play in a sports game because you may not be good at kickball, or basketball, or jump rope, or football. In either situation, the assertive behavior skills may help you ask to join in. But using the assertive behavior skill may not change the way the other children are leaving you out. So there are two other steps you can take:

1. Ask someone else to play.
2. Find something else you like to do.

If you are on the playground, there may be other children standing around by themselves. Maybe you could go up to them and ask them if they would like to toss a ball back and forth, or play tag, or jump rope, or swing. And, it's always a good idea for you to figure things out you can do to have fun if the other children won't let you play. Let's make a list of things children can do if they are being left out."

[Stop here and ask the children for some things they can do if being left out, on the playground, during recess, or in their neighborhood. Write their ideas on a chalkboard or flip chart.]

Let's see if you can figure out some more ways to use the assertive behavior skills of Body Language, I Statements, I Hear You Statements, Kill-Them-With-Kindness Sandwiches, Apologizing, Humor, Sound Bites, Nice Replies, and Broken Records when someone is being left out. And let's see how you can ask someone else to play or do something you like to do.

Discussion

Lead a discussion to help the group members understand how these assertive behavior skills can be used when being left out.

- Give an example of how to use Body Language when being left out.
- Give an example of how to use an I Statement when being left out.
- Give an example of how to use an I Hear You Statement when being left out.
- Give an example of how to use a Kill-Them-With-Kindness Sandwich when being left out.
- Give an example of how to use an Apology when being left out.
- Give an example of how to use Humor when being left out.
- Give an example of how to use a Sound Bite when being left out.
- Give an example of how to use a Nice Reply when being left out.
- Give an example of how to use a Broken Record when being left out.
- Give an example of how to ask someone else to play when being left out.
- Give an example of how to find something else you like to do when being left out.

Activity

Ask the children to take out Activity Sheet 8 (see page 161) from their folders. Tell them that these are situations where someone is being left out. They should look at each one and decide if they could use one of the assertive behavior skills to describe how they feel, ask to join in, or use one of the two steps:

1. Ask someone else to play.
2. Find something else you like to do.

Ask a child to read **Situation 1**, "The boys in your neighborhood are playing basketball. They won't let you play."

Ask each group member to say an assertive behavior skill they could use to describe how they feel, to ask to join in, to ask someone else to play, or to find something else they like to do. Repeat for each group member. If the children cannot think of any ideas, coach them to use one of the following, which you have written on a flip chart (see Preparation).

> **I Statement:** "I feel hurt that you won't let me go . . . (or play)." Reiterate that I Statements are good for telling how you feel if someone won't let you play or go with them.

> **Kill-Them-With-Kindness-Sandwich:** "I know that you don't want me to include me, but I would really like to join in. Won't you let me play (or go), too?" Kill-Them-With-Kindness Sandwiches are good ways to ask to join in.

> **Nice Reply:** "I would really like to play." Nice Replies are also good ways to ask to join in.

> **Broken Record:** "Please let me go along. Please let me go along. Please let me go along."

> Another example is "Please let me play, too. Please let me play, too. Please let me play, too." Broken Records are another good way to ask to join in.

> **Step One:** Ask someone else to play.
> **Step Two:** Find something else you like to do.

> Repeat the process for each situation.

Basic Facts

Ask the children to take out Basic Fact Worksheet 8 (see page 162) from their folders.

> 13. The assertive behavior skills help you **say** how you **feel** and **ask** to **join in** when you are being left out.

> 14. There are two other steps you can take if you are being left out:
>   a. **Ask** someone else to **play.**
>   b. **Find** something else you **like** to do.

Briefly discuss these facts, checking for understanding. Correct any misconceptions.

Give the children time to complete the bottom half of the worksheet by filling in the blanks. Then have the entire group read the facts out loud. Remind the children that you will be going over the basic facts learned so far at the beginning of each session, and that you will ask them to explain what each means. Have the children put their worksheets in their folders.

Homework Assignment

Ask the children to pull out Homework Assignment 8 (see page 163) from their folders. Ask one child to read it out loud. Tell the children that you want them to think of a way they can use one of these assertive behaviors when being left out to describe how they feel, or to ask to join in, every day for the next week, or to ask someone else to play, or find something else they like to do and to write down how.

Wrapping Up

Repeat the exercise from the beginning of the group, "The Rainbow" (see page 152).

Affirmation

Involve the group in an affirmation. Stand and join in a circle with the children, holding hands. Go around and have each child share an assertive behavior skill or one of the two other steps that he or she can use when being left out. Start the affirmation yourself: "One way I can use an assertive behavior skill when I'm being left out is . . ."

Closing

Remain standing in a circle with the children holding hands and lead the group in the closing activity, "Pass a Silent Wish" (see page 58).

Collect the folders and fill out a copy of the Process and Progress Form (see page 235) or the Progress Notes (see pages 236–237).

Handout 8
Assertive Behavior Skills to Use When Being Left Out

Body Language. Includes posture, eye contact, and tone of voice.

Posture: stand up straight, put your shoulders back, keep your head high, but not stuck up, and stand tall. *Eye contact:* look at the person to whom you are speaking, and look in a friendly way. *Tone of voice:* speak in a loud enough voice, clearly and distinctly. Speak in a friendly tone, so people can understand you and speak as though you mean what you say.

Example: When you say the following assertive behavior skills, stand tall, look at the person to whom you are speaking, and speak clearly, distinctly, and as though you mean what you say.

I Statements. A way to say what you feel without hurting anyone else. I Statements have three parts: " I feel (say how you feel) _____ when you (say what the other person did) _____ because (say why you feel the way you do) _____."

Example: "Tiffany, I feel sad and angry when you won't let me play because I am being left out."

I Hear You Statements. You repeat what the other person has said, not necessarily agreeing with them. By repeating what they have said, you let them know you heard them and understand what they said. An I Hear You Statement has two parts: "I can tell that you feel (or think) _____ because _____." An I Hear You Statement is a good way to cool off a fight instead of heating up the fight.

Example: "Tiffany, I can tell that you are probably angry at me because you won't let me jump rope."

Kill-Them-With-Kindness Sandwiches. First you say something nice to the other person. Then, you state your point of view, or you set a limit, or you say no. Then, you close by saying something nice again.

Example: "Tiffany, I know you like to jump rope with your friends. I just want to play too. I won't take your friends away."

Apologies. In an Apology, you admit you made a mistake and you say you're sorry. Sometimes you can say you're sorry that things don't go well for the other person, even if it's not your fault.

Example: "Tiffany, I'm sorry you don't want me to play, but the rules are that everybody gets a chance to play."

Humor. Sometimes, if you do or say something funny, or if you make a joke, it cools down what could become a fight instead of heating it up.

Sound Bites. A collection of short responses that you can use no matter what the other person says: "Yes"; "No"; "Oops"; "Oh, really!"; "Wow!"; and "Whatever."

Nice Replies. Nice Replies are just nice ways to say no without hurting the other person.

Broken Records. In a Broken Record, you just pretend you are a broken record and keep on repeating the same thing.

Example: "Tiffany, everybody gets to play. Tiffany, everybody gets to play. Tiffany, everybody gets to play."

Activity Sheet 8
Practice Situations for Being Left Out

Situation 1

The boys in your neighborhood are playing basketball. They won't let you play.

Situation 2

Your sister is playing your favorite board game with her friend. She won't let you play.

Situation 3

Your classmates are playing kickball during recess. You want to play.

Situation 4

Your brother is going to the movies with two friends. He won't let you go along.

Situation 5

Two students in your class are picking teams. You're the last to be selected.

Situation 6

The girls at the bus stop are in a circle talking. They won't let you join the circle.

Assertive behavior skills: Body Language, I Statements, I Hear You Statements, Kill-Them-With-Kindness Sandwiches, Apologizing, Humor, Sound Bites, Nice Replies, and Broken Records.

Steps:
1. Ask someone else to play.
2. Find something else you like to do.

Basic Fact Worksheet 8

13. The assertive behavior skills help you **say** how you **feel** and **ask** to **join in** when you are being left out.

14. There are two other steps you can take if you are being left out:

    a. **Ask** someone else to **play.**
    b. **Find** something else you **like** to do.

_____

13. The assertive behavior skills help you _____ how you _____ and _____ to _____ when you are being left out.

14. There are two other steps you can take if you are being left out:

    a. _____ someone else to _____.
    b. _____ something else you _____ to do.

Homework Assignment 8

Every day, see if you can find one way to use an assertive behavior skill of Body Language, I Statements, I Hear You Statements, Kill-Them-With-Kindness Sandwiches, Apologizing, Humor, Sound Bites, Nice Replies, or Broken Records when someone is being left out. You can use these skills to describe how you feel or to ask to join in. Or, see how you could use one of the other two steps you can take if you are being left out:

1. Ask someone else to play.
2. Find something else you like to do.

Write a short sentence.

Day 1 _____

_____

Day 2 _____

_____

Day 3 _____

_____

Day 4 _____

_____

Day 5 _____

_____

Session 9

Daniel the Dinosaur Learns Anger Management

Objectives

To help the students

- understand that anger management is a plan to handle anger in a nonviolent way
- learn a seven-step plan for managing anger
- discover helpful, nonviolent ways to express angry feelings

Preparation

- Display the posterboard copy of the group rules.
- Have available the toy Daniel and Mrs. Owl and Basic Fact Posters 1 to 14.
- For Daniel, print the steps of anger management (see number 15 on Basic Fact Worksheet 9, page 175) on one side of an index card. On the other side, print the following list of helpful ways to express anger: punch a pillow, do jumping jacks, hammer nails into old pieces of wood, sit in a time-out chair, roar when I'm by myself and it won't bother anybody, write or draw about my anger, run laps, and talk to someone I trust.
- Provide an index card for each child; for younger children, on each card write the list of seven anger management steps found on Basic Fact Worksheet 9.
- Make a poster. Across the top, print the title, "Anger Management Steps." Draw outlines of seven dinosaur footprints across the poster. (For a sample, see Activity Sheet 9, page 174.) With a marker write the steps of anger management in each footprint: Recognize, Accept, Relax, Think, Evaluate, Choose, Express.
- Add to each student's folder:

  –An index card (For younger children, on each card write the seven anger management steps found on Basic Fact Worksheet 9.)

–Activity Sheet 9 (Helpful Ways I Can Express Anger)
–Basic Fact Worksheet 9
–Homework Assignment 9
- Place each student's folder, pencil, and crayons or markers at his or her place.
- Read through the session plan before meeting.

Background and Guidelines

This session presents anger management steps that function as a cognitive behavioral technique; put simply, this session helps the children create a proactive plan to express their anger in helpful ways. The plan shows the children how to put thinking between feeling angry and expressing anger.

Even though the violent behavior of bullies is generally not to express anger but to attain power and dominance over others, the children who are their victims are often very angry. These children may be the provocative victims who themselves show aggressive behavior. This session is intended to help them deal in a proactive way with their anger.

As you lead the children through the session, help them become aware of the many different ways they can express their anger so they can let it go. Specific examples will be of great help: "One child I knew was angry about his parents' fighting, so he wrote them a letter, and he punched his pillow; in a little while, he didn't feel so angry." Or "One time when I felt angry, I cleaned the bathroom, top to bottom. Then I went out and jogged." To help children evaluate the consequences of their expressions of anger, teach them to ask themselves: "Will this particular action be helpful or harmful?" During the session, you may notice that some children will describe harmful ways to express anger. For instance, they might say they can hit someone or hit a wall, and they will feel better. Don't accept these harmful ways. Let the children know that it is not okay to express their anger in a way that hurts themselves or someone else. Rather, gently encourage and redirect the children to find helpful ways to express their anger.

Emphasize to the children that the anger management plan is something they can use in real life: at home, on the playground, on the bus, and in the classroom. Let the children know that it's hard to change behavior right away. In fact, most people change their behavior quite slowly. Chunking it down applies to learning anger management as well as to using assertive behavior skills. Tell the children that they can help themselves change their behavior by going through the anger management steps, even after they choose a harmful way to express anger. Doing so can help them figure out what would have been a more helpful choice to express their anger so they could let it go. It often takes people six to ten weeks of processing the steps retroactively before they form the habit of using the plan at the time of anger.

Since children with behavioral problems may have difficulty in remembering the plan and its steps and won't be able to change their behavior immediately, it's helpful to engage their teachers, principal, and student assistance team in using the plan. Work with teachers and children to set up a plan so that the children will know exactly what choices they have with regard to expressing their anger. Explosive children may benefit from a plan that includes helpful choices such as journal writing, playing with clay, drawing a picture, or sitting in a time-out chair in the office or with the guidance counselor. Help teachers to choose behavior that will work in a particular classroom and encourage them to help the children implement their plans when they feel angry.

Beginning the Session

Welcome the students. If necessary, begin with a quick review of the group rules (see page 51). Check for understanding before moving on.

Centering Exercise

Make certain that the children are comfortable and quiet. Ask them if any of them remembered to "Stop and Breathe to Five," "the Icicle," or "Defuse the Bomb" in the past week. Remind them that stopping and breathing to five, or tensing and relaxing muscles, and then thinking will help them make good decisions about how to get along with other children. Introduce the new centering exercise, "The Balloons." Tell the group members that this is another centering exercise that will help them to calm down, relax, and be able to think if they get angry or upset. They can use this exercise without anyone else knowing.

> In this centering exercise, you're going to experience some anger. Then you're going to express it in a helpful way. Finally, you'll be able to let it go.

> Imagine that you're very, very angry. Maybe you just had a terrible fight with your brother or sister. Maybe your parents were angry with you last night and hit you for no reason. Maybe your teacher said that you were talking in the classroom, but it was really the child who sits next to you.

> No matter the reason, imagine how angry you feel right now. You feel very hot; your blood is pumping fast; you feel as though you have a lot of energy; you are breathing fast, and you feel like you have a lot of air in your chest. You're going to express that anger by blowing up some balloons.

> The first balloon that you pick up is a long, red one. Start blowing into that balloon. Blow all the anger you feel in your chest into that red balloon. (Pause.) Soon the balloon is very large. You tie it up and put it down.

> Now pick up a round, blue balloon. You start to blow into it. You huff and puff. (Pause.) The balloon bets bigger and bigger as you blow a lot of air into it. Feel how much anger you are putting into the balloon. It is finally full and you tie it up.

> Pick up a very big purple balloon. Blow and blow into it. Keep on blowing. Put all of your anger into it. The purple balloon is getting bigger and bigger. When it gets large enough, you tie it up and put it down.

Now pick up a yellow balloon. You blow into it. You're not feeling so angry anymore, and your air has magically turned into helium. You feel much lighter because you've put all of your anger into the balloons, and you've let your anger go. You decide to let all of the balloons go. Watch all of them float away. Your anger is floating away, too.

Remind the students that they can use this technique in school, on the bus, during recess, and at home to help them relax so they can put thinking between their feelings and their behavior.

Feelings Check-in

Using the Feeling Daniel, do a feelings check-in with the students (see page 69). When the students finish, have a go-around.

Basic Facts Review

To help the students review their last session and the basic facts learned so far, show them Basic Fact Posters 1 to 14. The Basic Facts List and Questions to Help Clarify the Basic Facts are printed on pages 229–234.

Assignment Review

Ask the students if they brought their homework assignments from last week. Remind them of the assignment by reading it: "Every day, see if you can find one way to use an assertive behavior skill of Body Language, I Statements, I Hear You Statements, Kill-Them-With-Kindness Sandwiches, Apologizing, Humor, Sound Bites, Nice Replies, or Broken Records when someone is being left out. You can use these skills to describe how you feel or to ask to join in. Or, see how you could use one of the other two steps you can take if you are being left out: 1. Ask someone else to play. 2. Find something you like to do. Write a short sentence."

In a go-around, ask the children to share what they found. If the children forgot to do the assignment, in the go-around ask them to try to think of one way they could have used the assertive behavior skills of Body Language, I Statements, I Hear You Statements, Kill-Them-With-Kindness Sandwiches, Apologizing, Humor, Sound Bites, Nice Replies, or Broken Records when someone was being left out in the past week. If they can't think of anything they did, ask them what they could do in the next week to use one of these assertive behavior skills or the other two steps you can take if you are being left out.

Exploring the Story

Have the children get comfortable for today's story. Use the toy Daniel and Mrs. Owl and allow Daniel to tell the following:

Hi, boys and girls! Have you been practicing your assertive behavior skills and the other steps to take if someone is being left out? Today we're going to talk about the feeling of anger, and we're going to learn a plan to use our assertive behavior skills when we're angry.

Sometimes when Trevor was being violent with me—by making fun of me, calling me Brontostupid, making me give him my caveman pizza, tripping me during kickball—I got to be really angry. He kept messing with me, and I got angrier and angrier, and I had a good reason to be angry, I thought. I asked Mrs. Owl if I still had to use assertive behavior skills then. "Isn't it okay to be aggressive or violent if you are angry?" I asked Mrs. Owl. "Don't I have a right to be violent with Trevor if he is violent with me?" "Now Daniel," Mrs. Owl said, "remember that at Swamp School it's not okay for Trevor to be violent. But it's not okay for you to be violent either—remember violent behavior is mean and is not acceptable, even if you're angry. The only time it's okay to use violence is in self-defense—in a situation where your life is being threatened. Situations where somebody calls you a name, or hits you, or steals your lunch are not life-threatening situations. So, in situations like those, it's better to use nonviolent ways, helpful ways, to express your anger."

Mrs. Owl went on, "One of the things I like to teach young dinosaurs is that anger, like every emotion or feeling, has three parts—feeling, thinking, and behavior. It's always okay to have the feeling of anger. However, what you do with the anger, your behavior, can be good or bad. For instance, if you hit Trevor when he trips you, or don't let Tiffany jump rope, that behavior is violent and is bad. So, you need to think before you act, to make sure that your behavior is good, or helpful, and does not hurt anyone or anything. Anger management is a plan to help you choose a nonviolent way to express anger."

[Display the poster entitled "Anger Management Steps" and point out the seven dinosaur footprints. As Daniel explains the following anger management plan, point to the name of each step. If you do not make a poster, ask the children to retrieve Activity Sheet 9, Helpful Ways I Can Express Anger (see page 174), from their folder to follow along with Daniel.]

The first step in a plan for managing anger is to **recognize** that I'm angry. It's like I have to say to myself, "I'm not feeling sad. I'm not feeling lonely. I'm feeling angry." Sometimes I can tell I'm angry because my heart beats fast, I get red, and I breathe fast.

[Point to the word *Recognize* in the first footprint.]

The second step to take is to **accept** my anger. That means I have to see that anger is a normal feeling that dinosaurs and people have, and that it's okay for me to have it. It's not okay for me to behave in violent, angry ways, but it is okay to feel anger.

[Point to the word *Accept* in the second footprint.]

The third step is to practice a way to **relax**. This means that I have to do something that makes me feel relaxed. You know, like Stop and Breathe to Five or The Icicle. Calming down will help me think better.

[Point to the word *Relax* in the third footprint.]

The fourth step of the plan is to **think** about the different ways I could express my anger. I could kick someone or punch a pillow or slam a door.

[Point to the word *Think* in the fourth footprint.]

The fifth step is to **evaluate** the consequences of the different ways I thought about expressing my anger. Evaluate is a big word that means to think about what will happen after I express my anger—will it be helpful or will it be harmful? Like what might happen after I show my anger by kicking someone? Will it be helpful or harmful? Or what might happen after I show my anger by punching a pillow? Will it be helpful or harmful?

[Point to the word *Evaluate* in the fifth footprint.]

The sixth step is to **choose** a helpful way to express my anger.

[Point to the word *Choose* in the sixth footprint.]

The final step is to **express** my anger—to show it—in a helpful way.

[Point to the word *Express* in the seventh footprint.]

[As Daniel points to each step, encourage the children to read each aloud. Afterward, have Daniel point to the fourth step, **think**, and continue the story.]

Mrs. Owl and I spent a lot of time together thinking about ways I could express my anger. She asked me to make a list of things I can do when I feel angry. I'll share my **thinking** list with you, if you help me **evaluate** it. For each thing I tell you, show me a thumbs up if you think what might happen next would be helpful. But show me a thumbs down if what you think might happen next would be harmful.

These are some different ways I thought I could express my anger:

- Stomp around the house as loudly as I can. Helpful or harmful?
- Kick the kid at the bus stop who is always messing with me. Helpful or harmful?
- Punch a pillow. Helpful or harmful?
- Call somebody every bad name I can think of. Helpful or harmful?
- Do jumping jacks. Helpful or harmful?
- Break my sister's headphones. Helpful or harmful?
- Hammer nails into old pieces of wood. Helpful or harmful?
- Hammer nails into my mother's good furniture. Helpful or harmful?
- Sit in a time-out chair. Helpful or harmful?
- Use my loudest dinosaur roar in the classroom. Helpful or harmful?

- Use my loudest dinosaur roar in the middle of the swamp when I'm alone. Helpful or harmful?
- Write about how angry I am. Helpful or harmful?
- Swear at the teacher. Helpful or harmful?
- Draw a picture of my feelings. Helpful or harmful?
- Run dinosaur laps around my house. Helpful or harmful?
- Slam every door I can find. Helpful or harmful?
- Kick the principal. Helpful or harmful?
- Talk to someone I trust about how angry I am. Helpful or harmful?

Thanks for helping me evaluate my list of consequences of what might happen next. You helped me see that stomping, kicking, calling names, breaking things, hammering nails into my mother's good furniture, roaring in the classroom, swearing, slamming doors, and kicking the principal would be harmful and violent ways to express anger.

You also helped me see that punching a pillow, doing jumping jacks, hammering nails into old pieces of wood, sitting in a time-out chair, roaring when I'm by myself and it won't bother anybody, writing or drawing about my anger, running laps, and talking to someone I trust would be helpful and nonviolent ways to express my anger.

Before I go today, I'd like to tell about yesterday. Something happened that gave me a chance to practice my steps for anger management.

Recess was over, and Mrs. Dimetrodon asked me to go get the basketball at the edge of the playground. Trevor was there, and he kicked the basketball into the street. My teacher, Mrs. Triceratops, didn't know that Mrs. Dimetrodon had told me to get the ball. Instead, she punished me for being late to get back to the classroom—she took away recess for the rest of the week. She wouldn't even listen when I tried to explain. I started to feel hot and I was breathing fast and hard. I wanted to push over all the desks in the classroom.

Instead, I remembered the steps for managing anger. I recognized that I was angry and accepted that it was okay to feel that way. I was so angry that I had a hard time breathing, so I practiced a way of relaxing. I counted down from ten. Then I remembered my list. I decided to write a letter about what I was angry about. I used an Apology in my paragraph, and an I Statement. Here's what I said: "Mrs. Triceratops, I'm sorry that I was late getting back from recess, but Mrs. Dimetrodon asked me to get the basketball. I feel angry when I lose recess when I was just doing what another teacher asked me to do." After I wrote the letter, I decided to give it to Mrs. Triceratops. In a little while, I calmed down. I didn't feel so angry anymore. Then I decided to do something good for myself, so I went outside and practiced my long shots in basketball.

The plan for managing my anger worked really well last night. But Mrs. Owl warned me that sometimes I might forget to use the steps of my plan. Then I might express my anger in a harmful and violent way. But even if that happens, Mrs. Owl said that I should still go through the steps of the plan.

"It's hard for dinosaurs to change their behavior right away, Daniel, but practice makes perfect," Mrs. Owl said. "If you go through the steps often enough, it'll get easier and easier for you to remember to put thinking between feeling angry and expressing your anger in harmful and violent ways. Instead, you'll be able to express your anger in helpful ways, so you can let it go."

That's why I carry this card with me.

[Note: Have Daniel show the children an index card that lists the steps of anger management on one side and Daniel's helpful and nonviolent ways to express anger on the other side: punch a pillow, do jumping jacks, hammer nails into old pieces of wood, sit in a time-out chair, roar when I'm by myself and it won't bother anybody, write or draw about my anger, run laps, and talk to someone I trust. See Preparation section.]

On one side, I wrote the steps for anger management. There are a lot of steps, and this card helps me remember them. On the other side of the card is a list of the things I can do to express my anger in helpful ways: punch a pillow, do jumping jacks, hammer nails into old pieces of wood, sit in a time-out chair, roar when I'm by myself and it won't bother anybody, write or draw about my anger, run laps, and talk to someone I trust. I keep the list with me to help me remember what to do when I feel angry, so I can express my anger and let it go. Maybe you can make a card like this.

Until we meet next time, remember, if you feel yourself getting all steamed up and angry, take the right steps to manage your anger so you can let it go.

Now, let's discuss what we've learned so far.

Discussion

Lead a discussion to help the group members understand the plan for anger management.

- Is it okay to use violent or aggressive behavior when you are angry? (No. Violence is only justified in life-threatening situations, and they don't happen very often in elementary school.)
- Is it okay to feel angry? (Yes, everybody gets angry, and feeling angry is okay; but it's not okay to behave in a violent way. You may need to think to choose a helpful way to express your anger.)
- What does it mean to manage your anger? (It means having a plan to help you put thinking between feeling angry and doing angry things.)
- What are the steps of anger management? (Let the children use the poster you made, or Basic Fact Worksheet 9 (see page 175) as they respond: recognize

that you're angry; accept your anger; practice some form of relaxing; think about different ways to express your anger; evaluate the consequences; choose the best way; express the anger in a helpful way.)

- What are some ways you might recognize that you're feeling angry? (Accept all responsible replies; look for examples like the following: you might get hot, turn red, start to sweat, feel tense; feel your heart beating fast; breathe hard.)
- How do you accept your anger? (Tell yourself it's okay to feel angry.)
- What are some ways you can relax? (Practice one of the centering exercises: "Stop and Breathe to Five," "The Icicle," "Defuse the Bomb.")
- What are some ways to express anger? Are they helpful or harmful? (Accept all responsible replies; encourage the group to look to the examples in the story.)
- What does it mean to choose a helpful way to express your anger? (To pick a way that doesn't harm yourself or anyone or anything else.)
- What does it mean to express your anger in a helpful way? (To go ahead and act—to do your best choice.)
- Why should you always try to express your anger in a helpful way? (So you can let go of your anger in a way that won't hurt you or anyone else.)
- Should you expect to use these steps right away? (You should try. It's hard to change behavior right away. But if you keep using the steps, even after choosing a harmful way to express anger, doing so will help you to remember to put thinking between feelings and actions. Sooner or later, you'll use the steps when you're actually angry. But it may take two or three months and lots of practice. Don't give up.)

Activity

Ask the children to retrieve their copies of Activity Sheet 9 (see page 174). Read aloud the title at the top of the sheet: "Helpful Ways I Can Express Anger." Point out the seven footprints on the sheet. Read aloud the key words for anger management, which are found inside the footprints. Direct the children to list helpful ways they could express their anger next to the footprints. (Note: you may have to help younger children with writing.) Then ask them to choose one way they like and to illustrate it on the back of the sheet.

When the children finish, have a go-around. Invite each child to read from his or her list and to explain his or her drawing to the group. Don't accept harmful ways. Instead, gently encourage the children to choose helpful ways to express their anger. Afterward, have the children put their drawings in their folders.

Basic Facts

Ask the children to take Basic Fact Worksheet 9 (see page 175) and the index card out of their folders. This week, for older children, instead of filling in the Basic Fact worksheet ask the children to copy the main words in the anger management plan onto one side and their lists of helpful ways to express their anger on the other side of the card. Prepare the steps in advance for younger children, and offer them help with their helpful ways. Tell the children that they can keep their card and carry it in their pocket—just as Daniel does. Whenever they feel angry, they should look at the card to help them put thinking between feeling and action.

15. The anger management steps are:

    a. **Recognize** that you are angry.
    b. **Accept** your anger.
    c. Practice **relaxation.**
    d. **Think** about ways to express the anger.
    e. **Evaluate** the consequences.
    f. **Choose** the best way.
    g. **Express** the anger in a helpful way.

Briefly discuss each fact, checking for understanding. Correct any misconceptions.

Homework Assignment

Ask the children to pull out Homework Assignment 9 (see page 176) from their folders. Ask one child to read it out loud. Tell the children that you want them to try to use the steps for anger management every day and to write it down.

Wrapping Up

Repeat the centering exercise from the beginning of the group, "The Balloons" (see pages 166–167).

Affirmation

Involve the group in an affirmation. Stand and join in a circle with the children, holding hands. Go around and have each child share one time they felt angry and a helpful way they expressed—or could have expressed—their anger. Begin the affirmation yourself: "One time that I got angry was . . . A helpful way to express my anger would have been . . ."

Closing

Remain standing in a circle with the children holding hands and lead the group in the closing activity, "Pass a Silent Wish" (see page 58).

Collect the folders and fill out a copy of the Process and Progress Form (see page 235) or the Progress Notes (see pages 236–237).

Activity Sheet 9
Helpful Ways I Can Express Anger

Recognize _____
           _____

Accept   _____
           _____

Relax   _____
           _____

Think   _____
           _____

Evaluate   _____
           _____

Choose   _____
           _____

Express   _____
           _____

Basic Fact Worksheet 9

15. The anger management steps are:

    a. **Recognize** that you are angry.

    b. **Accept** your anger.

    c. Practice **relaxation.**

    d. **Think** about ways to express the anger.

    e. **Evaluate** the consequences.

    f. **Choose** the best way.

    g. **Express** the anger in a helpful way.

_____

15. The anger management steps are:

    a. _____ that you are angry.

    b. _____ your anger.

    c. Practice _____.

    d. _____ about ways to express the anger.

    e. _____ the consequences.

    f. _____ the best way.

    g. _____ the anger in a helpful way.

Homework Assignment 9

Every day, see if you can use the anger management steps. Write a short sentence.

1. **Recognize** that you are angry.
2. **Accept** your anger.
3. Practice **relaxation.**
4. **Think** about ways to express the anger.
5. **Evaluate** the consequences.
6. **Choose** the best way.
7. **Express** the anger in a helpful way.

Day 1 _____

_____

_____

Day 2 _____

_____

_____

Day 3 _____

_____

_____

Day 4 _____

_____

_____

Day 5 _____

_____

_____

Session 10

Daniel the Dinosaur Learns to Resolve Conflict

Objectives

To help the students

- prepare to present the basic facts in session 11
- understand that conflict resolution is a plan to solve conflicts in a nonviolent way
- learn a three-step plan for managing conflict

Preparation

- Display the posterboard copy of the group rules.
- Have available the toy Daniel and Mrs. Owl and Basic Fact Posters 1 to 15.
- Add to each student's folder:
  –Activity Sheet 10 (Scenarios for Conflict Resolution)
  –Basic Fact Worksheet 10
  –Homework Assignment 10
- Place each student's folder, pencil, and crayons or markers at his or her place.
- Read through the session plan before meeting.

Background and Guidelines

There are two main objectives for session 10. The first is preparation for the presentation in the next session, the last. The second main objective is to teach the students conflict resolution.

The presentation in session 11 serves several purposes. It is an easy, nonthreatening activity where the children merely read and explain the basic facts to an audience of your choosing—to a single person, such as another group leader, a counselor, or a principal, or to a class or a group of classes.

Children seem to learn the basic facts better when they explain them to someone else. And combining the presentation with the small party in the last session gives the children a sense of mastery, accomplishment, and celebration. Finally, presenting the facts to a class or group of classes has been effective in raising awareness of violent behavior and in giving these assertive behavior skills to other children so they can use them.

As suggested in the Background and Guidelines for session 8, you should find an audience appropriate for your experience level and for the children's maturity. New leaders might prefer giving their first presentation to a single person, such as a fellow group leader or to a counselor or principal. Experienced leaders will probably be comfortable preparing the presentation for as broad an audience as possible. Very young children, such as kindergartners and first-graders, will probably be most comfortable presenting to a single adult. Second-graders can present to a first- or second-grade class or group of classes. Third- to sixth-graders can also present to their own grade level and go up or down one or two grade levels.

As you start the rehearsal today, explain to the children the purposes of the presentation: to help them learn better, to give the group a sense of accomplishment as it comes to an end, and to help other children who have problems with violent behavior by teaching them basic facts.

Tell the children that all they need to do is read or repeat after you a basic fact, and, if they can, explain it. Assure the children that you will jump in to help them with words and ideas if they forget, by asking them questions to help them along. And if they don't want to explain it, tell them you will do the explaining yourself.

A good idea is to use the Basic Facts Review in this session as an easy rehearsal for the presentation. Ask the children to place their chairs in a row across the front of the room. Pass out the laminated Basic Fact Posters as though you were dealing cards from a deck. Ask the children to introduce themselves by saying their name, age, grade, and then something they like to do (play soccer, ride dirt bikes, play Nintendo games, and so on.). Then ask the child who has Basic Fact 1 to read it and explain it. The explanations for the Basic Facts are the same clarifications that you have been using for all of the Basic Facts Reviews, so this should be an easy process. Repeat for each Basic Fact until you get to Basic Fact 16, which will be presented today. When they finish, have the children take a bow. Tell them that next week, you will ask the audience if they have any questions. If you find a child who absolutely refuses to participate in the presentation, allow him or her to skip the presentation but join you for the small party at the end of session 11.

The second main teaching objective in this session is conflict resolution. As discussed in the Background and Guidelines for session 9, anger management and conflict resolution programs are usually not enough to make a child who exhibits bullying behavior change since bullies act out of a need for power and domination rather than anger. They have little motivation to change their behavior to resolve conflicts since they generally have few negative consequences. However, anger management and conflict resolution are included in this manual in the belief that some change has occurred by this point in the group—that the children have learned that their behavior has been violent, that violent behavior is unacceptable, and that they will probably have unhappy lives as adults unless they change their behavior. By now the children should be willing to learn how to resolve fights or disagreements.

There are many programs for peer mediation and conflict resolution. Most of these programs include steps such as the following described in *Peer Mediation: Conflict Resolution in Schools,* a program by Schrumpf, Crawford, and Usadel.

1. Open the session
   - Make introductions.
   - State the ground rules.
2. Gather information
   - Ask each person to tell what happened.
   - Ask each person whether he or she wants to add anything.
3. Focus on common interests
   - Determine and summarize shared interests.
4. Create options
   - Brainstorm solutions and ask disputants what can be done to resolve the problem.
5. Evaluate options and choose a solution
   - Ask each person what could be done to resolve the problem.
6. Write the agreement and close
   - Write up the agreement and have disputants sign it.
   - Shake hands.

The steps for conflict resolution in this manual are drawn from a video entitled *Conflict Resolution,* part of a two-part Anger Management set published by Hazelden. These steps are much more condensed than those above, and are simpler, making them more accessible for elementary-aged children.

In this manual, conflict is defined as a disagreement or a fight. Conflict resolution will work only if both parties are willing to solve the disagreement or fight. In today's story, Trevor admits that he usually uses excuses when he gets into a disagreement or fight. In the story he admits that he did something wrong (took Daniel's bike without permission) and is willing to do something about it (ask his dad to help him fix it.)

The three steps in this conflict resolution program are easy for children to understand and remember:

1. Think about it.
2. Talk about it.
3. Try to work it out.

In the first step, **Think about it,** the child works on his or her own to clarify the issues *before* discussing the problem with the other child. The child is to clarify who he or she is in conflict with and what the fight or disagreement is about. Then the child is to look at what his or her part in the fight or disagreement is. As in all the other activities, the group members take the characters in the scenarios of Activity Sheet 10 through the steps. Remember that they will probably be able to determine the part a character plays in a conflict more easily than their own part in a conflict in real life. Chunking it down applies to all the steps of conflict resolution. In the future, the children will probably need an adult's help to figure out an objective, nondefensive way to describe what the fight is about and what part they play in a conflict.

After the child is calm and has planned what he or she wants to say, the second step in conflict resolution is to **Talk about it.** The group members can use two assertive behavior skills—an I Statement and an I Hear You Statement—in this step. First, the child tells the other child his or her side and how he or she feels, using an I Statement. Then, he or she asks the other child to give their side and how he or she feels. Third, the child should use an I Hear You Statement to let the other child know he or she heard and understood (not necessarily agreed with) the other child.

In the third step of conflict resolution, **Try to work it out,** the child tells the other child what he or she wants, needs, or expects. Then the child asks the other child what he or she wants, needs, or expects. Finally, both children should be willing to give in a little to finally come to an agreement. There may be some instances where the children never do agree but can peacefully agree to disagree.

Session 10's activity gives two situations where the children can process the steps of conflict resolution. In each situation you will help the children go through the steps from each child's point of view. In the Trevor and Tiffany group, an entire session is devoted to teaching children how to stand in someone else's shoes. Children who participate in the Daniel group are usually able to put themselves in someone else's shoes.

Again, the children in your group will probably not be able to master the steps of a conflict resolution group after this brief introduction. If you are conducting this group as part of a schoolwide prevention plan that includes conflict resolution, then this session will probably be a review for the children. If not, remember that the more adults in the children's environment who can help them practice the steps of conflict resolution, the better.

Beginning the Session

Welcome the students. If necessary, begin with a quick review of the group rules (see page 51). Check for understanding before moving on.

Centering Exercise

Make certain that the children are comfortable and quiet. Begin the centering exercise, repeated from session 6, "Lower Your Temperature" (see page 126).

Feelings Check-in

Using the Feeling Dinosaur, do a feelings check-in with the students (see page 69). When the students finish, have a go-around.

Basic Facts Review

To help the students review their last session and the basic facts learned so far, show them Basic Fact Posters 1 to 15. Tell the students that they will be presenting the basic facts to the audience you have arranged. Tell the children that this will help them learn the basic facts better, will help the group have a sense of accomplishment as you end next week, and will also help other children learn how to change aggressive behavior to assertive behavior. To rehearse what you will do next week, ask the children to place their chairs in a row across the front of the room. Pass out the laminated Basic Fact Posters as though you were dealing cards from a deck. Ask each child to introduce him or herself by saying his or her name, age, grade, and something he or she likes to do. Then ask the child who has Basic Fact 1 to read it and explain it. Help the child with the clarification questions to plan what he or she will say next week. Assure the children that all they have to do is read the basic fact and explain it. Reassure them that you will help them if they have trouble reading, and you will also ask them, and the audience, questions to help explain the basic fact.

Repeat the procedure for the next basic fact.

As they read the basic facts and explain them, urge the children to use assertive body language: to stand up straight and tall, to make eye contact with the audience, and to speak clearly and distinctly.

The Basic Facts List and Questions to Help Clarify the Basic Facts are printed on pages 229–234.

Assignment Review

Ask the students if they brought their homework assignments from last week. Remind them of the assignment by reading it: "Every day, see if you can use the anger management steps. Write a short sentence."

In a go-around, ask the children to share what they found. If the children forgot to do the assignment, in the go-around ask them to try to think of one way they could have used the steps of anger management in the past week. If they can't think of anything they did, ask them for helpful ways they can express anger.

Exploring the Story

Have the children get comfortable for today's story. Use the toy Daniel and Mrs. Owl and allow Daniel to tell the following:

Hi, boys and girls! How did it go using helpful ways to express anger? Did you punch a lot of pillows last week? The assertive behavior skills we've learned, and the anger management steps, are tools that you can use by yourself if you're having trouble with an obnoxious dinosaur like Trevor. Today Mrs. Owl is going to teach us a plan to use if the other person is willing to work to fix the problem—it's called conflict resolution. Conflict is another word for fight or disagreement.

Conflict resolution has three parts to it. First, *Think about it*. In your own head, you ask, "Who am I fighting with; what am I fighting about; and what is my part in it?"

Second, *Talk about it*. You use the assertive behavior skill of an I Statement to tell the other person your side and how you feel. You ask the other person to give his or her side and how he or she feels, and then you use the assertive behavior skill of an I Hear You Statement to understand his or her point of view.

Third, *Try to work it out*. You tell the other person what you need, or want, or expect; then you ask the other person what he or she wants. Each of you should be willing to give in a little.

Conflict resolution is another great way that you can stand up for yourself instead of being passive or aggressive.

Let me give you an example of how it works. One time Trevor took my dinosaur bicycle and went riding into the swamp. He crashed on a log and smashed my bicycle. I went to Mrs. Owl and said, "Trevor has done something rotten again. He took my bicycle and crashed it." Mrs. Owl said, "I think I'll talk to Trevor. If he is willing to try to solve this problem, this will be a good one for conflict resolution."

Mrs. Owl came back with Trevor, and said that he was willing to talk. She asked each of us to take Step 1 and *Think about it*. I decided that I was angry because Trevor took my bicycle and crashed it.

Then, I took Step 2, *Talk about it*. I decided to use an I Statement, and I said, "Trevor, I feel angry because you took my bicycle and crashed it. What do you think?" Trevor said, "I didn't mean to crash your bicycle. I just wanted to ride it." I used an I Hear You Statement, and said, "Trevor, I hear that you didn't mean to crash it, but you did."

Then, I took Step 3, *Try to work it out*. I said, "What are you going to do to fix my bicycle?" Trevor said he would ask his father to help him fix my bike.

As you know, Trevor is usually mean and violent. This was the first time that he was willing to talk about a problem that we had. I felt good that at last he was willing to work problems out.

Now it's your turn to practice the three steps of conflict resolution.

Discussion

Lead a discussion to make sure the children understand the steps of conflict resolution. If you want, ask the children to take out Activity Sheet 10 (see page 187) from their folders to help them remember the steps of conflict resolution.

- What are the three steps of conflict resolution? (1. Think about it. 2. Talk about it. 3. Try to work it out.)
- What goes into Step 1, *Think about it?* (First, ask yourself who are you fighting with? Then ask what is the fight about? Then ask what is your part in the fight?)
- What goes into Step 2, *Talk about it?* (First, tell the other person your side of the fight and how you feel. Use an I Statement. Then ask the other person to give his or her side of the fight. Then use an I Hear You Statement to listen to what he or she says and repeat it back to the other person.)
- What goes into Step 3, *Try to work it out?* (First, tell the other person what you want, or need, or expect. Then ask the other person what he or she wants. Finally, be willing to give in a little.)

Activity

Ask the children to use their copies of Activity Sheet 10 for this activity, as well. Read aloud the title at the top of the sheet: "Scenarios for Conflict Resolution."

Ask a student to read Scenario 1.

1. David's team is losing at kickball. David is getting very angry. James is missing the ball a lot. David calls him stupid and tells him he should get out of the game.

Help the children go through the steps of conflict resolution for David. Under each step, ask the following questions. Example answers are provided in parentheses if the group members do not come up with any ideas.

Conflict Resolution Steps

Step 1. Think about it.
- Whom is David fighting with? (James)
- What is the fight about? (David is angry because his team is losing and James is missing the ball a lot.)
- What is David's part in the fight? (David is calling James stupid and telling him he should get out of the game.)

Step 2. Talk about it.
- How can David tell James his side of the fight and how he feels? (Use an I Statement: "James, I feel angry that you are missing the ball so much and our team is losing.")
- Then how can David ask James to give his side of the fight? ("James, what do you say?")
- Then how can David use an I Hear You Statement to listen to what

James says and repeat it back to James? ("James, I hear you say that you're playing the best you can.")

Step 3. Try to work it out.
- How can David tell James what he wants? ("James, I want our team to win.")
- How can David ask James what he wants? ("James, what do you want?")
- Finally, be willing to give in a little. ("Okay, I guess it's more important that everybody gets to play than that we win.")

Then help the children go through the steps of conflict resolution for James. Under each step, ask the following questions. Example answers are provided in parentheses if the group members do not come up with any ideas.

Conflict Resolution Steps

Step 1. Think about it.
- Whom is James fighting with? (David.)
- What is the fight about? (David is angry because James is missing the ball a lot and his team is losing.)
- What is James's part in the fight? (James doesn't seem to be adding to this fight.)

Step 2. Talk about it.
- How can James tell David his side of the fight and how he feels? (Use an I Statement: "David, I feel angry that you don't want me to play kickball just because our team is losing. The rules are that everybody gets a chance to play.")
- Then how can James ask David to give his side of the fight? ("David, what do you say?")
- Then how can James use an I Hear You Statement to listen to what David says and repeat it back to David? ("David, I hear you say that you're angry because our team is losing.")

Step 3. Try to work it out.
- How can James tell David what he wants? ("David, I want a chance to play, even if we lose.")
- How can James ask David what he wants? ("David, what do you want?")
- Finally, be willing to give in a little. ("Okay, I guess I'll wait till the tournament is over. Meanwhile, I'm going to practice my kicks.")

Repeat the process for Scenario 2.

2. Amy's best friend, Jessica, is angry at her because Amy is starting to play with Deanna, a new girl in the neighborhood. Jessica tells the girls at school not to play with Amy.

Go through the steps of conflict resolution for Amy.

Conflict Resolution Steps

Step 1. Think about it.
- Whom is Amy fighting with? (Jessica.)
- What is the fight about? (Jessica is probably hurt because Amy isn't play-ing with her anymore. Jessica is getting back at Amy by telling the girls not to play with Amy.)
- What is Amy's part in the fight? (Amy may be ignoring Jessica.)

Step 2. Talk about it.
- How can Amy tell Jessica her side of the fight and how she feels? (Use an I Statement: "I feel angry when you tell the girls not to play with me.")
- How can Amy ask Jessica to give her side of the fight? ("Jessica, what are you angry about?")
- How can Amy use an I Hear You Statement to listen to what Jessica says and repeat it back to her? ("I can hear that you are angry because I'm not playing with you anymore.")

Step 3. Try to work it out.
- How can Amy tell Jessica what she wants? ("I want you to stop telling the girls not to play with me.")
- How can Amy ask Jessica what she wants? ("What do you want?")
- Finally, how can Amy be willing to give in a little? ("I'll include you when I play with Deanna.")

Go through the steps of conflict resolution for Jessica.

Conflict Resolution Steps

Step 1. Think about it.
- Whom is Jessica fighting with? (Amy.)
- What is the fight about? (Jessica is probably hurt because Amy isn't play-ing with her anymore. Jessica is getting back at Amy by telling the girls not to play with Amy.)
- What is Jessica's part in the fight? (Jessica is telling the girls not to play with Amy.)

Step 2. Talk about it.
- How can Jessica tell Amy her side of the fight and how she feels? (Use an I Statement: "Amy, I feel hurt that you don't play with me anymore.")
- How can Jessica ask Amy to give her side of the fight? ("Amy, what do you say?")
- How can Jessica use an I Hear You Statement to listen to what Amy says, and repeat it back to her? ("Amy, I hear that you are angry that I told the girls not to play with you.")

Step 3. Try to work it out.
- How can Jessica tell Amy what she wants? ("Amy, I still want to be your friend.")
- How can Jessica ask Amy what she wants? ("Amy, what do you want?")
- Finally, how can Jessica be willing to give a little? ("Amy, I won't tell the girls not to play with you anymore.")

Basic Facts

Ask the children to take Basic Fact Worksheet 10 out of their folders (see page 188).

16. The conflict resolution steps are:
    a. **Think** about it.
    b. **Talk** about it.
    c. Try to **work** it out.

Briefly discuss each fact, checking for understanding. Correct any misconceptions.

Homework Assignment

Ask the children to pull out Homework Assignment 10 (see page 189) from their folders. Ask one child to read it out loud. Tell the children that you want them to try to use the steps for conflict resolution every day and to write about what they did.

Wrapping Up

Repeat the exercise from the beginning of the group, "Lower Your Temperature" (see page 126).

Affirmation

Involve the group in an affirmation. Stand and join in a circle with the children, holding hands. Go around and have each child share one time they could have used the steps of conflict resolution. Begin the affirmation yourself: "One time that I could have used the steps of conflict resolution was . . ."

Closing

Remain standing in a circle with the children, holding hands, and lead the group in the closing activity, "Pass a Silent Wish" (see page 58).

Collect the folders and fill out a copy of the Process and Progress Form (see page 235) or the Progress Notes (see pages 236–237).

Activity Sheet 10
Scenarios for Conflict Resolution

1. David's team is losing at kickball. David is getting very angry. James is missing the ball a lot. David calls him stupid and tells him he should get out of the game.

    —Go through the steps of conflict resolution for David.

    —Go through the steps of conflict resolution for James.

2. Amy's best friend, Jessica, is angry at her because Amy is starting to play with Deanna, a new girl in the neighborhood. Jessica tells the girls at school not to play with Amy.

    —Go through the steps of conflict resolution for Amy.

    —Go through the steps of conflict resolution for Jessica.

Conflict Resolution Steps

- Think about it.
    —Whom are you fighting with?
    —What is the fight about?
    —What is your part in the fight?

- Talk about it.
    —Tell the other person your side of the fight and how you feel. Use an I Statement.
    —Then ask the other person to give his or her side of the fight.
    —Then use an I Hear You Statement to listen to what he or she says and repeat it back to that person.

- Try to work it out.
    —Tell the other person what you want, or need, or expect.
    —Ask the other person what he or she wants.
    —Finally, be willing to give in a little.

Basic Fact Worksheet 10

15. The conflict resolution steps are:
    a. **Think** about it.
    b. **Talk** about it.
    c. Try to **work** it out.

---

15. The conflict resolution steps are:
    a. _____ about it.
    b. _____ about it.
    c. Try to _____ it out.

Homework Assignment 10

Every day, see if you can use the conflict resolution steps. Write a short sentence.

1. Think about it.
   - Whom are you fighting with?
   - What is the fight about?
   - What is your part in the fight?

2. Talk about it.
   - Tell the other person your side of the fight and how you feel. Use an I Statement.
   - Then ask the other person to give his or her side of the fight.
   - Then use an I Hear You Statement to listen to what he or she says, and repeat it back to that person

3. Try to work it out.
   - Tell the other person what you want, or need, or expect.
   - Ask the other person what he or she wants.
   - Finally, be willing to give in a little.

Day 1 _____

_____

Day 2 _____

_____

Day 3 _____

_____

Day 4 _____

_____

Day 5 _____

_____

Session 11

Daniel the Dinosaur Presents What He Has Learned and Says Goodbye

Objectives for the Presentation

To help the children as individuals

- demonstrate their understanding of the basic facts about standing tall
- grow in self-esteem

To help the children as a group

- share feelings of cohesiveness
- successfully complete a project

To help members of the audience

- learn a new, more inclusive definition of violence
- learn that violent behavior in schools is unacceptable
- learn assertive behavior skills

Objectives for the End of Group Celebration

To help the students

- close out their group experience

Preparation

- Allow one hour for this session.
- Have available the toy Daniel and Mrs. Owl and Basic Fact Posters 1 to 16.

For the Presentation
- Decide in advance on an appropriate audience to view the presentation. If this is the first time for such a presentation, or if the children are very young or very shy, you may wish to invite only the school principal or SAP staff. If you're an experienced leader, or if the group is part of a schoolwide intervention program, you may want to target a particular class or grade level.
- Have copies available of each of the sixteen Basic Fact Posters (see pages 213–228, laminated if possible.
- If presenting to students, make copies of the Audience Evaluation Form (see page 195) and have pens or pencils available for audience members.

For the End of Group celebration
- Make each child a copy of the Basic Facts List (see page 229). Mount on a piece of colored construction paper.
- Make copies of the Group Evaluation Form (see page 196).
- Make copies of the Certificate of Participation (see page 197). Complete a certificate for each group member and mount on construction paper.
- Make arrangements to serve refreshments of your choice after the presentation. Dinosaur cookies would be a big hit.
- Add to each student's folder:
  –the Basic Facts List, mounted on construction paper
  –the Group Evaluation Form
- Place each student's folder, pencil, and crayons or markers at his or her place.
- Read through the session plan before meeting.

Background and Guidelines

This session has two main objectives: (1) the students present what they have learned to an audience, as described in the Background and Guidelines for session 10; and (2) the children celebrate the end of the group with refreshments and a certificate and fill out a group evaluation.

By now the group members should be reporting how they are able to use the assertive behavior skills when other children tease them or call them names or when they are being left out. Children in the Daniel group are often eager to teach their siblings and friends some of these skills. Children who are provocative victims report that they are not getting into as much trouble and are not getting sent to the principal's office as often. They are usually proud of their new behavior.

Preparation for the presentation was described in the Background and Guidelines for the last session, which used the Basic Facts Review as a rehearsal. Notice that you introduce the presentation by saying you have been working with the group members to discuss how to stop mean and violent behavior at school. It would not be appropriate to identify these children as bullies, as children who are violent, or as children who are victims of bullies. However, most children think that the goal of stopping school violence is a good one.

If you give the presentation as an isolated program in a school that does not have a school-wide violence prevention program, you may find that classroom teachers and principals will be very interested in the information the children present. Be sure to offer teachers and principals a copy of the Basic Facts List and the Assertive Behavior Skills (Handouts 6, 7, or 8), and, if they want, show them activity sheets in the group manual so they can see how the skills are used. Remember that the presentation is a chance for you to spread the knowledge the children learn to other adults who can help them use their skills in potentially violent situations.

If you present to a class, the presentation also includes an audience evaluation, which you should pass out after the children finish. (Otherwise, some children in the audience may use the evaluations for paper airplanes.) This evaluation provides you with feedback about what the children in the audience learned from the presentation. It is also an opportunity for children to sign up to be in a Trevor and Tiffany or Daniel group themselves. Notice that they can sign up if they want to learn ways to stop violent behavior in their school. Be sure to screen these children and to talk to teachers or principals before putting them in a Trevor and Tiffany group or in a Daniel group to ensure that victims of bullies are not placed with bullies.

After the presentation, return to the group room and finish the session with a short story by Daniel, refreshments, and the group evaluations. Some children will need your help in filling out the evaluation. Remember that they can keep their name anonymous if they want.

At the end of the group, hand out the Certificates of Participation that you have prepared with each child's name on it. As you hand them out, say something personal about how much they have grown and how much you have enjoyed having them in your group. Remind the children to keep on practicing their assertive behavior skills and not to be shy about asking an adult for help about how to use them. The end of the group is sometimes a bittersweet experience. If so, acknowledge some sadness over the fact that you will not be working with the children in group anymore.

Beginning the Session

Welcome the students to the last session of the Daniel the Dinosaur group. If necessary, begin with a quick review of the group rules (see page 51).

Centering Exercise

Tell the students that you want to do a centering exercise to help them relax before giving the presentation. Make certain that the children are comfortable and quiet. Begin the centering exercise, repeated from session 2, "The Icicle" (see pages 68–69).

Assignment Review

Ask the students if they brought their homework assignments from last week. Remind them of the assignment by reading it: "Every day, see if you can use the conflict resolution steps. Write a short sentence."

In a go-around, ask the children to share what they found. If the children forgot to do the assignment, in the go-around ask them to try to think of one way they could have used the steps of conflict resolution in the past week.

Do the assignment review in private before the presentation if you are presenting to a class or a large group.

Presentation

If you are presenting in front of a classroom, have the children sit in chairs in a row in front of the class. Pass out the Basic Facts Lists.

With the toy Daniel and Mrs. Owl at hand, introduce the presentation using the following or similar words: "We're part of the counseling program at (name of school). We've learned some important facts about how to stop mean and violent behavior at school. Since this school is helping children learn not to be violent, we want to share what we have learned with you. The children are going to start by introducing themselves to you."

Have each child stand, face the audience, and say their name, age, grade, and something they like to do. Remind the children to concentrate on assertive body language: they should stand up straight, make eye contact with the audience, and speak in a clear tone of voice.

In turn, call on the children one at a time to present the Basic Facts. Have each child display his or her poster, read it aloud, and explain it. You can use the Questions to Help Clarify the Basic Facts (see pages 230–234) to help the children explain the Basic Facts if they cannot do so themselves.

Conclude the presentation by asking the audience members if they have any questions. Then have the children stand, face the audience, and take a bow. Lead the audience in applause.

Audience Evaluation

If the children are presenting to a class, pass out copies of the Audience Evaluation Form and pens or pencils to audience members. Encourage them to spend a moment completing the form. When audience members finish writing, ask them to fold the forms in half and collect them and the pens or pencils.

End of Group Celebration

Return to the group room and have the students sit in their usual seats. Use the toy Daniel and Mrs. Owl and allow Daniel to tell this short story:

Hi, boys and girls! You did a great job in presenting the basic facts. Well, I have really enjoyed getting to know you. I hope that like me you are standing tall. Every now and then Trevor still does some terrible Tyrannosaurus tricks, but now I have a lot of assertive behavior skills I use that help me feel better about myself. I hope you have someone like Mrs. Owl you can talk to in the future to help you remember how to use them. For now, remember to Stand Tall in your dinosaur footprints.

Refreshments, Group Evaluation, and Certificates

Pass out the refreshments you have brought. While the children are snacking, ask them to pull out the Basic Facts List that you placed in their folders. Tell them that they can take their folders home and show their parents what they have learned in the Daniel the Dinosaur group. Ask them to take out the Group Evaluation Form and to complete it. Point out that they do not need to put their names on the form. Older children may work on their own. Younger children, however, may require your assistance. For example, you may have to read each question aloud, or you may have to help with writing or spelling. When the children finish, collect the forms to help you evaluate the group program. After the children have finished the evaluation forms, pass out the Certificates of Participation. Tell the children that they can hang these on their wall at home if they want and that they should feel proud of what they have learned in the group.

Affirmation

Involve the group in an affirmation. Stand and join in a circle with the children, holding hands. Go around and have each child share one thing they liked about the presentation and what they liked best about the group. Begin the affirmation yourself: "One thing I liked about the presentation was . . . What I liked best about the group was . . ."

Closing

Remain standing in a circle with the children, holding hands, and lead the group in the closing activity, "Pass a Silent Wish" (see page 58).

Say a personal goodbye to the children.

Fill out a copy of the Process and Progress Form (see page 235) or the Progress Notes (see pages 236–237).

Audience Evaluation Form

1. The most interesting thing I learned from this presentation was

_____

_____

2. Did this presentation give you ways to change mean and violent behavior to assertive behavior?

             Yes   No

How will you use what you learned today?

_____

_____

If you're interested in being in a group like Daniel the Dinosaur because you'd like to learn ways to stop violent behavior in your school, please sign here. We will meet with you before starting the group.

Name: _____

Teacher's name or homeroom number:_____

Group Evaluation Form

1. What did you like best about this group?

_____

_____

2. What did you like least about this group?

_____

_____

3. What do you think should be done differently?

_____

_____

4. What would have made the group more helpful to you?

_____

_____

5. What do you think is the most important thing you learned from this group?

_____

_____

6. What is one good thing that's happened to you because you were in this group?

_____

_____

7. As a result of being in this group, how have you changed?

_____

_____

A Certificate of Participation
is awarded to

who has participated in a
Daniel the Dinosaur Group

Congratulations!

Leader's Name

Date   School

Part Four

Support Materials

This section of the manual includes the tools you'll need to develop and support the group program in your school. Each of the following materials is printed in blackline master form and is suitable for copying on most photocopy machines.

Activity Sheets, Handouts, and Homework Assignments. There are Activity Sheets, Handouts, and Assignments in each session, containing the puppets, scenarios, situations, assertive behavior skills, and assignments. (In the individual sessions.)

Audience Evaluation Form. This form may be used to evaluate the presentation in session 11. It is designed to provide important feedback regarding the presentation's effectiveness and to serve as a referral source for future groups. (In session 11, page 195.)

Basic Fact Posters. These sixteen sheets reproduce the basic facts in large print. They can be photocopied and laminated for use in the sessions (for the weekly Basic Facts Review and for the presentation in session 11). They can also be made into transparencies for larger presentations. (In this section, pages 213–228.)

Basic Fact Worksheets. The ten Basic Fact Worksheets will be used by the children in each session. (In the individual sessions.)

Basic Fact Worksheets with Answers Dotted In. These ten worksheets have the answers dotted in to help younger group members. (In this section, pages 203–212.)

Basic Facts List. The complete list of Basic Facts is to be copied and stapled to the left inside flap of the children's folders for easy reference. It can also be mounted on construction paper and given out in the last session. (In this section, page 229.)

Certificate of Participation. This award or participation certificate may be photocopied and given to each group member during session 11. (In session 11, page 197.)

Feeling Daniel. This sheet will aid you in doing a feelings check-in with the students. Each group member will need one copy. The students will use their copy of the Feeling Daniel in sessions 2–11. (In session 2, page 76).

Group Evaluation Form. This form is to be used in session 11 by the students to evaluate their experience in the group. (In session 11, page 196.)

Group Rules Contract. You'll need a copy of this contract for every group member. You will have all group members sign one in session 1. (In session 1, page 59).

Parental Consent Form. Once the students have been referred or self-referred to a group, you should seek parental consent by sending parents a copy of a form like the one provided here. (In this section, page 239.)

Process and Progress Form. This form is for you, the group leader. Make eleven copies of the form. After each session, fill out a copy of the form in order to evaluate the session and to keep timely notes on the progress of the group. (In this section, page 235.)

Progress Notes. This two-page form is a condensed version of the Process and Progress form and is suitable for the more experienced group leader. Simply copy each page and fill out the appropriate section after each group session. (In this section, pages 236–237.)

Questions to Help Clarify the Basic Facts. These questions will help you with the Basic Facts Review. Each week, review the Basic Facts that the children have already learned. (In this section, pages 230–234.)

References and Suggested Readings. This is a list of professional resources for your enrichment (In this section, pages 242–243.)

Screening Interview Outline. After referrals are obtained and categorized, the students need to be interviewed individually. The Screening Interview Outline will help you get basic, necessary information about the students and their daily lives. If a student seems like an appropriate referral, be sure to explain the group format and progression of themes and to show the student a copy of the Group Rules Contract. Make sure the students understand that they must attend every session and be willing to make up missed schoolwork. You might also show them a copy of the Parental Consent Form that you will send home. If you wish, you can ask the student to take it home. (In this section, page 240.)

Self-Referral Group Survey Form. This form should be made available to students after they've heard about the purpose of the support groups. Use the form in conjunction with a presentation at which available groups are explained to the students (see pages 33–35). When the students fill out the form, explain that if they want to be in more than one group, they should number their choices in priority. Also, make sure the students know that not everyone may be in the groups right away and that groups will be offered according to need and time. (In this section, page 238.)

Basic Fact Worksheet 1

1. **<u>Violence</u>** is any mean word, look, sign, or act that **<u>hurts</u>** a person's body, feelings, or possessions.
2. A consequence is what happens after you do something, and violent behavior almost always has the bad **<u>consequence</u>** of hurting someone.

---

1. ___Violence___ is any mean word, look, sign, or act that ___hurts___ a person's body, feelings, or possessions.
2. A consequence is what happens after you do something, and violent behavior almost always has the bad ___consequence___ of hurting someone.

Basic Fact Worksheet 2

3. **Children** who are mean and violent often grow up to be mean and violent as **adults.** They don't have very happy lives.

4. Children who are hurt by other children are often **afraid** to tell adults; then they let the other children **get away** with their mean and violent behavior.

---

3. ___Children___ who are mean and violent often grow up to be mean and violent as ___adults___ . They don't have very happy lives.

4. Children who are hurt by other children are often ___afraid___ to tell adults; then they let the other children ___get away___ with their mean and violent behavior.

Basic Fact Worksheet 3

5. Mean and violent behavior is **bad** and is not **acceptable** in our school; it is **never** okay for a child to hurt another child.

6. Children can have three rules to stop mean and violent behavior:

   a. We will **not** be mean and violent.

   b. We will try to **help** students who are being hurt by other children who are being mean and violent.

   c. We will **include** students who are being left out.

_____

5. Mean and violent behavior is __bad__ and is not __acceptable__ in our school; it is __never__ okay for a child to hurt another child.

6. Children can have three rules to stop mean and violent behavior:

   a. We will __not__ be mean and violent.

   b. We will try to __help__ students who are being hurt by other children who are being mean and violent.

   c. We will __include__ students who are being left out.

Basic Fact Worksheet 4

7. A child can react to another child's violent behavior by being **passive**, **aggressive**, or **assertive**.

8. The assertive behavior skills of **Body Language** include **posture**, **eye contact**, and tone of **voice** that help you stand up for yourself without hurting anyone else.

_____

7. A child can react to another child's violent behavior by being ___passive___ , ___aggressive___ , or ___assertive___ .

8. The assertive behavior skills of ___Body Language___ include ___posture___ , ___eye contact___ , and tone of ___voice___ that help you stand up for yourself without hurting anyone else.

Basic Fact Worksheet 5

9. Children can **ask** for **help** from an **adult** if another child is being violent toward them.

10. **I Statements** and **I Hear You Statements** are two good assertive behavior skills.

_____

9. Children can __ask__ for __help__ from an __adult__ if another child is being violent toward them.

10. __I Statements__ and __I Hear You Statements__ are two good assertive behavior skills.

Basic Fact Worksheet 6

11. **Kill-Them-With-Kindness Sandwiches**, **Apologizing,**
    Humor, Sound Bites, Nice Replies, and **Broken Records**
    are more good assertive behavior skills to use.

    _____

11. ___Kill-Them-With-Kindness Sandwiches___ , ___Apologizing___ ,
    ___Humor___ , ___Sound Bites___ , ___Nice Replies___ , and
    ___Broken Records___ are more good assertive behavior skills
    to use.

Basic Fact Worksheet 7

12. The assertive behavior skills help you **stand** up for yourself when someone is teasing you or calling you names.

_____

12. The assertive behavior skills help you __stand__ up for yourself when someone is teasing you or calling you names.

Basic Fact Worksheet 8

13. The assertive behavior skills help you **say** how you **feel** and **ask** to **join in** when you are being left out.

14. There are two other steps you can take if you are being left out:

    a. **Ask** someone else to **play.**

    b. **Find** something else you **like** to do.

---

13. The assertive behavior skills help you __say__ how you __feel__ and __ask__ to __join in__ when you are being left out.

14. There are two other steps you can take if you are being left out:

    a. __Ask__ someone else to __play__ .

    b. __Find__ something else you __like__ to do.

Basic Fact Worksheet 9

15. The anger management steps are
    a. **Recognize** that you are angry.
    b. **Accept** your anger.
    c. Practice **relaxation.**
    d. **Think** about ways to express the anger.
    e. **Evaluate** the consequences.
    f. **Choose** the best way.
    g. **Express** the anger in a helpful way.

---

15. The anger management steps are
    a. __Recognize__ that you are angry.
    b. __Accept__ your anger.
    c. Practice __relaxation__.
    d. __Think__ about ways to express the anger.
    e. __Evaluate__ the consequences.
    f. __Choose__ the best way.
    g. __Express__ the anger in a helpful way.

Basic Fact Worksheet 10

16. The conflict resolution steps are
    a. **Think** about it.
    b. **Talk** about it.
    c. Try to **work** it out.

---

16. The conflict resolution steps are
    a. __Think__ about it.
    b. __Talk__ about it.
    c. Try to __work__ it out.

<u>Violence</u> is any mean word, look, sign, or act that **<u>hurts</u>** a person's body, feelings, or possessions.

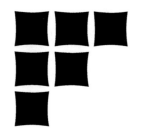

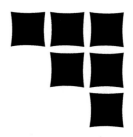

A consequence is what happens after you do something, and violent behavior almost always has the bad **<u>consequence</u>** of hurting someone.

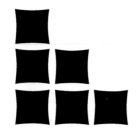

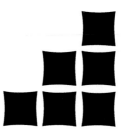

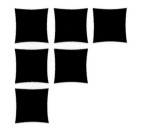

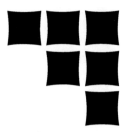

<u>Children</u> who are mean and violent often grow up to be mean and violent as **<u>adults</u>.** They don't have very happy lives.

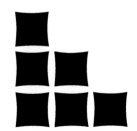

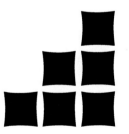

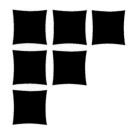 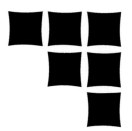

Children who are hurt by other children are often **afraid** to tell adults; then they let the other children **get away** with their mean and violent behavior.

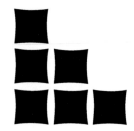 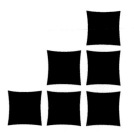

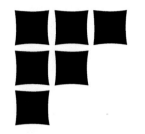

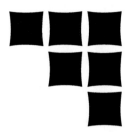

Mean and violent behavior is **<u>bad</u>** and is not acceptable in our school; it is **<u>never</u>** okay for a child to hurt another child.

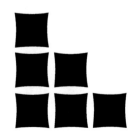
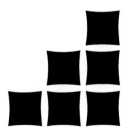

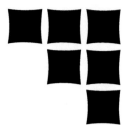

Children can have three rules to stop mean and violent behavior:

1. We will **<u>not</u>** be mean and violent.

2. We will try to **<u>help</u>** students who are being hurt by other children who are being mean and violent.

3. We will **<u>include</u>** students who are being left out.

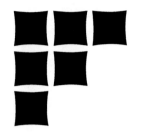

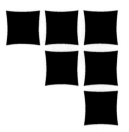

A child can react to another child's violent behavior by being **passive**, **aggressive**, or **assertive**.

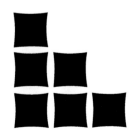

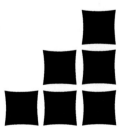

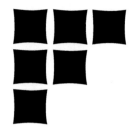 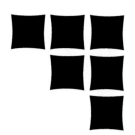

8

The assertive behavior skills of **Body Language** include **posture**, **eye contact**, and **tone of voice** that help you stand up for yourself without hurting anyone else.

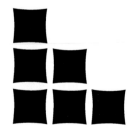 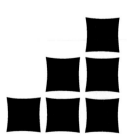

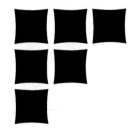

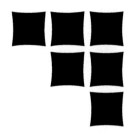

Children can **<u>ask</u>** for help from an adult if another child is being violent toward them.

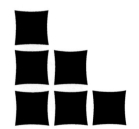

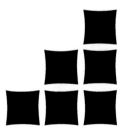

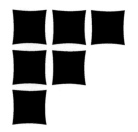
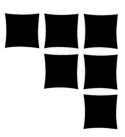

<u>I Statements</u> and **<u>I Hear You Statements</u>** are two good assertive behavior skills.

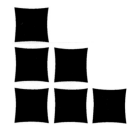
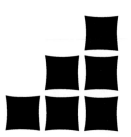

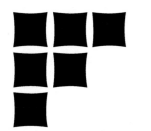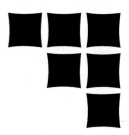

<u>Kill-Them-With-Kindness Sandwiches</u>, <u>Apologizing</u>, <u>Humor</u>, <u>Sound Bites</u>, <u>Nice Replies</u>, and <u>Broken Records</u> are more good assertive behavior skills to use.

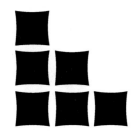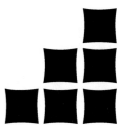

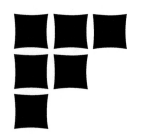

12

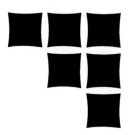

The assertive behavior skills help you **stand up** for yourself when someone is teasing you or calling you names.

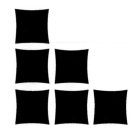

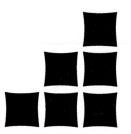

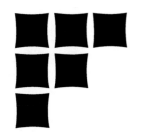

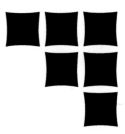

The assertive behavior skills help you **say** how you **feel** and ask to **join in** when you are being left out.

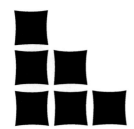

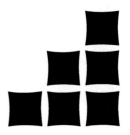

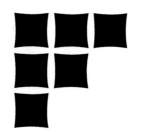

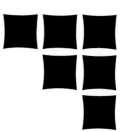

There are two other steps
you can take if you are
being left out:
a. **<u>Ask</u>** someone else
to **<u>play</u>**.
b. **<u>Find</u>** something else
you **<u>like</u>** to do.

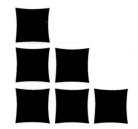

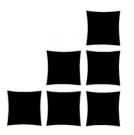

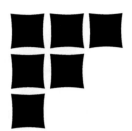 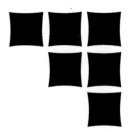

The anger management steps are:
a. **<u>Recognize</u>** that you're angry.
b. **<u>Accept</u>** your anger.
c. Practice **<u>relaxation</u>**.
d. **<u>Think</u>** about ways to express the anger.
e. **<u>Evaluate</u>** the consequences.
f. **<u>Choose</u>** the best way.
g. **<u>Express</u>** the anger in a helpful way.

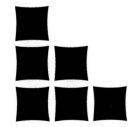 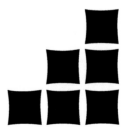

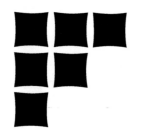

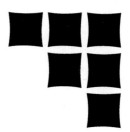

The conflict resolution
steps are:
a. **Think** about it.
b. **Talk** about it.
c. Try to **work** it out.

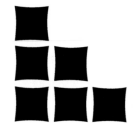
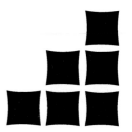

Basic Facts List

1. **Violence** is any mean word, look, sign, or act that **hurts** a person's body, feelings, or possessions.
2. A **consequence** is what happens after you do something, and violent behavior almost always has the bad consequence of hurting someone.
3. **Children** who are mean and violent often grow up to be mean and violent as **adults.**
4. Children who are hurt by other children are often **afraid** to tell adults; then they let the other children **get away** with their mean and violent behavior.
5. Mean and violent behavior is bad and is not **acceptable** in our school; it is **never** okay for a child to hurt another child.
6. Children can have three rules to stop mean and violent behavior:
   a. We will **not** be mean and violent.
   b. We will try to **help** students who are being hurt by other children who are being mean and violent.
   c. We will **include** students who are being left out.
7. A child can react to another child's violent behavior by being **passive**, **aggressive**, or **assertive**.
8. The assertive behavior skills of **Body Language** include **posture**, **eye contact**, and **tone of voice** that help you stand up for yourself without hurting anyone else.
9. Children can **ask** for **help** from an **adult** if another child is being violent toward them.
10. **I Statements** and **I Hear You Statements** are two good assertive behavior skills.
11. **Kill-Them-With-Kindness Sandwiches, Apologizing, Humor, Sound Bites, Nice Replies,** and **Broken Records** are more good assertive behavior skills to use.
12. The assertive behavior skills help you **stand up** for yourself when someone is teasing you or calling you names.
13. The assertive behavior skills help you **say** how you **feel** and **ask** to **join in** when you are being left out.
14. There are two other steps you can take if you are being left out:
    a. **Ask** someone else to **play.**
    b. **Find** something else you **like** to do.
15. The anger management steps are:
    a. **Recognize** that you're angry.
    b. **Accept** your anger.
    c. Practice **relaxation**.
    d. **Think** about ways to express the anger.
    e. **Evaluate** the consequences.
    f. **Choose** the best way.
    g. **Express** the anger in a helpful way.
16. The conflict resolution steps are
    a. **Think** about it.
    b. **Talk** about it.
    c. Try to **work** it out.

Questions to Help Clarify the Basic Facts

1. **Violence** is any mean word, look, sign, or act that **hurts** a person's body, feelings, or possessions.

Clarification: If a child uses a gun, is that being mean and violent? (Yes.) If a child accidentally kicks someone while playing ball, is that being violent? (Probably not: the child who kicked wasn't being mean; it was an accident.) If a child sits in back of someone and constantly kicks the desk of the person in front of him or her, is that being violent? (Probably: the child is being mean by repeating the kicking, which hurts the child in front of him.) If a child spreads rumors about another child, is that being violent? (Yes. They are using mean words that hurt someone.) If a group of children do not let another child play with them, is that being violent? (Yes. They are hurting that child with their mean behavior of not letting him or her play.) Repeat that violence is not just using a gun or knife or killing someone. It is a form of violence to kick, call names, threaten, spread rumors, or refuse to let someone play with you.

2. A consequence is what happens after you do something and violent behavior almost always has the bad **consequence** of hurting someone.

Clarification: What is a consequence? (What happens when someone does something—the result of a behavior.) Can consequences be good? (Yes.) For example, if you study hard for a test, what will the consequence be? (You will probably get a good grade.) But consequences can be bad if the behavior is bad. What is the consequence of a child hitting another child? (The child who is hit will be hurt; the child who hits may get into trouble.) What is the consequence of calling names? (The child who calls names may not get into trouble, but the child who is called names will have hurt feelings.) So, when a child is mean or violent, even if they're calling names, then someone usually gets hurt in their feelings, or their body, or their possessions.

3. **Children** who are mean and violent often grow up to be mean and violent as **adults**. They don't have very happy lives.

Clarification: What are the kinds of behaviors an adult who is mean and violent might have? (They might beat their wives; they might have trouble on their jobs; they might end up in jail for crimes; they seldom take responsibility for what they do; they blame others.) So if a child is mean and violent, he or she might want to stop the mean and violent behavior. Then, he or she can grow up to have a happier life.

4. Children who are hurt by other children are often **afraid** to tell adults; then they let the other children **get away** with their mean and violent behavior.

Clarification: Why don't children who are hurt by other children tell adults? (The don't want to be tattletales; they might be ashamed or afraid the adult will be mad at them; they might be afraid they will get hurt more by the other children.) What happens when children don't tell? (The children who are mean and violent keep on with their behavior because they can get away with it.)

> 5. Mean and violent behavior is **bad** and is not **acceptable** in our school; it is **never** okay for a child to hurt another child.

Clarification: A lot of children think it's okay to call names, or threaten other kids, or boss them around to get their way. But we're learning in this group that behavior like that is bad, and not permitted here, and that it's not okay for a child to hurt another child. The only time it is okay to use violence is when your life is in danger, and life-threatening situations don't happen very often in elementary school.

> 6. Children can have three rules to stop mean and violent behavior:
>   a. We will **not** be mean and violent.
>   b. We will try to **help** students who are being hurt by other children who are being mean and violent.
>   c. We will **include** students who are being left out.

Clarification: How can children in your class not be mean and violent? (By not calling names or making fun of other children. By not kicking the desk, not pushing other children in the rest room so they can go first.) How can children help students who are being hurt by other children who are being mean and violent? (They can stand by them if someone is calling them names or threatening to hit them. There is often safety in numbers.) How can children include students who are being left out? (They can ask them to play.)

> 7. A child can react to another child's violent behavior by being **passive, aggressive**, or **assertive**.

Clarification: What is passive behavior? (Passive behavior is when you do nothing. Sometimes passive behavior is a good way to handle a situation.) What is aggressive behavior? (Some people say that aggressive behavior is when you play your hardest in sports. Here, we say that aggressive behavior is any mean word, look, sign, or act that hurts another person's body, feelings, or possessions. Aggressive behavior is mean. It may make you feel better but it hurts someone else.) What is assertive behavior? (Assertive behavior is standing tall, standing up for yourself, without hurting anyone else. Assertive behavior may not change the other person's behavior, but it will help you feel better about yourself.)

> 8. The assertive behavior skills of **Body Language** include **posture, eye contact**, and **tone of voice** that help you stand up for yourself without hurting anyone else.

Clarification: How can you have assertive posture? (You can stand up straight, put your shoulders back, keep your head high, but not stuck up, and stand tall.) How can you have assertive eye contact? (You can look at the person to whom you are speaking and look in a friendly way.) How can you have an assertive tone of voice? (You can speak in a loud enough voice, clearly and distinctly. You can speak in a friendly tone, so people can understand you and speak as though you mean what you say.)

9. Children can ask for **help** from an adult if another child is being violent toward them.

Clarification: What should you do if someone is being physically violent toward you? (You should get to a safe place and tell an adult.) What should you do if someone trips you over and over, or threatens to take your lunch or your lunch money, or never lets you play? (You should tell an adult; you should also use assertive behaviors skills to help you stand up for yourself.) What should you do if someone is hurting your feelings? (You should try an assertive behavior skill. If you still feel bad, you should talk to an adult so the adult can tell the child that violent behavior is not acceptable and teach the child how to replace violent behavior with assertive behavior.)

10. **I Statements** and **I Hear You Statements** are two good assertive behavior skills.

Clarification: What is an I Statement? (It's a way to be assertive, to say what you feel without hurting anyone else. I Statements have three parts: "I feel (say what you feel) _____ when you (say what the other person did) _____ because (say why you feel the way you do _____).") Example: "Trevor, I feel angry when you trip me when we play Dinosaur Dodge Ball."

What is an I Hear You Statement? (Another way to be assertive. You repeat what the other person has said, not necessarily agreeing with them. By repeating what they have said, you let them know you heard them and understand what they said. I Hear You Statements have two parts: "I can tell that you feel (or think) _____ because _____." I Hear You Statements are a good way to cool off a fight instead of heating up the fight.) Example: "Trevor, I can tell that you are angry that I missed the basketball shot."

11. **Kill-Them-With-Kindness Sandwiches, Apologizing, Humor, Sound Bites, Nice Replies,** and **Broken Records** are more good assertive behavior skills to use.

What is a Kill-Them-With-Kindness Sandwich? (Another good way to say what you want without hurting anyone else. First, you say something nice to the other person. Then, you state your point of view, or you set a limit, or you say no. Then, you close by saying something nice again.) Example: "Trevor, I'd like to give you the answer to the math homework, but I don't have it myself, so maybe we can figure it out together."

What is an Apology? (In an Apology, you admit you made a mistake and you say you're sorry. Sometimes you can say you're sorry that things don't go well for the other person, even if it's not your fault.) Example: "Trevor, I'm sorry our team lost the game in Dinosaur Dodge Ball."

How can you use Humor as an assertive behavior skill? (Sometimes, if you do or say something funny or if you make a joke it cools down what could become a fight instead of heating it up.) Example: if someone calls you a chicken, start flapping your arms and make clucking noises. You probably won't fight.

What are some Sound Bites you could use to cool off a potential fight? (A collection of short responses that you can use no matter what the other person says.) Example: "Yes"; "No"; "Oops!"; "Oh, really!"; "Wow!"; and "Whatever." If someone says they're going to hit you, you can say "Oh really!"

What are Nice Replies? (Nice Replies are just nice ways to say no without hurting the other person.) Example: "I'm sorry, but you're too small for me to fight."

What is the Broken Record technique? (In a Broken Record, you just pretend you are a broken record and keep on repeating the same thing.) Example: "I can't lend video games. I can't lend video games. I can't lend video games."

12. The assertive behavior skills help you **stand up** for yourself when someone is teasing you or calling you names.

Clarification: The assertive behavior skills will give you a way to respond without being passive or aggressive if someone is calling you a name or teasing you. Using these skills will help you feel better and stand up for yourself, even if they don't change the person who is calling you names or teasing you. If the person who is calling you names doesn't stop, you should tell an adult so the adult can intervene and can teach the child that calling you names is violent and not acceptable, and can teach the child how to replace violent behavior with assertive behavior.

13. The assertive behavior skills help you **say** how you **feel** and **ask** to **join in** when you are being left out.

Clarification: The assertive behavior skill of an I Statement is good for saying how you feel. The skills of Kill-Them-With-Kindness Sandwiches, Nice Replies, and Broken Records are good for asking to join in.

14. There are two other steps you can take if you are being left out:
    a. **Ask** someone else to **play**.
    b. **Find** something else you **like** to do.

Clarification: If using the assertive behavior skills doesn't work in getting the other children to let you play, you don't have to sit around and do nothing. You can always ask someone else to play, or you can find something you like to do by yourself.

15. The anger management steps are
    a. **Recognize** that you're angry.
    b. **Accept** your anger.
    c. Practice **relaxation**.
    d. **Think** about ways to express the anger.
    e. **Evaluate** the consequences.
    f. **Choose** the best way.
    g. **Express** the anger in a helpful way.

Clarification: If you are angry, it is okay to feel angry, but it is not okay to behave in an angry or violent way. The anger management steps help you put thinking between feeling angry and expressing the anger. We teach children to express their anger in helpful ways. What are some helpful ways to express anger? (Punch a pillow, run laps, do jumping jacks, shoot hoops, draw or write what you are angry about, talk to someone you trust, hammer nails into old pieces of wood.)

16. The conflict resolution steps are
    a. **Think** about it.
    b. **Talk** about it.
    c. Try to **work** it out.

Clarification: Conflict resolution has three parts to it. First, *Think about it.* In your own head, you ask, who am I fighting with; what am I fighting about; and what is my part in it. Second, *Talk about it.* You use the assertive behavior skill of an I Statements to tell the other person your side and how you feel. You ask the other person to give his or her side and how he or she feels, and then you use the assertive behavior skill of an I Hear You Statement to understand their point of view. Third, *Try to work it out.* You tell the other person what you need or want or expect; then you ask the other person what he or she wants. Each of you should be willing to give in a little.

Process and Progress Form

Leader's Name:_____ Session #:_____ Date:_____

Children (group members) present:_____

_____

Processing the Session

1. What were the objectives of this session? _____

_____

_____

2. How were they met? _____

_____

_____

3. What concepts must the leader understand to facilitate this session effectively?_____

_____

_____

4. What happened during the session?

Highs:_____

_____

_____

Lows: _____

_____

_____

5. What did you see as your strengths as you facilitated this session?_____

_____

_____

6. What changes would you make for next time?_____

_____

_____

Noting progress:

_____

_____

Progress Notes

Group: _____

Members of Group:_____

_____

Session 1: Date: _____

Notes: _____

_____

_____

Session 2: Date: _____

Notes: _____

_____

_____

Session 3: Date: _____

Notes: _____

_____

_____

Session 4: Date: _____

Notes: _____

_____

_____

Session 5: Date: _____

Notes: _____

_____

Session 6: Date: _____

Notes: _____

_____

_____

Session 7: Date: _____

Notes: _____

_____

_____

Session 8: Date: _____

Notes: _____

_____

_____

Session 9: Date: _____

Notes: _____

_____

_____

Session 10: Date: _____

Notes: _____

_____

_____

Session 11: Date: _____

Notes: _____

_____

_____

Self-Referral Group Survey Form

Dear Student:

The Pupil Services Staff of _____
School is pleased to be able to offer groups to the students.

These groups will meet once a week during the school day for eleven weeks. Group meetings last about forty-five minutes to one hour. We offer groups on many different subjects, and we hope you will be interested in joining.

Please put an "X" on the group or groups you would like to join. If you are interested in more than one group, please number them in priority, with 1 being the highest.

_____ Della the Dinosaur Group (if your parent uses harmful ways to show anger)

_____ Trevor and Tiffany Group (if you would like to learn how to stop school violence and learn how to replace aggressive behavior with assertive behavior)

_____ Daniel the Dinosaur Group (if you would like to learn how to stand up for yourself politely, without hurting anyone else)

Name _____

Teacher or homeroom number _____

We will meet with students individually before starting the groups.

_____
Signature of Guidance Counselor or School Social Worker

Parental Consent Form

School address _____

Date_____

Dear Parent:

The counseling staff of _____ School is happy to be offering several groups this year. One group that we will be offering is a group for students who have problems handling the behavior of other children who are aggressive. We will use a stuffed animal called Daniel to teach the children how to change their own behavior from passive or aggressive behavior to assertive.

In the group, we will be discussing the definition of violence, which includes mean words as well as physical violence, the value judgment that violence is unacceptable unless the situation is life-threatening, and that violence will not be tolerated in school. We will teach them many assertive behavior skills, ways they can stand up for themselves without hurting anyone else. We will also be teaching anger management and conflict resolution plans.

The group will be held during the school day, one day a week, for one class period, for eleven weeks. As a teaching technique, we like the students to present what they have learned in session 11. We think that this group will be very beneficial in helping students develop assertive behavior, and we are happy to offer it.

We would like your permission for your child, _____, to participate in this group. If you do give permission, please sign the permission form below and return it to us. Please call us at _____ if you have any questions.

Sincerely,

_____

_____

I give permission for my child, _____, to participate in the Daniel the Dinosaur group to be held at _____ School.

_____

Name   *Date*

Screening Interview Outline

Name: _____ Date: _____

Age: _____ Date of birth: _____

Grade: _____

Do you like school? _____

What is your school adjustment? _____

   Grades: _____

   Behavior: _____

Home Address? _____ Phone? _____

Who lives in your house? _____

If parents are divorced, where do they live? _____

Visitation? _____

What do you do after school? _____

_____

Typical daily schedule: _____

_____

Hobbies, sports, clubs: _____

_____

What are your strengths? _____

_____

What are your weaknesses? _____

_____

What are the stresses in your life? _____

_____

References and Suggested Readings

Cicchetti, D., and V. Carlson, eds. 1989. *Child maltreatment: Theory and research on the causes and consequences of child abuse and neglect*. New York: Cambridge University Press.

Cicchetti, D., and P. W. Howes. 1991. Developmental psychopathology in the context of the family: Illustrations from the study of child maltreatment. *Canadian Journal of Behavioral Science* 23 (July).

Coleman, J. C., and L. Hendry. 1990. *The Nature of adolescence*. New York: Routledge.

Crittenden, P. M., and M. D. S. Ainsworth. 1989. Child maltreatment and attachment theory. In Cicchetti and Carlson, eds. *Child maltreatment: Theory and research on the causes and consequences of child abuse and neglect*. New York: Cambridge University Press.

Garbarino, J. 1989. Troubled youth, troubled families: the dynamics of adolescent maltreatment. In Cicchetti and Carlson, eds. *Child maltreatment: Theory and research on the causes and consequences of child abuse and neglect*. New York: Cambridge University Press.

Gravitz, H. L., and J. D. Bowden. 1985. *Recovery: A guide for adult children of alcoholics*. New York: Simon & Schuster.

Greenbaum, S., B. Turner, and R. Stephens. 1989. *Set straight on bullies*. Malibu, Calif.: National School Safety Center.

Olweus, D. 1994. *Bullying at school*. Cambridge, Mass.: Blackwell Publishers.

Reiss, J., and J. Roth, eds. 1993. *Understanding and preventing violence*. Washington, D. C.: National Academy Press.

Remboldt, C. 1995. *Solving violence problems in your school: Why a systematic approach is necessary*. Minneapolis: Johnson Institute.

———. 1995. *Violence in schools: The enabling factor*. Minneapolis: Johnson Institute.

Remboldt, C., and R. Zimman. 1996. *Respect and protect: A practical, step-by-step violence prevention and intervention program for schools and communities*. Center City, Minn.: Hazelden.

Schaefer, D. 1987. *Choices and consequences*. Minneapolis: Johnson Institute.

Schmidt, T. 1993. *Anger management and violence prevention: A group activities manual for middle and high school students*. Minneapolis: Johnson Institute.

———. 1994. *Changing families: A group activities manual for middle and high school students from separated, divorced, single-parent families or stepfamilies*. Minneapolis: Johnson Institute.

Schmidt, T., and T. Spencer. 1991. *Della the dinosaur talks about violence and anger management (Grades K–6)*. Building Trust, Making Friends. Minneapolis: Johnson Institute.

———. 1991. *Peter the puppy talks about chemical dependence in the family (Grades K–6)*. Building Trust, Making Friends. Minneapolis: Johnson Institute.

———. 1991. *Tanya talks about chemical dependence in the family (Grades K–6)*. Building Trust, Making Friends. Minneapolis: Johnson Institute.

———. 1991. *Thomas Barker talks about divorce and separation (K–6)*. Building Trust, Making Friends. Minneapolis: Johnson Institute.

Schrumpf, F., D. Crawford, and H. Usadel. 1991. *Peer mediation: Conflict resolution in schools*. Champaign, Ill.: Research Press Company.

Sharp, S., and P. Smith, eds. 1994. *Tackling bullying in your school*. New York: Routledge.